For
Not to be taken
from the room.
reference

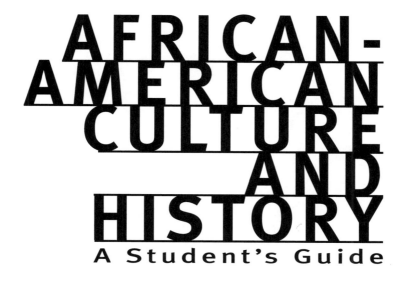

AFRICAN-AMERICAN CULTURE AND HISTORY
A Student's Guide

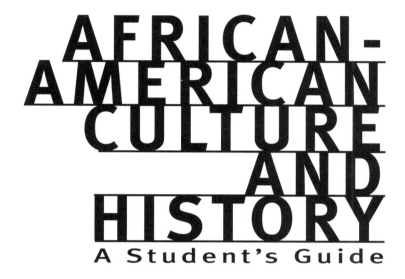

AFRICAN-AMERICAN CULTURE AND HISTORY
A Student's Guide

JACK SALZMAN
Editor-in-Chief

James S. Haskins
Consulting Editor

Evelyn Bender
Kathleen Lee
Advisors

volume **3**
J-P

Macmillan Reference USA
an imprint of the Gale Group
New York • Detroit • San Francisco • London • Boston • Woodbridge, CT

Macmillan Reference USA
1633 Broadway
New York, NY 10019

Gale Group
27500 Drake Rd.
Farmington Hills, MI 48331

Editorial and Production Staff

David Galens, *Project Editor*
Kelle Sisung, *Developmental Editor*
Kathy Droste, *Illustration Editor*
Shalice Shah, *Permissions Associate*
Mark Milne, Pam Revitzer, and Larry Trudeau, *Contributing Editors*
Tim Akers, Rebecca Blanchard, Elizabeth Bodenmiller, Anne Marie Hacht, and
    Tara Atterberry, *Proofreaders*
Robert Griffin, *Copyeditor*
Tracey Rowens, *Senior Art Director*
Randy Bassett, *Imaging Supervisor*
Pam A. Reed, *Imaging Coordinator*
Dan Newell, *Imaging Specialist*
Kay Banning, *Indexer*
Geraldine Azzata, *Further Resources Compiler*

Elly Dickason, *Publisher, Macmillan Reference USA*
Jill Lectka, *Associate Publisher*

Printing number
1 2 3 4 5 6 7 8 9 10

LIBRARY OF CONGRESS CATALOGING-IN-PUBLICATION DATA

African-American culture and history: a student's guide / Jack Salzman, editor-in-chief.
    p. cm.
    Adapted from the five-volume Encyclopedia of African American culture and history published by Macmillan in 1996; revised for a sixth- to seventh-grade, middle school audience.
    Includes bibliographical references and index.
    ISBN 0-02-865531-1 (set : hardcover : alk. paper) – ISBN 0-02865532-X (vol. 1 : alk. paper) – ISBN 0-02-865533-8 (vol. 2 : alk. paper) – ISBN 0-02-865534-6 (vol. 3 : alk. paper) – ISBN 0-02-865535-4 (vol. 4 : alk. paper)
Afro-Americans—Encyclopedias, Juvenile. 2.
Afro-Americans—History—Encyclopedias, Juvenile literature. [1.
Afro-Ameridans—Encyclopedias.] I. Salzman, Jack. II. Encyclopedia of African-American culture and history.

E185 .A2527 2000
973'.0496073—dc21

Table of Contents

VOLUME 1

Table of Contents

VOLUME 2

Table of Contents

VOLUME 3

Table of Contents

VOLUME 4

Preface

The history and culture of African Americans is to a great extent the history and culture of the United States. But as much as we may now accept this as a truism, it was not always so. It was not until the second half of the twentieth century that students and historians of the American experience began to document and carefully study the lives of people of African descent. Until then our knowledge of a people who comprise almost 15 percent of this country's population was shamefully inadequate. In 1989 Macmillan Publishing Co. decided to redress this situation by publishing a major reference work devoted to the history and culture of African Americans. I was asked to serve as editor of the new work, and in 1996 the five volume *Encyclopedia of African-American Culture and History* was published.

The encyclopedia contains close to two million words and covers all aspects of the African-American experience. In the few years since its publication it has come to be recognized as a mainstay in most high school, public, and academic libraries. *Rettig on Reference* (April 1996) found the set to be "scholarly yet accessible and immeasurably informative." *CHOICE* (1996) praised its "clear and succinct writing style" and its "breadth of coverage of general biographical and historical data." It received a Dartmouth Award Honorable Mention and appeared on every list of 1996 best reference sources. After spending six years compiling the encyclopedia it was gratifying to read, in *American Libraries* (May 1997), that the work "is of enduring value and destined to become a standard reference source."

The enthusiastic response to *Encyclopedia of African-American Culture and History* convinced us that students would benefit from a work with similar scope but one rewritten for a wider audience. *African-American Culture and History: A Student's Guide* is that work. It incorporates the same editorial criteria we used for the original encyclopedia : articles include biographies of notable African Americans, events, historical eras, legal cases, areas of cultural achievement, professions, sports, and places. Readers will find entries on all 50 states, 12 major cities, and 15 historically black colleges.

This comprehensive four-volume Student's Guide has 852 articles—arranged alphabetically—of which 597 are biographies and 255 are events, eras, genres, or colleges, states, or cities. Although for the most part articles in this set are based on entries from the original encyclopedia, our Advisory

Board recommended that we also cover several contemporary popular topics and figures. Entries were chosen to reflect the school curriculum and have been updated through Summer 2000.

African-American Culture and History: A Student's Guide has been carefully designed for younger readers, and professional writers have crafted the articles to make them accessible for the intended audience. In addition, readers will find that articles are enhanced with numerous photographs and sidebar materials. Lists, quotations, extracts from primary sources, interesting facts, and chronologies are to be found in the margins. A system of cross-references makes it easy to explore the Student's Guide. Within the text, terms and names set in boldface type indicate that there is a separate entry for this subject. Additional cross-references appear at the end of many entries. A comprehensive index for the entire set appears at the end of volume 4. A list of "Further Resources" in Volume Four includes books, articles, and web sites and will provide a starting point for students who are beginning to explore the extraordinary history and accomplishments of African Americans.

Many people have provided invaluable help with *African-American Culture and History: A Student's Guide*. In particular, I would like to single out Jill Lectka and David Galens of the Gale Group and Kelle Sisung. I would also like to thank our editorial advisors, Evelyn Bender, Librarian, Edison High School in Philadelphia; and Kathleen Lee, Librarian, John P. Turner Middle School in Philadelphia. Thanks, too, to Jim Haskins, Professor of Education, University of Florida and author of numerous books for young adults. These three professionals provided valuable guidance as I developed the article list and helped design the margin features. It was at their urging that we included curriculum-related web sites in the resources list. Finally, to Becca, Phoebe, Jonah, and Libby, who soon will be able to make use of these volumes: thank you for being as wonderful as you are and for bringing so much to me and Cec.

Jack Salzman
New York City

Contributors

The text of *African-American Culture and History: A Student's Guide* is based on the Macmillan *Encyclopedia of African-American Culture and History*, which was published in 1996. We have updated material where necessary and added new entries. Articles have been condensed and made more accessible for a student audience. Please refer to the Alphabetical List of Articles on page xi of the first volume of *Encyclopedia of African-American Culture and History* (also edited by Jack Salzman) for the names of the authors of the articles in the original set. Their academic affiliations are noted in the Directory of Contributors. This title also includes entries from the Supplement to *Encyclopedia of African-American Culture and History* published by Macmillan late in 2000. The Supplement has its own Alphabetical List of Articles and Directory of Contributors. Here we wish to acknowledge the writers who revised entries from those two publications and wrote new articles for this set:

Sheree Beaudry
Craig Collins
Stephanie Dionne
Rebecca Ferguson
David Galens
Robert Griffin
Cathy Dybiec Holm
Paul Kobel
Paula Pyzik-Scott
Ann Shurgin
Kelle Sisung
Larry Trudeau

Jack, Beau ▪▪▪

BOXER
April 21, 1919–February 9, 2000

Beau Jack was a raw street fighter who made it into professional boxing at a time when blacks were heavily discriminated against (early 1940s) in the United States. He learned how to fight in "battle royals," where a group of young blacks fought until one man was left standing. Born in Augusta, Georgia, Jack's real name was Sidney Walker. In 1943 he won the equivalent of the lightweight championship, joining **Joe Louis** as the first two blacks to win championship titles. Jack was the most popular fighter at New York's Madison Square Garden in the early 1940s. He finished his career with eighty-three wins, twenty-four losses, and five draws. After boxing, Jack worked as a bootblack (shoe shiner) in Miami, Florida, as a boxing trainer, and as a wrestling referee. Late in life Jack suffered from Parkinson's disease, which claimed his life in February 2000.

Jackson, Angela ▪▪▪

POET, PLAYWRIGHT
July 25, 1951–

Born in Greenville, Mississippi, Angela Jackson grew up in Chicago, Illinois, the fifth of nine children. Her first work of note was a leadership role in the Organization of Black American Culture Writers Workshop in the 1970s. Her work has been admired for its beautiful language, which combines the African-American conversational style with a literary discipline. Her poetry books include *Voo Doo/Love Magic* (1974), *Solo in the Boxcar Third Floor E* (1985), and *And All These Roads Be Luminous* (1992), her collected poems. Jackson's best-known play, *Shango Diaspora*, was first staged in Chicago in 1980. Jackson has received numerous literary awards and has taught at Stephens College and Columbia College of Chicago, where she continues to reside.

Jackson Family, The

MUSIC FAMILY

A major influence on American popular music since the 1960s, the Jackson family consists of nine brothers and sisters. Five brothers began singing in the early 1960s: Sigmund "Jackie" (May 4, 1951–), Toriano "Tito" (October 15, 1953–), Jermaine (December 11, 1954–), Marlon (March 12, 1957–) and Michael (August 29, 1958–). In the 1970s Maureen "Rebbie" (May 29, 1950–), LaToya (May 29, 1956–), Steven "Randy" (October 29, 1962–), and Janet (May 16, 1966–) began entertaining with the others. By the 1980s, they were generating a nonstop stream of recordings, music videos, movies, television shows, and concerts that were hugely popular among both African-American and white audiences.

All of the Jackson children were born and raised in the midwestern industrial city of Gary, Indiana. The five oldest sons were driven by their father, a steel mill crane operator and one-time guitarist, to practice music three hours a day. As The Jackson Five, they began to perform in local talent contests in the early 1960s. In 1967 Michael's lead singing and dance moves helped the brothers win the famed amateur night contest at the **Apollo Theater** in New York.

After recording two single records that failed to create a stir, the group was signed by Berry Gordy and **Motown Records** of **Detroit, Michigan**. After Gordy took control of The Jackson Five, they immediately produced the popular singles "I Want You Back" (1969) and "ABC" (1970).

In 1970 the family moved to Los Angeles, and in the years that followed The Jackson Five made numerous television appearances, including a cartoon series. Their recordings from this time include the albums *Lookin' Through The Windows* (1972) and *Get It Together* (1973). Michael recorded his first solo album, *Got To Be There*, in 1971. His second solo recording, *Ben*

The Jackson 5 in performance; (left to right) Tito, Marlon, Michael, Jackie, and Jermaine (AP/Wide World Photos. Reproduced by permission)

MICHAEL JACKSON: POP SUPERSTAR

While the Jackson Five's success as a musical act was tremendous, lead singer Michael Jackson's solo career would far surpass the fame he had found singing with his brothers. While Michael had solo hits in the early 1970s with songs like "Got to Be There" and "Ben," it was not until 1979's *Off the Wall* album that he gained attention as an artist separate from the Jackson Five. In 1982, Jackson released *Thriller,* which became the biggest selling album of all-time (boasting seven top ten singles) and established Michael as the predominant musician of the 1980s. Songs such as "Billy Jean" and "Beat It" dominated radio playlists as a diverse audience embraced Jackson's music. With *Thriller* Michael became the first artist to top the Dance, R&B, and Pop charts simultaneously.

Jackson soon became one of the most famous and recognizable figures in the world. While Michael continued to record and tour with his brothers on and off, it was solo albums such as *Bad* and *Dangerous* that propelled him to greater fame, fortune, and notoriety. While his music established his celebrity status, Jackson became equally well-known for his eccentric behavior. He named his sprawling California estate "Neverland" and kept a large zoo of animals on the property. Numerous rumors arose, including one that alleged that Michael had attempted to buy the remains of John Merrick, the famed "Elephant Man." An admitted recluse who felt more comfortable in the company of children than adults, Michael was seen as a somewhat strange though essentially harmless person. That image changed in 1993 when Jackson was accused of molesting a young boy with whom he had been spending time. The case never went to court, but Jackson made a monetary settlement with the boy's family in 1994. Perhaps in an effort to distance himself from these events, Michael married Lisa Marie Presley, daughter of rock and roll legend Elvis Presley, in 1994. Rumors continued to plague Jackson, however, with many claiming the marriage was a fake, little more than a transparent attempt to hide the singer's strange, possibly criminal behavior. Jackson and Presley divorced in 1996. He subsequently married a former nurse, Debbie Rowe, with whom he had two children—though rumors persisted that he and Rowe conceived the children artificially. Rowe and Jackson divorced in 1999, with Michael gaining custody of the two children, Prince Michael Jr. and Paris.

Despite the trials of his very public private life, Jackson's music has remained a powerful force. His albums continue to sell millions of copies and his infrequent concert performances routinely sell out. In 2000, he was named the best-selling artist of the millenium at the World Music Awards in Monaco. His accomplishments as a musician have earned him other awards, including numerous Grammy and American Music Awards.

(1972), went to number one and received an Academy Award nomination. In 1974 the Jacksons produced "Dancing Machine," a feverish dance hit. The next year, Michael recorded another solo album, *Forever, Michael.*

In 1975 The Jackson Five broke ties with Motown and signed with Epic Records; with Epic, the group was promised much more in royalties and more creative control. Because Motown "owned" the name "The Jackson Five," the group changed its name to "The Jacksons." In 1977 the Jacksons came out with the album *Destiny*, featuring Michael's intense, gospel-style vocals. In 1976 and 1977 Randy joined Michael, Jackie, Tito, and Marlon in a television variety show, *The Jacksons*. Rebbie, LaToya, and Janet also joined the cast, performing in both musical and comedy sketches. In 1978 Michael appeared as the Scarecrow in the film *The Wiz*.

In 1979 Michael again went solo and appeared in a tuxedo and glowing white socks on the cover of his smash album, *Off The Wall*. A collaboration with producer **Quincy Jones** (1933–), the album yielded four Top Ten singles and sold eleven million copies. In 1982 Michael again teamed up with Jones to make *Thriller*, a rock-oriented album that yielded seven Top Ten singles, including "Thriller" and "Beat It." *Thriller* sold more than 40 million copies, making it the best-selling album of all time.

The Jacksons got together again in 1980 for the very successful Victory tour and album. Since then, they have been less active as a group and have concentrated on solo careers. They are still the most productive family in African-American popular music.

Jackson, George Lester

ACTIVIST
September 23, 1941–August 21, 1971

George Jackson is known as the man who brought political activism to prisoners in the 1960s. In 1960, after years of small crimes and jail sentences, Jackson was accused of stealing $71 from a gas station and received a sentence of one year to life. After he served the statutory minimum of one year, his case was reconsidered yearly. Jackson was never granted parole, and he spent the rest of his life in prison. He was imprisoned in Soledad State Prison in Salinas, California, where he began to study the writings of revolutionary political thinkers. He used this knowledge to educate black and Chicano prisoners about politics. Partly because of his prison activities, he was placed in solitary confinement for extended periods of time.

On January 16, 1970, in response to the death of three black inmates in Soledad Prison, a white guard, John Mills, was killed. Jackson, John Clutchette, and Fleeta Drumgo were accused of the murder. All three were regarded as black militants by prison authorities; they came to be known as the Soledad Brothers. The extent of their involvement in the murder has never been clear. The treatment of Jackson and his fellow prisoners became an international cause that focused attention and publicity on the treatment of black inmates. Jackson's dignity made him a symbol of pride and defiance, and rallies and protests were held to support him and focus public attention on the problems of the prisoners.

The publication in 1970 of *Soledad Brother: The Prison Letters of George Jackson* greatly contributed to Jackson's fame. The book traces his personal and political experiences and the relationship he saw between the condition of black people inside prison walls and those outside. Jackson believed that

creating political awareness among imprisoned people was the first step in the overall development of a movement that would change society for the better.

During 1970 the Soledad Brothers were transferred to San Quentin Prison. On August 21, 1971, three days before his case was due to go to trial, Jackson was killed by prison guards. The official report said that Jackson was armed; that he had participated in a prison revolt earlier in the day, which had left two white prisoners and three guards dead; and that he was killed in an apparent escape attempt. However, accounts of this incident are conflicting, and many argue that Jackson was set up for assassination and had nothing to do with the earlier riot. In March 1972 the remaining two Soledad Brothers were acquitted of the original charges.

Jackson, Jesse Louis

MINISTER, POLITICIAN, CIVIL RIGHTS ACTIVIST
October 8, 1941–

Jesse Jackson has been the most prominent civil rights leader and African-American national figure since the death of **Martin Luther King Jr.** In 1959 Jackson accepted a scholarship to play football at the University of Illinois. When he discovered that African Americans were not allowed to play quarterback, he enrolled at North Carolina Agricultural and Technical College in Greensboro.

Jackson's leadership abilities and charisma earned him a considerable reputation by the time he graduated with a degree in sociology in 1964. He then moved to Illinois to attend the Chicago Theological Seminary. Jackson left the seminary in 1965 and returned to the South to become a member of Martin Luther King Jr.'s staff of the **Southern Christian Leadership Conference (SCLC).**

In 1966 King appointed Jackson to head the Chicago branch of the SCLC's Operation Breadbasket, which was formed to force various businesses to employ more African Americans. In 1967 King made Jackson the national director of Operation Breadbasket. Jackson arranged a number of boycotts of businesses refusing to hire African Americans and successfully negotiated employment agreements.

Jackson was with King and a group of King's supporters when King was assassinated in Memphis, Tennessee, in 1968. After King's death, Jackson's relationship with the SCLC became increasingly strained over disagreements about his independence. Finally, in 1971, Jackson left the SCLC and founded Operation PUSH (People United to Save Humanity). As head of PUSH, he continued a program of negotiating black employment agreements with white businesses, as well as promoting black educational excellence and self-esteem.

In 1983 Jackson became a candidate for president of the United States. His campaign stressed voter registration and carried a message of empowerment to African Americans, poor people, and other minorities. This support of the "voiceless and downtrodden" became the foundation for what Jackson termed the "Rainbow Coalition" of Americans—the poor, struggling farmers, feminists, and others who historically, according to Jackson, had lacked

representation. Jackson called for a halt to military spending, programs to stimulate full employment, and political empowerment of African Americans through voter registration. Jackson got almost 3.3 million votes of the approximately 18 million cast.

Jackson again ran for president in 1988. He campaigned on the themes he first advocated in 1984. He once again promoted voter registration drives and urged voters to join the Rainbow Coalition, which by this time had become a structured organization closely overseen by Jackson. His campaign also called for national health care and aid to farmworkers. Jackson won almost 7 million votes out of the 23 million cast in 1988. His performance indicated a growing national respect for his skills.

Since 1988 Jackson has crusaded for various causes, including the institution of a democratic government in South Africa, statehood for the District of Columbia, and the banishment of illegal drugs from American society. On his 1991 television talk show, Jackson sought to widen his audience, addressing pressing concerns faced by African Americans. In 1996 he was a supporter of the successful congressional campaign of his son, Jesse Jackson, Jr. In 1998, he became a close adviser to President Bill Clinton

(1993–2001). In 2000 Clinton bestowed on Jackson the nation's highest civilian honor, the Presidential Medal of Freedom, for his many years of service to the country, including negotiating for the release and personally retrieving three U.S. soldiers held as prisoners in Yugosolavia.

Jackson, Laurence Donald "Baby Laurence"

TAP DANCER

1921–1974

Tap dancer "Baby Laurence" used **jazz** music to influence his dancing. He was born in Baltimore, Maryland, and first performed at age eleven with a leading big band. After the death of his parents, Jackson ran away to **New York**, where he found a job at the Harlem nightclub owned by Dickie Wells, who nicknamed him "Baby." Jackson soon turned to dancing, absorbing ideas and techniques from such tap-dancing performers as Eddie Rector (1898–1962) and Pete Nugent (c. 1910–). In the mid-1930s Jackson sang and danced with The Four Buds, later known as The Harlem Highlanders. These six performers dressed in kilts and sang Jimmie Lunceford arrangements.

In the 1940s Jackson expanded his technique in jazz dancing. Sometimes working with **Art Tatum** (1909–1956), he would duplicate with his feet what Tatum played on the piano, creating a sound of explosions, machine-gun rattles, and jarring thumps. Increasingly his dancing was influenced by the complex rhythms of bebop jazz. In 1961 he played an engagement with **Count Basie** at the **Apollo Theater** in New York; the next year he appeared at the Newport Jazz Festival with **Duke Ellington** (1899–1974). In the 1970s, with his home base in Baltimore, Baby Laurence headed the Sunday afternoon tap sessions at the Jazz Museum. He died in 1974.

Jackson, Mahalia

GOSPEL SINGER

October 26, 1911–January 27, 1972

When sixteen-year-old Mahala Jackson (as she was named at birth) moved to Chicago, Illinois, in 1927, she had already developed the vocal style that was to win her the title of "the world's greatest gospel singer." Although her New Orleans, Louisiana, family was extremely religious, Jackson repeatedly listened to recordings of blues singers **Bessie Smith** (1894–1937) and **Ma Rainey** (1886–1939), and she adopted a sound similar to theirs rather than the sound of the early **gospel** singers.

In Chicago, Jackson joined the Johnson Singers, one of the city's better-known gospel groups. Now calling herself Mahalia, she eventually became a soloist. In 1935 she became gospel composer **Thomas Andrew Dorsey**'s (1899–1993) official song demonstrator, a position she held until 1945.

Jackson made her first recordings in 1937, but it was not until the mid-1940s that she established a national reputation. Her 1947 recording of "Move On Up a Little Higher" made her a superstar and won her one of the first two Gold Records for sales in gospel music. As a result, she became the official soloist for the **National Baptist Convention.**

Soon Jackson was becoming known to a wide audience. In 1954 CBS made Jackson the first gospel singer with her own network radio show. That same year, she had a hit with listeners outside the gospel audience with the recording "Rusty Old Halo." She appeared on the Ed Sullivan and Dinah Shore television shows, and at New York's Carnegie Hall. On world tours, Jackson was praised in France, Germany, and Italy. She also appeared in such films as *St. Louis Blues* (1958) and *Imitation of Life* (1959).

In 1961 Jackson sang at one of President John F. Kennedy's (1917–1963; president 1961–63) inaugural parties. In 1963 she sang "I've Been Buked and I've Been Scorned" before Rev. Dr. **Martin Luther King Jr.** delivered his famous "I Have a Dream" speech at the March on Washington.

Before her death in 1972, Jackson suffered from heart trouble but continued to sing. She appeared on a U.S. postage stamp in 1998.

Jackson, Michael. *See* Jackson Family, The

Jackson, Reginald Martinez "Reggie"

BASEBALL PLAYER
May 18, 1946–

Reginald "Reggie" Martinez Jackson was one of the most exciting hitters in the history of professional baseball. When Reggie Jackson came to the plate, baseball fans held their breath, waiting for the slugger to send the ball soaring over the fence.

Born in Wyncote, Pennsylvania, Jackson went to Arizona State University on a football scholarship. After a year of football, he decided his true calling was baseball. In 1967 he began his twenty-one-year career in the major leagues with the Kansas City Athletics (who later moved to Oakland, California). Jackson then joined the New York Yankees, where he earned the nickname "Mr. October" for his clutch play in the postseason. The highlight of Jackson's stellar career came in the 1977 World Series when he hit three home runs in a row off three different pitchers, all on the first pitch.

Jackson next played for the California Angels (1982–86) and finished his career in Oakland with 563 home runs; but he also finished with the unfortunate record of most career strikeouts (2,597). Jackson played in five World Series, was voted the league's Most Valuable Player (1973), and was elected to the Hall of Fame in 1993. After baseball, Jackson became involved with the Big Brothers and Big Sisters program, started a car dealership, and helped advise the New York Yankees (1993). In March 2000 Jackson entered into a business venture, becoming chief communications officer for an Internet company called SportsHabitat.com (http://www.sportshabitat.com).

Jackson, Shirley Ann

PHYSICIST
AUGUST 5, 1946

In 1973 Shirley Ann Jackson became the first African-American woman to receive a doctorate (Ph.D.) degree in physics from the Massachusetts Institute of Technology (MIT), considered one of the top engineering and technology colleges in the world. She had received a bachelor of science degree from MIT in 1968. A native of Washington, D.C., Jackson worked at physics laboratories in the United States and abroad during the 1970s. From 1976 until 1991 she taught physics at Rutgers University (New Brunswick, New Jersey).

In 1991 Jackson was appointed a commissioner of the Nuclear Regulatory Commission, a government agency that oversees nuclear activities in the United States. In 1995 she became chair of the commission. She resigned from that position in 1998 to become president of the Rensselaer Polytechnic Institute in Troy, New York.

Jacobs, Harriet Ann

SLAVE NARRATOR, REFORMER
1813–March 7, 1897

Harriet Jacobs's major contribution is her book, *Incidents in the Life of a Slave Girl: Written by Herself* (1861). Jacobs tells the story of her life in the South as a slave and of her life as a fugitive slave in the North.

After her 1842 escape to New York City, Jacobs moved to Rochester, New York, where she became part of the circle of abolitionists around **Frederick Douglass**'s newspaper the *North Star*.

Supported by Quaker groups and the newly formed New England Freedmen's Aid Society, Jacobs and her daughter, Louisa, moved to Alexandria, Virginia, in 1863, where they provided emergency supplies and medical care to Union (Northern) army soldiers during the **Civil War** (1861–65). In 1865 mother and daughter moved to Savannah, Georgia, where they continued their work. Throughout the war years, Harriet and Louisa Jacobs reported on their Southern relief efforts in the Northern press and in newspapers in England, where Jacobs's book had appeared as *The Deeper Wrong: Incidents in the Life of a Slave Girl: Written by Herself* (1862). In 1868 they sailed to England and raised money for Savannah's black orphans and aged.

In the face of increasing violence in the South, Jacobs and her daughter moved to Massachusetts. In Boston they were connected with the newly formed New England Women's Club. They next moved to nearby Cambridge, Massachusetts, where for several years Jacobs ran a boarding-house for Harvard faculty and students. She and Louisa later moved to Washington, D.C., where she continued to work among former slaves and Louisa was employed at Howard University.

"O, what days and nights of fear and sorrow that man caused me! Reader, it is not to awaken sympathy for myself that I am telling you truthfully what I suffered in slavery, I do it to kindle a flame of compassion in your hearts for my sisters who are still in bondage, suffering as I once suffered."

(Source: Harriet Ann Jacobs. Excerpts from *Incidents in the Life of a Slave Girl*.)

In 1896, when the National Association of Colored Women held its organizing meetings in Washington, Harriet Jacobs was confined to a wheelchair. The following spring, she died at her Washington home. She is buried in Mount Auburn Cemetery, Cambridge, Massachusetts. (*See also*: **Slave Narratives**)

Chappie James sitting in the cockpit of a jet fighter plane (AP/Wide World Photos. Reproduced by permission)

James, Daniel Jr. "Chappie"

GENERAL
February 25, 1920–

Daniel "Chappie" James Jr. was the first African American to become a four-star general. James was a firm believer that a strong individual could overcome any obstacle, even racism.

James joined the black Army Air Corps in 1937 and led a fighter group during **World War II** (1939–45). He earned the Distinguished Service Medal for designing a way for military aircraft to assist ground troops. James also served in the **Vietnam War** (1959–75), earning the Legion of Merit award for his efforts. He later commanded the important North American Air Defense, for which he earned his fourth medal for monitoring air and missile attacks.

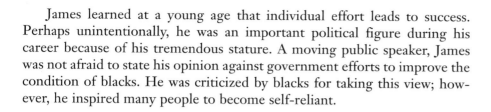

James learned at a young age that individual effort leads to success. Perhaps unintentionally, he was an important political figure during his career because of his tremendous stature. A moving public speaker, James was not afraid to state his opinion against government efforts to improve the condition of blacks. He was criticized by blacks for taking this view; however, he inspired many people to become self-reliant.

James, Etta

RHYTHM-AND-BLUES SINGER
January 5, 1938–

Etta James, born Jamesetta Hawkins in Los Angeles, California, sang in a church choir as a child and began to sing professionally at the age of fourteen. Her first recording, "Roll With Me Henry" (1954), was originally banned by radio stations because of its sexual content. However, the record became a hit, and it was re-released in 1955 under the title "Wallflower."

In the mid-to-late 1950s James was one of the most popular singers in **rhythm-and-blues (R&B)** and toured with stars such as **Little Richard** and **James Brown**. Her gospel-influenced voice could be either sweet, pouting, or rough. Among her hit records were "W-O-M-A-N" (1955), "How Big a Fool" (1958), "Stop the Wedding" (1962), and "Something's Got a Hold On Me" (1964).

Heroin addiction forced James to quit recording in the mid-to-late 1960s, but she eventually entered a rehabilitation program and returned to music in 1973 with the album *Etta James*, which won a Grammy Award. James then recorded numerous albums, including *Mystery Lady*, a collection of **Billie Holliday** songs that earned James another Grammy in 1995. In 1990 James won an **NAACP** Image Award, and in 1993 she was inducted into the Rock and Roll Hall of Fame. She published an **autobiography,** *Rage to Survive: The Etta James Story*, in 1995.

Jamison, Judith

DANCER
May 10, 1943–

Dancer Judith Jamison studied piano and violin as a child. She was enrolled in dance classes at about age six so that she would gracefully handle her above-average height. She later decided on a career in dance after briefly taking classes in psychology at **Fisk University** (Nashville, Tennessee). Jamison completed her education at the Philadelphia Dance Academy in Pennsylvania.

In 1964 Jamison was invited to appear in choreographer Agnes de Mille's *The Four Marys* at the New York-based American Ballet Theatre. The next year, she moved to New York and joined the **Alvin Ailey** American Dance Theater (AAADT).

Judith Jamison (center) performing with the Alvin Ailey Dance Company (AP/Wide World Photos. Reproduced by permission)

Jamison performed with AAADT on tours of Europe and Africa in 1966. She became a principal dancer with the company, dancing roles that showcased her technique, beauty, and statuesque height of five feet ten inches. Jamison and Ailey began creating dances together, including a solo in his

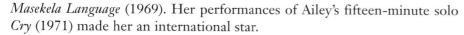

Masekela Language (1969). Her performances of Ailey's fifteen-minute solo *Cry* (1971) made her an international star.

In 1976 Jamison danced with ballet star Mikhail Baryshnikov in Ailey's *Pas de Duke*, set to music by **Duke Ellington.** Her growing fame led to appearances around the world, including roles with the San Francisco Ballet, the Swedish Royal Ballet, and the Vienna State Ballet.

In 1980 Jamison left the Ailey company to star in the Broadway musical *Sophisticated Ladies.* She later began doing choreography (dance composition) and founded her own dance company, the Jamison Project.

Alvin Ailey's failing health caused Jamison to rejoin the AAADT as artistic associate in 1988. In December 1989 Ailey died, and Jamison was named artistic director of the company. In 1999 she was awarded a Kennedy Center Honor for her lifetime of contributions to dance.

Jarreau, Alwyn Lopez "Al"

JAZZ AND POP SINGER
1940–

Al Jarreau is known for his distinctive style of **jazz** singing. He was born in Wisconsin and received his degrees in the Midwest. Jarreau worked in San Francisco as a rehabilitation counselor until 1968. After some success singing part-time in local clubs, Jarreau turned professional with a band named The Indigos. He next worked with George Duke's trio, playing the club circuit in San Francisco.

Jazz standards formed the major part of his music. He released his first album in 1975. The following year he toured Europe, where he was quite popular. Jarreau claims to have been influenced by **Nat "King" Cole** (1919–1965), **Billy Eckstine** (1914–1993), and **Sarah Vaughan** (1924–1990), among others. Jarreau's intonation and vocal range are impressive; his vocal "library" includes tongue clicks, gasps, and unique "Oriental"-sounding nonsense syllables. He has received many awards for his work. He is generally considered to be one of the foremost jazz singers of his generation.

Jarreau's music was generally less well accepted by younger fans in the 1990s, and he claimed that a revolution was happening within **rhythm-and-blues** music. He called the new music "alive and angry." His home was damaged by an earthquake in 1995, just when a long-term contract with a record studio ended. However, he remained upbeat about his future career, looking forward to "serious success."

Al Jarreau: Selected Albums

We Got By
(1975)

Look to the Rainbow
(1977)

Breakin' Away
(1981)

Jazz

Jazz is a musical style with African-American roots. It is played throughout the world and was perhaps the most influential music of the twentieth-century in the United States.

Early Jazz

Jazz became well known around 1900 in cities such as **New Orleans, Louisiana**; **Chicago, Illinois**; and **Memphis, Tennessee**. Two forms of African-American folk and popular music—**the blues** and **ragtime**—gave rise to jazz. Both types of music began during the late 1800s in towns along the Mississippi River. The first jazz masters—including Buddy Bolden (1877–1931), **Edward "Kid" Ory** (c. 1889–1973), **"Jelly Roll" Morton** (1890–1941), and **Sidney Bechet** (1897–1959)—came from New Orleans.

New Orleans was culturally rich, with French, Spanish, Haitian, Native American, and African-American peoples, as well as Creoles, people of mixed black and French or Spanish ancestry. Each group contributed its music, and by 1910 these had evolved into a style known as New Orleans jazz. Jazz was also influenced by traveling minstrel shows (stage entertainment by white performers in black facial makeup) and by marching bands that played for funerals and parades.

Improvisation, or creating parts of a musical piece as it is played, always had an important role in jazz. Early jazz performers improvised solo (playing alone) or with two or more instruments. This "collective" improvisation was the key feature of New Orleans jazz and, later, Chicago Dixieland-style jazz.

Big-Band Jazz in the Swing Era

By the early 1920s jazz was being played by dance-band orchestras with trumpets, trombone, saxophones, clarinets, drums, piano, string bass, and guitar. In these "big bands," instrumental sections traded off playing with a soloist. The soloist was probably the most important development of the big-band era, and one of the greatest was trumpet player **Louis Armstrong** (1901–1971). He transformed dance-band sounds to the New Orleans-influenced style that would eventually become known as "swing." By singing the same way he played the trumpet, Armstrong became the model for "scat" singing, which uses nonsense syllables instead of words.

By the mid-1930s New York City's large African-American neighborhood, **Harlem**, became the center of the jazz world, and the swing era began. Both black and white audiences enjoyed dancing to big-band swing at Harlem's famous nightclubs, like the **Cotton Club** and the **Savoy Ballroom**. Starting in the late 1920s, dance bands led by African Americans **Duke Ellington** (1899–1974), **Count Basie** (1904–1984), **Cab Calloway** (1907–1994), and others competed with white bands like those led by Benny Goodman (1909–1986), Tommy Dorsey (1905–1956), and Glenn Miller (1904–1944). The big-band era also created black tenor saxophonist stars such as **Coleman Hawkins** (1904–1969) and jazz vocalists like **Billie Holiday** (1915–1959) and **Ella Fitzgerald** (1918–1996).

Bebop

African-American saxophonist **Charlie Parker** (1920–1955) was among the first musicians to play in the new style of jazz known as "bebop," named for the two notes that often ended bebop solos. All of the early bebop giants drew on their experience playing with swing musicians in big bands. One of the first great bebop groups was a big band led by **Dizzy Gillespie** (1917–1993) in the mid-1940s.

Jazz drummers like **Kenny Clarke** (1914–1985) and **Max Roach** (1924–) set the rhythm for bebop as they began keeping time on the high-hat cymbal rather than on the bass drum. Parker and Gillespie, along with musicians like **Charles Mingus** (1922–1979) and **Thelonious Monk** (1917–1982), began playing a complex music with new songs that were unsuitable for swing-era dancing. Bebop was most popular in small Harlem nightclubs, where it was played by groups of piano, bass, drums, and two or three horns.

Cool Jazz and Hard Bop

Pianist John Lewis and trumpeter **Miles Davis** (1926–1991) soon forged a new style known as "cool jazz." Davis formed a nine-piece band that played elegant-but-complex music that greatly influenced white musicians like Dave Brubeck and Stan Getz.

Davis also helped launch another major trend of the 1950s, "hard bop," with longer, more emotional solos, similar to those of gospel and blues. Mingus, **Art Blakey** (1919–1990), Monk, and others were major hard-bop performers, as were later musicians **Cannonball Adderley** (1928–1975) and **Jackie McLean** (1932–).

Avant-Garde and Fusion Jazz

During the 1960s musician **John Coltrane** (1926–1967) and others developed a new style of jazz with longer solos and more difficult pieces. A new generation of avant-garde (innovative) musicians known as "free jazz" musicians, including **Archie Shepp** (1937–), **Sun Ra** (1914–1993), and Don Cherry (1936–), played a style similar to the old New Orleans jazz. Inspired by the **Civil Rights movement**, they addressed race issues in their music.

Avant-garde jazz was not as popular with the black audience in the United States, and by the late 1960s free-jazz musicians sought ways to recapture this audience. Once again, it was Miles Davis who led the way, using electric instruments and adding funk, **rhythm-and-blues**, and rock rhythms to his jazz recordings. This fusing of different kinds of music led to a new style known as "fusion" or "jazz-rock fusion." Members of Davis's electric groups, such as **Herbie Hancock** (1940–) and white composer Chick Corea (1941–), later enjoyed tremendous success.

The Chicago-based Association for the Advancement of Creative Musicians (AACM) and the St. Louis-based Black Artists Group were responsible for important developments in jazz after the mid-1970s. The Art Ensemble of Chicago, pianist Muhal Richard Abrams (1930–), and saxophonists like Anthony Braxton (1945–) were important to a new "creative music" that draws on everything from ragtime to free jazz.

Jazz in the Late Twentieth Century

Since the 1970s, music-school training has resulted in innovative arists like **Anthony Davis** (1951–) and David Murray, as well as traditionalists

AFRICAN-AMERICAN JAZZ MUSICIANS WINNING GRAMMY LIFETIME ACHIEVEMENT AWARDS

The Grammy Award is the recording industry's most prestigious award, presented annually by the Recording Academy. During the 1990s African-American jazz artists **Wayne Shorter**, Herbie Hancock, **Lena Horne**, **Etta James**, Miles Davis, **Quincy Jones, Bobby McFerrin**, Dizzy Gillespie, and Ella Fitzgerald, among others, won Grammy Awards. Dozens of others have won since the first jazz Grammy was given to Fitzgerald in 1958.

A special award given by the Recording Academy's National Trustees is the Lifetime Achievement Award, for performers who have made creative contributions of outstanding artistic significance to recording. Following are some African-American jazz musicians who have received this award.

Duke Ellington
(1966)

Ella Fitzgerald
(1967)

Louis Armstrong
(1972, posthumously)

Charlie Parker
(1984, posthumously)

Benny Carter
(1987)

Billie Holiday
(1987, posthumously)

Lena Horne
(1989)

Art Tatum
(1989, posthumously)

Sarah Vaughan
(1989)

Dizzy Gillespie
(1989)

Miles Davis
(1990)

John Coltrane
(1992, posthumously)

Thelonious Monk
(1993, posthumously)

Charles Mingus
(1997, posthumously)

with a bebop background—like trumpeter and composer **Wynton Marsalis** (1961–)—who have brought mainstream jazz back to public popularity.

In 1997 Marsalis's composition *Blood on the Fields* was awarded the Pulitzer Prize for music, and in 1999 Duke Ellington was honored posthumously (after death) with a Pulitzer Special Award on the one-hundredth anniversary of his birth.

As jazz enters its second century, a new generation of musicians, including pianist Geri Allen and tenor saxophonist Joshua Redman, continue to define jazz styles.

Jefferson, Lemon "Blind"

BLUES GUITARIST, SINGER
July 1897–December 1929

The circumstances of his birth are uncertain, but "Blind" Lemon Jefferson's birthplace is often given as Couchman, Texas. He is thought to

Blues legend Blind Lemon Jefferson pictured with his guitar (Archive Photos. Reproduced by permission)

have been born blind, but several of his songs indicate he lost his sight in childhood. Jefferson learned to play guitar as a teen, played spirituals in the family church, and performed on the streets and at parties.

Jefferson, a heavyset man, moved to Dallas in 1912 and for a brief time earned money as a novelty wrestler in theaters. He met **Hudson "Leadbelly" Ledbetter** in Dallas's Deep Ellum neighborhood, and they played and traveled together throughout East Texas until Leadbelly was jailed for murder in 1918. Jefferson also performed for spare change on Dallas streets, at times assisted by bluesmen T-Bone Walker and Josh White. In the early 1920s Jefferson married and had a son.

Jefferson's first recordings were spirituals, made under the name Deacon L. J. Bates. "Long Lonesome **Blues**" (1926), his first popular success, displayed his clear, high-pitched voice, accented by hums and moans. Like many East Texas and Delta bluesmen, Jefferson sang of day-to-day life and travel. In the late 1920s Jefferson's recordings made him a wealthy, nationally recognized figure. He traveled throughout the South and Midwest, and even kept an apartment in Chicago. But his popularity lasted only briefly, and by 1929 he was no longer performing and recording as often. In December 1929 Jefferson froze to death in a Chicago blizzard.

Jehovah's Witnesses

The Jehovah's Witnesses is a religious group that believes that Armageddon (the end of the world as described in the Bible) is "imminent," or ready to occur some time in the near future. In fact, the second president of the Jehovah's Witnesses believed Armageddon was so near that many of its current members would never die, but would be taken directly to heaven. For this reason, the group requires total commitment from its members. It does not permit involvement in any other organization.

African-Americans have made up 20–30 percent of the membership of the Jehovah's Witnesses throughout most of its history. Although the church has had some racist policies in its past, in general the Jehovah's Witnesses has led in recruiting members from all races. Because of its message of self-sufficiency, the religion appeals to people on the fringes of society, including minorities and the poor.

Throughout its history the church's policies toward African-American members have been inconsistent. On the one hand, the group condemned racial divisions as early as 1952 and accepted minority members more openly than most other religious groups. On the other hand, the group also condemned interracial marriage (1953) and supported segregated (racially separated) congregations in the South well into the 1960s. Still, the Witnesses's aggressive recruitment of African-Americans has made it one of the fastest-growing religious groups in the United States.

Jemison, Mae Carol

ASTRONAUT
October 17, 1956–

Astronaut Mae C. Jemison was the first African-American woman to fly in space. She was born in Alabama but grew up in Chicago, Illinois. In 1977 she graduated from Stanford University, in Palo Alto, California. She earned an M.D. from Cornell University Medical College in 1981. After interning, she worked in private practice until January 1983, when she joined the Peace Corps. She served in Sierra Leone and Liberia—both in Africa—as a Peace Corps medical officer for two and a half years, returning in 1985 to Los Angeles, California, to work as a general practitioner.

In 1987 Jemison's application to NASA's astronaut-training program was accepted, and she was named the first African-American woman astronaut. After completing the one-year program, she worked as an astronaut officer representative at the Kennedy Space Center in Florida. In September 1992 Jemison became the first black woman in space when she flew as a payload specialist aboard the space shuttle *Endeavor*. During the seven-day flight, Jemison conducted experiments to determine the effects of zero gravity on humans and animals.

In March 1993 Jemison resigned from NASA in order to form her own company, the Jemison Group, which specializes in adapting technology for use in underdeveloped nations. Her historic spaceflight brought her much

Mae Jemison during a parachute training course (AP/Wide World Photos. Reproduced by permission)

fame. A 1993 television special focused on her life story, and *People* magazine named her one of the year's "50 Most Beautiful People in the World." Jemison once claimed that she was inspired to become an astronaut by the actress Nichelle Nichols, who portrayed the black Lieutenant Uhura on the original *Star Trek* television series.

Jemison received several awards throughout her career. In addition to running her company, she is a professor of environmental studies at Dartmouth College (Hanover, New Hampshire).

Jennings, Wilmer Angier

ARTIST
November 13, 1910–June 25, 1990

Artist Wilmer Jennings was born in Atlanta, Georgia. He graduated from Atlanta's **Morehouse College** in 1933 and later studied with the noted artist **Hale Woodruff**, painting in oils, experimenting with wood and steel engraving, and learning other printmaking techniques. Jennings worked for the federal Works Project Administration (a program to help people find employment during the **Great Depression**) in Atlanta, where he painted a mural for **Booker T. Washington** High School. During the 1930s Jennings's work was exhibited in New Jersey, Texas, Illinois, Maryland, and New York. In the 1940s Jennings moved to Providence, Rhode Island.

Jennings's wood engravings (a print made from a design cut into wood) and linocuts (a print made from a design cut into linoleum, a floor covering) are known for their rich textures and vigorous designs and the bold contrast created by their black and white elements. Jennings won the National Silversmith Award for designing jewelry and an honorary doctorate in 1978 from Rhode Island College. Works by Jennings were shown at the Newark (New Jersey) Museum's exhibition "Against the Odds" in 1990. His paintings and engravings are held by the Smithsonian Institution in Washington, D.C., the Newark Museum, the National Center for Afro-American Artists (Boston), and the Rhode Island School of Design.

Jet Magazine

Jet magazine is the leading African-American weekly news publication. By 1990, 8.7 million people were reading the magazine and it was distributed throughout the United States and in forty foreign countries.

Founded in 1951 by John H. Johnson, *Jet* was designed by Johnson Publishing Company to complement the popular magazine *Ebony*. The name of the magazine represents dark skin color (as in the expression "jet black") and a fast plane. It was designed to be a "speedy" source of black news. *Jet* is known for providing precise and to-the-point news. It is made for people on the run who want to get a quick glance at what is happening in the world and in the African-American community in particular.

Jim Crow

The term "Jim Crow" originally came from a popular minstrel show song from the early 1800s. Minstrel shows were performed by white entertainers who painted their faces black and pretended to be black people. The shows portrayed blacks as stereotyped (all alike) characters wearing loud-colored clothes and wide grins. Such performances helped to reinforce negative images of African Americans.

Abolitionists (people who fought to end slavery) began to use the term in the 1840s to describe separate accommodations and separate railroad cars for blacks and whites. Eventually, Jim Crow referred to the laws that were in effect in the southern United States from the 1880s until the early 1950s that made segregation (separation of blacks and whites) legal.

Prior to the **Civil War** (1861–65), although blacks were free in most parts of the northern United States, they were still treated unfairly and were segregated in all forms of transportation: they were excluded from cabins and dining rooms on steamboats, forced to ride on the outside of stage-coaches, and to travel in special Jim Crow coaches on trains. In the South, since the majority of blacks were slaves, there was no need for special laws to separate blacks and whites; it was a part of everyday life.

After the Civil War, segregation became less severe in the North, but in the South it was fully enforced. And in 1896, when the Supreme Court ruled in *Plessy v. Ferguson* that segregation was constitutional, laws were passed again and again in the South that reinforced segregation and discrimination. Signs were posted everywhere in the South that read "White Only" and "Colored." There were separate public parks, cemeteries, hospitals, public bathrooms, water fountains, telephone booths, and elevators. There were separate entrances and exits to theaters and movie houses. There were even separate textbooks for black and white children. Some of the laws encouraged not only separation, but exclusion. For example, many areas had only one public library, and blacks usually were not allowed.

These laws continued until the 1950s and 1960s, when a new generation of African Americans fought to gain equal rights. During this period many laws were passed that overturned the old segregation laws and ended Jim Crow. In 1954 *Brown v. Board of Education of Topeka, Kansas* ruled that public schools could not be segregated. *Brown* was followed by the Civil Rights Act of 1964, which prohibits discrimination based on color, race, religion, or place of origin; the Voting Rights Act of 1965, which ensures equal voting rights; and the Civil Rights Act of 1968, which covers fairness in housing.

Joans, Ted

POET, PAINTER, JAZZ MUSICIAN
July 4, 1928–

Poet Ted Joans was born in Illinois. Influenced by his father, a riverboat entertainer, Joans played the trumpet from an early age, developing a lifelong interest in **jazz.** In 1951 he received a degree in fine arts. Shortly afterward, he moved to New York City to study art. Joans quickly became a part of the arts community of Greenwich Village and set up a studio. Over the next few years, he became acquainted with a number of notable jazz musicians and with many poets. In 1958 Joans began giving public readings of his poetry, which integrated jazz rhythms, social protest, imagery (mental images), and satire (ridicule). In 1959 he published his first volume of poetry.

Joans soon became dissatisfied with the commercialism (emphasis on making money) that he felt had taken over the poetry scene. In 1961 he moved to Paris, France. After brief residences there and in Africa, Joans spent most of each year in Timbuktu, Mali (West Africa), with long seasonal visits to Europe and the United States. His later work shows the influence of African culture while maintaining ties to both jazz and surrealism (a movement in art that attempts to interpret the subconscious mind).

Joans has published over thirty collections of poems. He has also worked as an essayist and critic. In the 1990s he established a full-time residence in Paris.

John Brown's Raid at Harper's Ferry, Virginia

John Brown was an abolitionist who believed that **slavery** in America would come to an end only through warfare. As a result, he supported armed attacks against the South as a way to start a war that would force the South to abandon slavery. His last and most famous attack began and ended at the military armory (a place where weapons are stored) at Harper's Ferry, Virginia, in 1859.

Two years earlier, in 1857, Brown had begun raising money and making plans for his attack. He contacted many abolitionists, both black and white, for support, providing few details about his planned attack on Virginia. Many of the African Americans he contacted supported his cause but did not support his violent plans. Other African Americans did support a violent uprising against slavery but did not trust Brown (a white man) to carry it out.

By July 1859, however, Brown had raised enough money to buy weapons. He rented a farmhouse close to Harper's Ferry to serve as his headquarters, and by October he had gained the support of several African Americans. Too impatient to wait for additional help from black militia units in Ohio and Canada, Brown launched his attack on October 16.

After quickly seizing the armory, Brown stalled and waited. He expected that word of the uprising would attract nearby slaves to his cause. Instead, his inaction allowed the state of Virginia to organize a military response and alert President James Buchanan, who sent a group of Marines to end the rebellion. After only thirty-six hours, Brown was captured. Ten of his followers, including two of his sons, were killed.

Brown used his trial to publicize his cause. Newspapers across the country reported his courtroom speeches, winning him the admiration of thou-

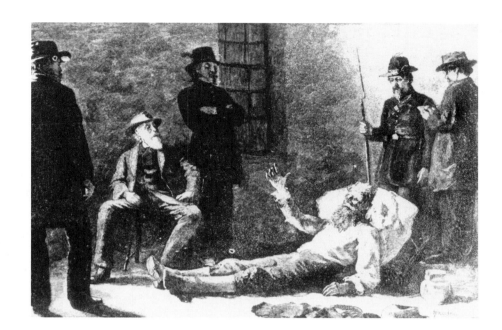

A depiction of John Brown following his capture at Harper's Ferry

sands. Even his bitterest enemies could not deny Brown's courage and devotion to his principles. Even though he was sentenced to execution, Brown succeeded in capturing the attention of the nation. Ralph Waldo Emerson, the famous poet and essayist, stated that Brown's death would "make the gallows glorious like the cross." Brown's attack also convinced most Americans that compromise on the issue of slavery was impossible. Although his raid failed miserably, Brown succeeded in focusing the nation's attention on slavery.

John Henry

John Henry is a legendary figure from the late 1800s. He is the central character in a folktale about the human cost of industrialization and African-American resistance to white control of workers. The legend may be based on events surrounding the construction of the Chesapeake & Ohio railroad in Summers County, West Virginia, in the 1870s.

In the legend, John Henry is an enormously strong black man who competes against a steam drill intended to replace workers. Wielding only a hammer, Henry drills holes along fifteen feet of granite, compared to the machine's nine feet, but the effort kills him.

The story has been told in song many times; some versions have different melodies and words. Among hundreds of recordings about John Henry, the first was done by country music pioneer Fiddlin' John Carson in 1924. The first recording by black musicians was by the Francis and Sowell duo in 1927. Other versions have been released by **"Leadbelly" Ledbetter, Paul Robeson, Odetta,** Mississippi John Hurt, and **Harry Belafonte,** among others.

EXCERPT FROM "JOHN HENRY"

De man dat invented de steam drill,
Thought he was mighty fine.
John Henry drove his fifteen feet,
An' de steam drill only made nine,
Lawd, Lawd, an' de steam drill only made nine.
De hammer dat John Henry swung',
It weighed over nine pound;
He broke a rib in his lef'-han' side,
An' his intrels fell on de groun',
Lawd, Lawd, an' his intrels fell on de groun'.

Johns, Vernon

MINISTER
1892–June 11, 1964

The minister Vernon Johns preached about political and social justice. Born and raised in Virginia, Johns ran away from home and traveled to Ohio, where he talked his way into a seminary graduate program despite not having a bachelor's degree. After graduating, Johns enrolled in the University of Chicago.

Johns left Chicago in the early 1920s and preached in black **Baptist** churches throughout the Midwest and the South. Toward the end of the decade he returned to Virginia and lectured in black schools and churches along the East coast. Johns became one of the most important African-American religious leaders encouraging Christians to work for social reform. But Johns's fame came primarily from his oral sermons. During **World War II** (1939–45) he became known as a scholar and an eccentric, dramatic speaker.

In 1940 Johns was recruited as minister of the Dexter Avenue Baptist Church in Montgomery, Alabama. He quickly took the opportunity to deliver his message of social justice. According to Johns, the Bible condemned segregation (separate public facilities for blacks and whites). Johns stirred controversy by calling whites "anti-Christian" and black ministers "elitist opportunists" (snobs looking out for opportunities to improve their social or economic interests). He helped local victims of racist violence press charges in court and carried out one-man protests against segregated buses and restaurants. Johns embarrassed a large part of the Dexter membership by selling farm produce in front of the church. He hoped to demonstrate that ministers had a duty to live like the common people and that black freedom could only be won through earnest, independent labor.

Johns's political and confrontational tactics created controversy in his church, and he resigned in 1952. He returned to Virginia, and Dexter Avenue Baptist later hired as minister the Reverend Dr. **Martin Luther King Jr.** (1929–1967), who considered himself a student of Johns's. Johns spent the rest of his life alternately tending to his farm, preaching, and lecturing. He

died in 1964 shortly after delivering a lecture. In 1994 the actor James Earl Jones (1931–) portrayed Johns in the television film *The Vernon Johns Story*.

Johnson, Earvin Jr. "Magic"

BASKETBALL PLAYER
August 14, 1959–

Earvin Johnson Jr., best known as "Magic" Johnson, was one of the best **basketball** players in the history of the game. On the court he was known for his agility, quick thinking, and scoring ability. Off the court he is known for his lovable personality and business sense.

Born in Lansing, Michigan, Johnson showed extraordinary athletic promise at a young age. Although he would later dominate games with apparent ease, he devoted tremendous energy to learning the fundamentals of basketball. He led his high school team to a state championship, and in college at Michigan State University he led the Spartans to a national championship. In 1979 Johnson left college to play for the Los Angeles Lakers; he led the team to five National Basketball Association (NBA) championships in the 1980s. Johnson was both an individual and team player, holding the record for most assists (9,921) and winning the Most Valuable Player award three times during his career (1980, 1982, and 1987). In 1992 Johnson came out of retirement to help the United States win an Olympic gold medal. Johnson's dazzling play and endearing personality contributed to the success of the NBA as well as the Lakers.

Johnson retired from basketball in 1991, at which point he revealed the news that he had contracted the virus that causes AIDS (acquired immune deficiency syndrome). However, with his positive outlook and tireless work ethic, he began fund-raising programs and generating awareness of the disease. He was appointed to the President's National Commission on AIDS, but he resigned shortly afterward because he did not believe the government was doing enough to advance AIDS research. He then established the Magic Johnson Foundation, an organization devoted to the fight against AIDS, and published a book called *What You Can Do to Avoid AIDS*. In addition to his work on health issues, Johnson has encouraged business development in inner-city neighborhoods.

In 1997 Johnson started a television talk show, but the show was not successful. Johnson has become a living example that one can continue to live a full, active life while suffering from the AIDS virus. In July 2000 he unveiled the Magic Johnson AIDS Clinic in Oakland, California, which is open to anyone suffering from the disease.

Johnson, James Weldon

SONGWRITER, WRITER, POLITICAL LEADER
June 17, 1871–June 26, 1938

James Weldon Johnson was an influential writer and political activist whose poetic voice fueled the movement for racial equality. Johnson argued for a distinctive African-American creative expression generated by both professional black artists and blacks engaged in everyday work pursuits. He believed this cultural identity was necessary to achieve social progress for African Americans. Johnson is known for writing the lyrics to what is considered the Negro National Anthem ("Lift Every Voice and Sing")

Born in Jacksonville, Florida, Johnson was the son of hardworking parents who valued education. He developed his love of knowledge through reading in his father's private library and through his mother's teaching. He graduated from **Atlanta University** (1894) in Georgia, an all-black college that stressed to students the importance of helping other blacks. After graduating, he returned to Florida, where he became the principal for the largest school for African Americans. In 1902 Johnson moved to New York with his brother and began writing songs. The songwriting team they created with Robert Cole became the most successful in the country at that time.

Johnson then decided to get involved in New York City politics. He became the treasurer of the Colored Republican Club, for which he was rewarded with a consular position by the Republican Party. He served as consul (U.S. representative) to Venezuela and Nicaragua.

The election of Democratic president Woodrow Wilson (1856–1924) in 1914 brought an end to his consular activities, after which he got involved with the **National Association for the Advancement of Colored People (NAACP)**. His work with the NAACP led to the creation of an anti-**lynching** law and established the NAACP as a powerful force in the fight for racial equality. In 1930 Johnson began a teaching career at **Fisk University** in Nashville, Tennessee, and continued to work on his literary career before a car accident took his life in 1935.

Johnson, John Arthur "Jack"

BOXER
March 31, 1878–June 10, 1946

Jack Johnson was the first African-American boxer to win the World Heavyweight **Boxing** Championship, a title he held from 1908 to 1915. Disliked by many whites of his day but a hero to many blacks, Johnson was inducted into the Boxing Hall of Fame in 1954.

Jack Johnson was born in 1878 in Galveston, Texas, to Henry and Tiny Johnson. After holding a series of jobs, including janitor and cotton picker, he turned to fighting. These early fights, called "battle royals," were fierce and bloody competitions. The last fighter standing received only a few coins. In 1897, at age nineteen, Johnson became a professional fighter. Six feet tall and weighing two hundred pounds, he was known as a powerful defensive boxer with quickness, style, and grace.

Johnson's first fights as a professional were mostly against other African Americans. In 1903 he became champion of the unofficial Negro heavyweight division. Johnson then turned his sights to winning the official world championship, even though blacks were not allowed to participate in the competition at that time.

JOHNSON PUSHES THE COLOR BARRIER

Jack Johnson further pushed the color barrier by marrying three white women during the early 1900s; his first marriage took place in 1911. In some states at that time, it was against the law for two people of different races to marry. Whether it was against the law or not, a marriage between a black person and a white person was considered "taboo" (unacceptable in society). It was especially unacceptable for black men to marry white women. The federal government charged Johnson with violating the Mann Act (1910), also called the "white-slavery act," which forbade taking white women across state lines for "unlawful purposes." The law was seldom enforced, but the federal government chose to prosecute Johnson, even though he was not involved in procuring. He was only guilty of flaunting his relationships with white woman. Johnson was convicted in 1913 and fled to Canada and then to Europe, South America, and Mexico to avoid serving a prison sentence. In 1920 he returned to the United States and served one year in prison.

In 1908 a promoter arranged a match between Johnson and world champion Tommy Burns in Australia. The fight was so violent that the police stopped the fight in the fourteenth round and Johnson was declared the winner, the first black boxer to win a world heavyweight championship. After the fight, journalists began calling Johnson "a huge primordial ape." This prompted a search for "the Great White Hope," a fighter who would restore the championship to whites.

In 1910 Johnson fought and defeated former world champion Jim Jeffries. This started a wave of racial violence, as gangs of whites and blacks fought in cities across the United States. News writers called boxing a vicious sport; many people wanted to see it banned.

After Johnson lost the heavyweight title to challenger Jess Willard in Havana, Cuba, in 1915, no African American was given a chance to fight for the title again until **Joe Louis** (1914–1981) in 1937. After his defeat, Johnson continued to fight periodically, gave exhibitions, trained and managed fighters, and lectured. He died in an automobile accident in North Carolina in 1946.

Johnson's **autobiography**, *Jack Johnson: In the Ring and Out*, first appeared in 1927. A new edition, with new material, was published in 1969. Howard Sackler's play *The Great White Hope* (1969) tells the story of Johnson's life. It was made into a movie in 1971.

Johnson, Joshua

PORTRAIT PAINTER

c. 1765–c. 1830

Little is known about the early life of portrait painter Joshua Johnson. Johnson's name first appeared in Baltimore, Maryland, city records in the 1790s. During the late eighteenth and early nineteenth centuries, Baltimore was home to a vibrant community of **free blacks** and wealthy abolitionists (those who worked to end **slavery**), a situation that surely favored Johnson's early career. Nonetheless, in 1798 Johnson claimed he "experienced many obstacles in his studies."

Johnson described himself as an amateur, part-time portrait painter. His portrait subjects included members of the working and middle classes, but he is best known for his depictions of well-to-do Baltimore families and children, whom he painted on gracefully curved sofas and chairs, with domestic objects like pet dogs, red shoes, coral jewelry, and white dresses.

Only two Johnson paintings of African Americans have been identified. One of these, *Portrait of Daniel Coker* (1805–10), is considered Johnson's most important work and portrays the prominent black Methodist and advocate of African immigration.

Johnson used a restrained painting style, and his works have a silvery quality that captures the light of Baltimore's seaport. He applied paint thinly, focusing with a fine line on costume, facial features, hair, and props. In his later works Johnson was especially skilled at portraying human relationships through his subjects' poses and gestures.

Johnson may have died after 1824, since that is the last year he appears in Baltimore municipal records; no date of death or burial records have been found. He was married twice and had several children. Johnson's achievements came to wider public attention during the 1940s with the publication of a series of articles about the artist. By the 1990s more than eighty paintings had been credited to him. (*See also*: **painting and sculpture**)

Johnson, Magic. *See* Johnson, Earvin

Johnson, Robert Leroy

BLUES GUITARIST, SINGER
May 8, c. 1911–August 16, 1938

The year of Robert Johnson's birth in Hazelhurst, Mississippi, is uncertain. He grew up in the upper Mississippi Delta, and in the mid-1920s he studied guitar and learned about music with Delta bluesmen such as Willie Brown, Charley Patton, and Son House. In 1929 Johnson married Virginia Travis. She died the next year, and in 1931 Johnson married Calletta Craft. By the early 1930s Johnson was performing professionally at parties, juke joints (small rural clubs), and nightclubs. He spent most of the rest of his life traveling and performing. During visits to Texas in 1936 and 1937, he made his only recordings—twenty-nine songs in all.

During his lifetime Johnson's career was surrounded by an aura of danger and wickedness. His superiority as a singer and guitarist, combined with powerful appetites for alcohol, sex, and fighting, caused a story to circulate that one night, at a lonely Delta crossroads, he had sold his soul to the devil. The myth was fueled by the mysterious circumstances of his death; while uncertain, most biographers generally agree that he was poisoned by the jealous husband of a woman he had met at a party in Mississippi.

After his death Johnson came to be called "the king of the Delta **blues**." In his lifetime Johnson's influence came largely through the musicians who heard him and adopted parts of his unusual style—some elements, such as the "walking" bass line, became standard blues features. His songs contained observations about life and travel in the Delta ("Ramblin' on My Mind"), as well as haunting visions of loneliness and almost supernatural emotional torment ("Hellhound on My Trail").

Johnson was "rediscovered" in the 1960s, and his songs became standards of 1960s rock and roll. The 1990 release *Robert Johnson: The Complete Recordings* was a huge success.

Johnson, William Julius "Judy"

BASEBALL PLAYER
October 26, 1899–June 15, 1989

William Julius "Judy" Johnson is considered by many to be the best black third baseman in the history of **baseball**. He was known for having a powerful throwing arm and excellent fielding abilities. Although records of Negro league play are scarce, those that exist indicate that Johnson was also an outstanding batter. Born in Wilmington, Delaware, Johnson was the son of a seaman. He played on three different teams during his eighteen years in the Negro leagues. At the peak of his career Johnson was a player and manager for the Homestead Grays (Pittsburgh, Pennsylvania, and Washington, D.C.) in 1930 and played for what may have been the greatest Negro league team ever, the Pittsburgh Crawfords. Later in life, he worked as a scout for major league teams. Johnson was inducted into the Baseball Hall of Fame in 1975.

Jones, Absalom

MINISTER, COMMUNITY LEADER
1746–1818

Absalom Jones made important contributions to black community building when the first urban free black communities of the United States were taking form. Born a slave in Delaware, Jones was taken from the fields into his master's house as a young boy and began his education. When his master moved to Philadelphia, Pennsylvania, in 1762, Jones worked in his master's store but continued his education in a night school for blacks. In 1770 he married, and he was able to buy his wife's freedom in about 1778 and his own in 1784.

Jones rapidly became one of the main leaders of the growing free black community in Philadelphia. He began to discuss a separate black religious society with other prominent black Methodists such as **Richard Allen** (1760–1831). They formed the Free African Society of Philadelphia, probably the first independent black organization in the United States. The Free African Society was partly religious; beyond that, it was an organization where people emerging from slavery could gather strength, develop their own leaders, and begin living a free life.

Jones then established the African Church of Philadelphia, the first independent black church in North America. It was designed as a racially separate, nondenominational (open to people of all religious backgrounds), and socially oriented church. Jones became its minister when it opened in 1794 and served until his death in 1818. In his first sermon Jones put out the call to his fellow African Americans to "arise out of the dust and shake ourselves, and throw off that fear, thatoppression and bondage trained us up in." Jones's church became a center of social and political as well as religious activities, and a fortress from which to struggle against white racial hostility.

Jones became a leading educator and reformer in the black community. In 1797 he helped organize the first petition of African Americans against **slavery,** the **slave trade,** and the federal Fugitive Slave Law of 1793. Three years later, he organized another petition to President Thomas Jefferson (1743–1826) and the Congress against slavery and the slave trade. He was responsible in 1808 for informally establishing January 1 (the date on which the slave trade ended) as a day of thanksgiving and celebration.

Jones functioned far beyond his pulpit. Teaching in schools established by the Pennsylvania Abolition Society and by his church, he helped train a generation of black youths in Philadelphia. He struggled to advance the self-respect and enhance the skills of the North's largest free African-American community. He would long be remembered for his ministry among the generation emerging from slavery.

Jones, Bill T.

DANCER, CHOREOGRAPHER
February 15, 1952–

Dancer and choreographer Bill Jones was born and raised in rural Steuben County in upstate New York. He began his dance training at the State University of New York (SUNY) at Binghamton, where he was a theater major on an athletic scholarship. After living briefly in Amsterdam, the Netherlands, Jones returned to SUNY in 1973, where he and Lois Welk formed the American Dance Asylum.

Two years earlier, Jones had met his long-time partner and companion Arnie Zane. The two choreographed (created dance routines) and performed innovative solos and duos in the 1970s, often using openly gay choreography. In 1982 they founded Bill T. Jones/Arnie Zane and Company.

A tall, powerful dancer, Jones was considered an outstanding soloist and often mixed video, text, and autobiographical material with his choreography. Jones and Zane gained recognition as choreographers with large-scale, abstract dance pieces that used contemporary sets, costumes, and body painting to dramatic effect. Their works were performed in such well-known places as the Brooklyn Academy of Music and New York's City Center theater.

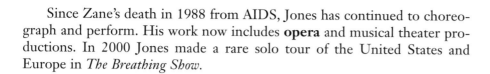

Since Zane's death in 1988 from AIDS, Jones has continued to choreograph and perform. His work now includes **opera** and musical theater productions. In 2000 Jones made a rare solo tour of the United States and Europe in *The Breathing Show*.

Jones, Gayl

NOVELIST, POET, CRITIC
November 29, 1949–

Born in Lexington, Kentucky, Gayl Jones grew up listening to the African-American oral tradition that is prominent in her narratives. Jones received several prizes for poetry while an English major at Connecticut College, and she went on to study creative writing at Brown University (Providence, Rhode Island). Later, while teaching creative writing and African-American literature at the University of Michigan, Jones met her future husband, Bob Higgins, and became involved in an apparently troubled relationship that would come to play a devastating role in her life.

All of Jones's early novels, including the celebrated *Corregidora*, (1975) are disturbing accounts of black women ruined by sexual and racial exploitation. Beginning in the 1980s, Jones published poetic volumes presenting the history of blacks in the New World, while still focusing on the suffering of black women. In 1983, when Bob was arrested on a weapons charge, Jones resigned from the university and fled with him to Europe, where they lived before returning to Lexington. For a period of fifteen years, family members believe she was trapped in an emotionally abusive relationship with a disturbed man, and it was twenty years after the publication of her first novel before she published her second. Her career was dramatically revived in 1998 with *The Healing*, a sweet and engaging book that she claimed to be a rejection of her earlier work. The novel was nominated for a National Book Award.

Not long after *The Healing* was published, Jones was involved in a bizarre and tragic event—the suicide of her husband—who had barricaded himself and Jones into their apartment as the police approached to arrest him on the old weapons charge. After recovering from his death, Jones set to work on her next novel, *Mosquito*, which was published in 1999.

Jones, James Earl

ACTOR
January 17, 1931–

James Earl Jones, an actor renowned for his broad, powerful voice and acting range, was born in Arkabutla, Mississippi. He was raised by his grandparents, who moved to Michigan when Jones was five. Soon afterward, Jones developed a bad stutter and remained largely speechless for the following eight years. When he was fourteen, a high school English teacher had him read aloud a poem he had written, and Jones gradually regained the use of his voice. He subsequently starred on the school's debating team.

In 1949 Jones entered the University of Michigan as a premedical student but soon switched to acting, receiving his bachelor's degree in 1953. Two years later, he moved to New York City and studied at the American Theater Wing. Jones first became well known in the early 1960s when he became a member of Joseph Papp's New York Shakespeare Festival.

In 1967 Jones received his first widespread critical and public recognition when he was cast as a boxer in the play *The Great White Hope*. He also starred in the 1970 film based on the play and was nominated that year for an Oscar. During the 1970s Jones appeared in a variety of stage and screen roles. He also provided the voice of Darth Vader in *Star Wars* (1977) and its sequels. In 1977 Jones appeared on Broadway in a one-man show in which he portrayed singer-activist **Paul Robeson.** The play's Broadway run and subsequent appearance on public television served to revive public interest in Robeson's life and career.

During the 1980s and 1990s Jones continued to act in various media. On stage, he starred in several dramatic plays. He also appeared in more than thirty films during this period.

Jones also has had considerable experience in television. In 1965 his role on *As the World Turns* made him one of the first African Americans to regularly appear in a daytime drama. In 1973 he hosted the variety series *Black Omnibus*. Jones played author **Alex Haley** in the television miniseries *Roots: The Next Generations* in 1978. He also has starred in two short-lived dramatic series, *Paris* (1979-80) and *Gabriel's Fire* (1990-1992), for which he won an Emmy in 1990. In 1993 Jones published a memoir, *Voices and Silences*.

Throughout his career, Jones's distinctive voice has made him a favorite spokesperson for several companies and products. In 2000, in his role as spokesperson for Bell Atlantic Yellow Pages, Jones participated in several literacy events sponsored by the company.

Jones, LeRoi. *See* Baraka, Imamu Amiri

Jones, Lois Mailou

PAINTER, DESIGNER
November 3, 1905–June 9, 1998

Born and raised in Boston, Lois Jones studied art from childhood and trained at the School of the Museum of Fine Arts of Boston. As a professor in the **Howard University** (Washington, D.C.) art department in 1930, she taught several generations of artists until her retirement in 1977.

Initially trained as a textile designer, Jones produced many works of art. Wishing to receive further recognition, she studied landscape **painting** in Paris, France, in 1937–38. During the 1940s she painted scenes of black life, both ordinary and striking. In the 1950s, visits to her husband's homeland of Haiti influenced her painting with vibrant colors and abstract (symbolic) shapes. After a trip to Africa in the 1960s, Jones developed a distinctive style that combined her strong sense of design with images of African people, art,

and culture. Lois Mailou Jones's work reveals her natural, inborn responsiveness to changing times and places.

Jones has shown her work in numerous exhibitions in the United States, France, and Haiti. Her work is represented in collections in all three countries. She has been decorated by the government of Haiti and received honorary doctorates from the Massachusetts College of Art and Howard University. Jones died on June 9, 1998.

Jones, M. Sissieretta "Black Patti"

SINGER
January 5, 1869–June 24, 1933

M. Sissieretta Jones was born in Virginia and in 1876 moved to Rhode Island, where she began formal music training. She studied voice at the Providence Academy of Music and the New England Conservatory of Music and took private lessons. Her public debut occurred on April 5, 1888, at Steinway Hall, New York. In July 1888 she embarked on a six-month tour of the West Indies with the Tennessee Jubilee Singers. On that tour she acquired the name "Black Patti" (taken from the name of Spanish soprano Adelina Patti), which she kept for the rest of her career.

Jones sang as a soloist from 1890 to 1895 in the United States, Canada, the West Indies, and Europe. She attracted considerable national attention from well-publicized performances. Her career as a soloist ended abruptly in 1896 when she became the leading soprano of Black Patti's Troubadours, a newly organized company. The company's performances combined elements of vaudeville shows, including song and dance, skits, and comedy acts. It also featured a special finale that starred Jones with a supporting cast of soloists, chorus, and orchestra performing staged scenes from operas and musical comedies.

Jones enjoyed celebrity status at a time when most blacks with classical training found professional opportunities limited in American music because of racial prejudices. Endowed with a natural voice of phenomenal range and power, she brought musicality, artistry, and dramatic flair to the stage. Her repertory included classical songs, sentimental ballads, popular tunes, and roles in such operas as *Carmen* and *Lucia di Lammermoor*.

Jones, Quincy Delight Jr. "Q"

MUSIC PRODUCER, COMPOSER
March 14, 1933–

Born in Chicago, Illinois, Quincy Jones learned to play trumpet in the public schools of the Seattle, Washington, area, where his family had moved in 1945. Jones sang in church groups from an early age and wrote his first composition at the age of sixteen. While in high school he played trumpet in **rhythm-and-blues** groups with his friend **Ray Charles.** After graduating from high school, Jones attended Seattle University, and then Berklee School of Music in Boston.

In 1951 Jones was hired by **Lionel Hampton** and toured Europe, soloing on the band's recording of his own composition, "Kingfish" (1951). After leaving Hampton in 1953, Jones turned to studio composing and arranging, and also led his own big bands on albums such as *This Is How I Feel About Jazz* (1956). In 1956 Jones helped **jazz** trumpeter **Dizzy Gillespie** organize his first state department big band, then worked as the music director for Barclay Records in Paris, France, until 1960.

After returning to the United States, Jones began working as a producer at Mercury Records in 1961, becoming Mercury's first African-American vice president in 1964. That year he scored and conducted an album for Frank Sinatra and **Count Basie,** *It Might As Well Be Swing.* Jones also branched into concert music with his *Black Requiem,* a work for orchestra (1971). Jones was the first African-American **film** composer to be widely accepted in Hollywood, and he scored dozens of films such as *The Pawnbroker* and *In Cold Blood.*

In 1974, shortly after recording *Body Heat,* Jones suffered a cerebral stroke. He underwent brain surgery, and after recovering he formed his own record company, Qwest Productions. Throughout the 1970s Jones remained in demand as an arranger and composer. He wrote or arranged music for **television** shows such as *The Bill Cosby Show* and *Sanford and Son,* and for films (*The Wiz,* 1978). In 1985 he co-produced and wrote the music for the film *The Color Purple* and served as executive music producer for **Sidney Poitier**'s film *Fast Forward* (1985). Collaborations with **Michael Jackson** on *Off The Wall* (1979) and *Thriller* (1984) resulted in two of the most popular albums of all time. In 1985 Jones conceived USA for Africa, a famine-relief organization that produced the album and video *We Are The World* (1985).

By 1994, with twenty-two Grammy Awards to his credit, Jones was the most honored popular musician in the history of the awards. He also had enormous artistic and financial power and influence in the entertainment industry and was a masterful discoverer of new talent. In 1990 his album *Back on the Block,* which included **Miles Davis** and **Ella Fitzgerald** in addition to younger African-American musicians such as Ice-T and Kool Moe Dee, won six Grammy Awards. He also produced the hit television series *Fresh Prince of Bel Air,* which began in 1990.

Joplin, Scott

RAGTIME COMPOSER
c. 1867/68–April 1, 1917

Widely known as "the king of ragtime composers," Scott Joplin is honored for his piano "rags," even though he also aspired to be a classical composer and wrote two operas, a symphony, and a musical. "Rags" are pieces in the musical style **ragtime,** which uses a rhythm called "syncopation" for an uneven, ragged effect.

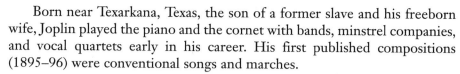

Born near Texarkana, Texas, the son of a former slave and his freeborn wife, Joplin played the piano and the cornet with bands, minstrel companies, and vocal quartets early in his career. His first published compositions (1895–96) were conventional songs and marches.

In 1894 Joplin settled in Sedalia, Missouri, where he attended George R. Smith College. His "Maple Leaf Rag" (1899), inspired by a black social club in Sedalia, became the most popular piano rag of the era, making him famous by 1901. He moved to St. Louis, Missouri, where he worked as a composer, and in 1903 he formed a company to stage his first opera, *A Guest of Honor*. Joplin spent all of his money on the unsuccessful **opera** tour and then returned to composing piano rags.

Joplin moved to New York City in 1907 and found that major music publishers were eager to publish his rags. Altogether, Joplin had fifty-two piano pieces published; forty-two are rags. He also had twelve songs and an instructional piece published. Joplin self-published his second opera, *Treemonisha*, in 1911. Several other songs and rags, a symphony, his first opera, a musical, and a variety-show piece were never published and are now lost.

Joplin never succeeded in producing *Treemonisha* for the stage. Its first full performance was held in 1972 in Atlanta, Georgia. In 1975 the opera was performed on Broadway in New York City. In *Treemonisha* Joplin expressed the view that African Americans could overcome many of their racial problems through education.

A Scott Joplin revival began in the 1970s when Nonesuch Records issued a recording of Joplin's rags played by classical pianist Joshua Rifkin (1944–). In 1971 the New York Public Library issued the *Collected Works of Scott Joplin*, and afterward classical concert artists began including Joplin's music in their recitals.

In 1974 the award-winning film *The Sting* featured several of Joplin's rags, with his piece "The Entertainer" (1902) as the movie's theme song. It became one of the most popular pieces of the mid-1970s.

Joplin was honored posthumously (after death) in 1976 with a Pulitzer Special Award for his contribution to American music. In 1983 a Scott Joplin U.S. postage stamp was issued.

Jordan, Barbara Charline

CONGRESSWOMAN, PROFESSOR
February 21, 1936–January 17, 1996

Barbara Jordan was the first African-American woman to be elected to the U.S. House of Representatives and one of the most influential women in U.S. history. In addition to her many political achievements, she was known for her respect and devotion to the U.S. Constitution.

Born in Houston, Texas, Jordan spent her childhood in that state and earned a bachelor's degree from Texas Southern University (1956) and a law degree from Boston University (1959). In 1966 Jordan became the first black

An African-American FIRST

In 1972 Barbara Jordan became the first female African American to serve in Congress. Her election to Congress was greatly attributed to congressional redistricting, which allowed more blacks to vote. Before the Civil Rights movement, many districts in the South had been drawn to keep black populations from obtaining a majority in any one area, which prevented blacks from becoming elected to public office. When districts began to be drawn more fairly, it opened the door for many African Americans to obtain political positions.

Barbara Jordan giving a speech (AP/Wide World Photos. Reproduced by permission)

since 1883 to be elected to the Texas senate. Her election was helped by a series of black voter registration drives. At the time, few blacks bothered to register to vote because measures such as the poll tax and literacy tests prevented them from casting their ballots. However, the reforms of the **Civil Rights movement** eliminated many of the formal and informal obstacles to black voting. In 1967 Jordan became the first female president of the Texas senate, and in 1972 she was elected to the U.S. House of Representatives.

Jordan enjoyed a prestigious career in Congress, beginning with her election to the House Judiciary Committee, where she voted to impeach President Richard Nixon during the Watergate scandal. Jordan was a gifted speaker and during the Watergate hearings used her ability to convey to the public the importance of protecting the Constitution. While in Congress she spoke out against the **Vietnam War** (1959–75) and increasing the U.S. military budget. She also supported environmental reform and advanced programs designed to help people in need. Despite her achievements in Congress, Jordan believed she could make more of an impact through other activities. She left Congress in 1978 and became a professor, holding the prestigious Lyndon B. Johnson Centennial Chair in Public Policy at the University of Texas.

In 1992, confined to a wheelchair because of multiple sclerosis, Jordan gave a speech at the Democratic National Convention that moved many in the large crowd. In 1996 she received the Presidential Medal of Freedom for her lifetime commitment to public service. She died in 1996.

Jordan, June

WRITER
July 9, 1936–

Born in Harlem, New York, to Jamaican immigrants, June Jordan grew up in Brooklyn. In her family, literature was important, and by age seven she was writing poetry. She attended an exclusive white high school and went to Barnard College (New York City) in 1953, both of which she found to be alienating experiences. Jordan married in 1955, had a son, and divorced in 1965. A single working mother, she took part in and wrote about African-American political movements in New York. Her first book-length publication, *Who Look at Me* (1969), her poems in *Some Changes* (1971), and her later works clearly show her belief that politics directly affect individuals— and that poetry is political action.

Jordan's writing workshop for children in Brooklyn in 1965 resulted in the collection *Voice of the Children* (1970) and hinted at the many books for children she would publish throughout her career. In 1964 she worked with famed architect Buckminster Fuller to create an urban design for Harlem, which won an international prize in 1970, a year she spent in Rome and Greece.

Jordan's reflections on her mother's suicide in 1966 are the origin of many of the black feminist poems she wrote throughout the 1970s and 1980s, gradually widening her vision to include oppression in politically troubled areas of the world, such as South Africa. She also began to write

Michael Jordan, holding his MVP trophy, and Chicago Bulls coach Phil Jackson, holding the NBA championship trophy; Jordan helped lead the team to a record three consecutive championships (Archive Photos. Reproduced by permission)

plays during the 1980s, became a regular magazine columnist, and in 1991 launched a program known as "Poetry for the People," which encourages poetry as a way to educate children about other cultures. Her first attempt at writing an opera, *I Was Looking at the Ceiling and Then I Saw the Sky*, about the political troubles in early 1990s Los Angeles, California, was produced in New York in 1995. She continued to write several volumes of protest poetry throughout the 1990s, and in 2000 her memoir *Soldier: A Poet's Childhood* was published.

Jordan, Michael Jeffrey

BASKETBALL PLAYER
February 17, 1963–

Michael Jordan is widely considered to be one of the most exciting—and gifted—**basketball** players in history. On the court, Jordan was known for his ability to take command of a game, propelling his team to victory through his skill and leadership. Off the court, Jordan became an ambassador for the game of basketball and a beloved role model for millions of young athletes.

Born in Brooklyn, New York, Jordan grew up in North Carolina, where his talents went undiscovered for some time. Jordan attended the University of North Carolina (UNC), where his basketball skills began to emerge. Jordan first achieved wide recognition when he made the winning shot that brought UNC its first national championship in twenty-five years. After leading the 1984 Olympic team to a gold medal, he entered the National Basketball Association (NBA) as a first-round draft pick of the Chicago Bulls.

At the time Jordan joined the Bulls, the team could barely compete in the NBA. Jordan made an immediate impact, winning the NBA's Rookie of the

MICHAEL JORDAN'S BRIEF BASEBALL CAREER

In October 1993, to the dismay of his fans, Jordan announced a premature retirement. He indicated in a nationally televised news conference that he had lost his love for the game of basketball and was mentally exhausted from the pressures of being a celebrity. In addition, Jordan's life was shaken by the murder of his father in a car-theft incident. Jordan turned to baseball in an apparent effort to escape the pressures that came along with being a celebrity of enormous stature. He signed with the Chicago White Sox in 1994 and threw himself into batting and fielding practice. However, the sport turned out to be a poor match for his talents, and, to the delight of his fans, he returned to basketball in 1995.

Year award his first year on the team. Jordan began turning the Bulls around with his extraordinary offensive and defensive play. In 1987, he won the first of six successive scoring titles averaging 37.1 points per game, and became the first player to win the Most Valuable Player and Defensive Player of the Year awards in the same season (1987-1988). In addition to becoming one of the most popular athletes in the world, Jordan became a marketing wonder. His radiant smile and endearing personality led to multimillion-dollar endorsements from Nike, McDonald's, Quaker Oats (Gatorade), and General Mills (Wheaties). He complemented his commercial success with the popular animated film *Space Jam* (1996), which marked his acting debut.

Although Jordan was criticized by some for being too individualistic, he responded to his critics by leading the Bulls to three consecutive NBA championships (1990-93). After retiring from basketball for two years, Jordan returned to the Bulls and led them to championships in 1996, 1997, and 1998. Among his several achievements, Jordan finished his career third on the NBA's all-time scoring list (29,277 points) and first in scoring average (31.5 points per game), with six championships and two Olympic gold medals. In 1999 Jordan announced his second and final retirement, having accomplished everything he set out to accomplish as a player. After his retirement Jordan entered into various business ventures, concentrated on his golf game, and devoted more time to his family. Jordan is an exceptional golfer and has become friends with golfing superstar **Tiger Woods**. In early 2000 Jordan got reinvolved with basketball, becoming the director of basketball operations with the Washington Wizards.

Jordan, Vernon Eulion Jr.

LAWYER, CIVIL RIGHTS LEADER
August 8, 1935–

Vernon Jordan Jr. is a civil rights leader and prominent attorney who nearly lost his life fighting for racial equality. He is perhaps best known for being one of President Bill Clinton's (1993–2001) closest friends, testifying on behalf of the president during a grand jury investigation for improper conduct.

Born in Atlanta, Georgia, Jordan lived his first thirteen years in university housing projects. He earned a bachelor's degree from DePauw University (Greencastle, Indiana) in 1957 and a law degree from **Howard University** (Washington, D.C.) in 1960. In 1961 he practiced law with a civil rights firm, helping to open the University of Georgia's doors to African Americans. In 1970 he was named executive director for the United Negro College Fund, for which he conducted highly successful fund-raising programs. Jordan was later hired as the executive director for the **National Urban League**, whose budget he doubled with his fund-raising activities.

On May 29, 1980, Jordan was the target of a racial attack. After making a speech in Fort Wayne, Indiana, he was shot in the back by a sniper. After spending more than ninety days in the hospital, Jordan fully recovered. By the time of his trial for shooting Jordan, however, his attacker was already serving four consecutive life sentences for the earlier murder of two black joggers.

After the murder attempt, Jordan resigned from the Urban League and began practicing law in Washington, D.C. Throughout the 1980s he served as a lobbyist (representative) for corporations and foundation boards. Although he was accused of forsaking the black struggle for personal advantage, his supporters point to his contributions to the passage of the 1991 Civil Rights Act. In 1998 Jordan came to President Bill Clinton's defense in the highly publicized grand jury investigation that unveiled Clinton's relationship with a White House intern. In early 2000 Jordan began working as an investment banker for the prestigious Washington, D.C., firm Lazard Freres & Company.

Joyner-Kersee, Jacqueline "Jackie" ▪▪▪

TRACK AND FIELD ATHLETE
March 3, 1962–

Jacqueline "Jackie" Joyner-Kersee is an athletic superstar. She is known for her tremendous Olympic achievements and being an inspiration for young athletes.

Born in East Saint Louis, Missouri, Joyner-Kersee showed athletic promise at an early age, entering **track-and-field** competitions at the age of nine. Five years later she won four junior pentathlon (an athletic competition with five different events) championships. In high school her athleticism and disciplined study habits earned her a **basketball** scholarship to the University of California at Los Angeles (UCLA). She played basketball all four years in college and continued entering track and field events. After winning the National Collegiate Athletic Association (NCAA) heptathlon (an athletic competition with seven different events) titles (1982 and 1983) she won a silver medal in the 1984 Olympics for the same event.

In 1986 Joyner-Kersee shattered the world record for the heptathlon event by two hundred points, scoring 7,148 (each event in the competition

One of the greatest athletes of all time, Jackie Joyner-Kersee competes in a hurdling event (AP/Wide World Photos. Reproduced by permission)

is worth a certain point value). A year later Joyner-Kersee became the first woman to win gold medals in multi-sport and individual events at the Olympic level. Throughout the 1990s she continued to dominate the heptathlon event in Olympic competitions. Joyner-Kersee established a foundation to help young athletes realize their dreams of becoming Olympic champions. In July of 2000 Joyner-Kersee tried out for her fifth Olympic appearance at the age of thirty-eight. She failed to qualify for the long-jump event.

Julian, Percy Lavon

CHEMIST
April 11, 1899–April 21, 1975

Percy L. Julian was born in Alabama to parents who stressed academic achievement. He attended the private State Normal School for Negroes in Montgomery. Julian was admitted to DePauw University in Indiana and graduated at the head of his class.

DePauw usually awarded fellowships (or financial assistance) for chemistry students planning to pursue a Ph.D. degree. After all of his classmates

received graduate fellowships, Julian became concerned. The department head informed him that because of his race no graduate school had granted him a fellowship. Left with few options Julian took a position as a chemistry teacher at **Fisk University** in Nashville, Tennessee.

After two years at Fisk, Julian received an Austin Fellowship to attend Harvard University, where he earned a master's degree. He then taught at West Virginia State College for Negroes and later at **Howard University** (Washington, D.C.). He received a fellowship to pursue his Ph.D. at the University of Vienna in Austria. After earning his doctorate, Julian taught at Howard and DePauw. At DePauw he became internationally known for his research on the structure and synthesis of physostigmine, a drug used in the treatment of glaucoma (an eye disease).

Julian was offered a research position at the Institute of Paper Chemistry in Appleton, Wisconsin, until company officials discovered that the city had an old law prohibiting the housing of an African American overnight. Fortunately, the vice president of the Glidden Company (Chicago, Illinois)—also the president of the Institute of Paper Chemistry—heard of the incident and offered Julian the position of chief chemist and director of research at the company. Julian joined the staff of Glidden in 1936. It was a turning point in the hiring of African-American scientists in U.S. industry, and it opened opportunities for other talented African-American scientists who had been denied employment because of their race.

At Glidden, Julian developed a new process for isolating and commercially preparing soybean protein to be used in coating and sizing paper (filling in pores and applying a protective coating to the paper), in cold-water paints, and in textile sizing. This new process was cheaper than the existing one, and of equal quality. It was a huge commercial success for Glidden.

In 1953 Julian founded his own companies in Chicago and Mexico City. These firms grew to be among the world's largest producers of drugs processed from wild yams. By the early 1960s Julian had sold his laboratories for a considerable profit. At the time of his retirement, he held more than 130 chemical patents (licenses for inventions).

Julian was also a prominent civil rights leader. In 1967 he and the president of the black-owned North Carolina Mutual Life Insurance Company headed a group of influential African Americans in raising a $1 million to finance lawsuits to enforce civil rights legislation. He was the recipient of numerous awards. Julian was featured on a U.S. postage stamp in 1996.

Just, Ernest Everett

ZOOLOGIST, EDUCATOR
August 14, 1883–October 27, 1941

Ernest Just was born in South Carolina in 1883. In 1896 he entered the teacher-training program at South Carolina State College in Orangeburg. Later, he attended Dartmouth College (Hanover, New Hampshire), where he majored in biology, graduating with high honors in 1907.

There were two career options available to an African American with Just's academic background: teaching in a black institution or preaching in a black church. Just began teaching in 1907 as an instructor in English and rhetoric at **Howard University** (Washington, D.C.). In 1909 he taught English and biology and a year later taught zoology full-time. He also taught physiology in the medical school. A devoted teacher, Just served as faculty adviser to a group that was trying to establish a nationwide fraternity of black students. The Alpha chapter of Omega Psi Phi was organized at Howard in 1911, and Just became its first honorary member. In 1912 he married a fellow Howard faculty member, Ethel Highwarden; they had three children.

Just later began pursuing scientific research. In 1909 he started studying at the Marine Biological Laboratory at Woods Hole, Massachusetts, under the eminent scientist Frank Rattray Lillie. Their relationship quickly blossomed into a full and equal scientific collaboration. By the time Just earned a Ph.D. degree in zoology at the University of Chicago in 1916, he had already coauthored a paper with Lillie and written several on his own. The two worked on fertilization in marine animals. In 1915 the **National Association for the Advancement of Colored People (NAACP)** awarded Just the first Spingarn Medal, its highest honor, in recognition of his scientific contributions and "foremost service to his race."

Just deeply enjoyed science and research and looked forward to doing it each summer as a welcome break from his heavy teaching and administrative responsibilities at Howard. His productivity was extraordinary. Within ten years he published thirty-five articles, mostly relating to his studies on fertilization. Though proud of his output, he yearned for a position or environment in which he could pursue his research full-time.

In 1928 Just received a large grant that allowed more time for his research. He traveled to Europe ten times over the course of the next decade, staying for periods ranging from three weeks to two years. In Europe, Just wrote a book describing many of the scientific theories, philosophical ideas, and experimental results of his career. Just died in 1941 and was featured on a U.S. postage stamp in 1996.

Kansas

First African-American Settlers: The first documented African Americans in Kansas arrived in the 1820s. Some were free and others purchased their freedom, but most were enslaved and in the service of army officers, fur traders, missionaries, or **American Indians.**

Slave Population: The passage of the Kansas-Nebraska Act in 1854 allowed people in the territories to decide for themselves whether or not to allow **slavery** within their borders. Violence erupted between proslavery and antislavery forces, resulting in the nickname "Bleeding Kansas." Eventually, antislavery settlers became the majority, and a new constitution was drawn up. In January 1861, just before the start of the Civil War (1861–65), Kansas was admitted to the Union as a free state.

Free Black Population: The state's 1860 constitution, which prohibited slavery, resulted in an influx of African Americans. As a result, the number of **free blacks** jumped from 192 in 1855 to 625 in 1860.

Civil War: During the **Civil War** Kansas remained a major destination for African Americans from the South. By 1865 the black population had increased to 12,537. Many newcomers found work as farm laborers, domestic servants, or soldiers. About one out of every six blacks in Kansas served in the Northern army. In 1862 in Missouri, black troops from Kansas making up the 1st Regiment of Kansas Colored Volunteers were the first African-American soldiers to engage the enemy in military action.

Reconstruction: African Americans continued to move to Kansas after the Civil War, and in 1877 a second wave of black immigration began. Over the next four years, between 40,000 and 70,000 blacks migrated to the state. When **Reconstruction** ended, political repression and poverty became widespread, and many blacks left. In the late 1800s advertisements depicting Kansas as peaceful and idyllic, filled with free land, triggered "Kansas Exodus Fever." By 1880 the black population stood at 48,000; in 1900, 52,000; and in 1920, 58,000.

The Great Depression: Stimulated by job opportunities in the state's defense industries, Kansas's black population reached 65,138 in 1940. With population growth came renewed civil rights activism, particularly in towns with branches of the **National Association for the Advancement of Colored People (NAACP).**

Civil Rights Movement: Beginning in the 1960s, black political representation increased substantially in Kansas. Legislative reapportionment was ordered by the Supreme Court in 1962 and effectively shifted legislative seats from rural to urban areas.

Current African-American Population: According to U.S. Census Bureau estimates, the total black population in Kansas was 154,750 (nearly 6 percent of the state population) as of July 1, 1998.

Key Figures: George Washington Carver (c. 1864–1943), scientist and educator; poet **Langston Hughes** (1902–1967); artist **Aaron Douglas** (1899–1979); Eva Jessye (1895–1992), original choral director of composer George Gershwin's *Porgy and Bess.*

(SEE ALSO SIT-INS.)

Karamu House

Founded in 1915 in Cleveland, Ohio, Karamu House became world famous as an interracial (for blacks and whites) center for theater and the arts. It was founded by white Oberlin College (Oberlin, Ohio) graduates Russell and Rowena Jelliffe, who wanted to help African Americans migrating from the rural South. The Jelliffes at first worked with neighborhood children, providing recreational activities. Some of this work continues today, but since the 1920s Karamu House has focused on the theater. It was given its present name in 1927—Karamu means "a place of joyful meeting" in the African language Swahili.

In 1930 *The Crisis* magazine called Karamu House the "most successful Negro Little Theatre in the United States." During the 1930s Karamu received federal funding through the Works Progress Administration (WPA) and became known for its visual arts programs. The best-known black playwright associated with Karamu was **Langston Hughes** (1902–1967), who grew up in Cleveland and knew the Jelliffes. Between 1936 and 1939 the theater produced several plays by Hughes, including *Mulatto* (1935).

The Karamu House was destroyed by fire in 1939, but it was rebuilt in 1949 through contributions from Cleveland residents and the Rockefeller Foundation and others. The new complex had two theaters and visual arts and dance studios. Karamu House presented experimental black theater, dance, and music during the 1950s, as well as art and sculpture exhibits.

During the 1970s Karamu focused on black theater for black audiences, but in 1982 it went back to its interracial roots, keeping a strong African-American influence. In the 1990s it also provided lessons in crafts, from jewelry making to wood carving, but it is still primarily known for its performing arts theater.

Karenga, Maulana Ronald McKinley Everett

ACTIVIST, EDUCATOR
1941–

Maulana Karenga, best known in the late twentieth century as the creator of the African-American cultural celebration **Kwanzaa,** has been active in civil rights and black cultural movements from the mid-1960s.

Born Ronald McKinley Everett, the youngest of fourteen children of a Baptist minister, in Parsonsburg, Maryland, Karenga moved to Los Angeles, California, in 1959. He received degrees in political science from the University of California at Los Angeles in 1963 and 1964. He helped rebuild the African-American Watts community of Los Angeles in 1965, following riots earlier that year.

He adopted the African name Maulana (master teacher) Karenga (keeper of the tradition) and in 1966 founded the organization US (referring to all African Americans), based on the belief that a black cultural renewal is the first step in the struggle for black power. US members wore traditional African clothing and promoted the teaching of the African language Swahili. With fewer than one hundred members, US played an important role in building independent schools and creating black-studies departments.

Karenga was deeply influenced by Pan-Africanists (people who believe that all African nations should work together as one) such as Ghana's president Kwame Nkrumah (1909–1972), Kenya's president Jomo Kenyatta (c. 1894–1978), and African-American educator and writer **W. E. B. Du Bois** (1868–1963). Karenga argued that African Americans should embrace their African heritage and reject white cultural values. He developed a new philosophy, which he called **Kawaida.**

Maulana Karenga: Selected Books

Race, Ethnicity and Multiculturalism: Issues in Domination, Resistance and Diversity
(2000)

Kawaida Theory: An African Communitarian Philosophy
(New edition, 2000)

Odu IFA: The Ethical Teachings
(1999)

Kwanzaa: A Celebration of Family, Community and Culture
(New commemorative edition 1998)

The Book of Coming Forth by Day: The Ethics of the Declarations of Innocence
(1990)

Selections from the Husia: Sacred Wisdom of Ancient Egypt
(1984)

Introduction to Black Studies
(1982)

Kwanzaa: Origin, Concepts, Practice
(1977)

Kawaida is based on seven African values: Umoja (unity); Kujichagulia (self-determination); Ujima (collective work and responsibility); Ujamaa (cooperative economics); Nia (purpose); Kuumba (creativity); and Imani (faith). In 1966 Karenga founded Kwanzaa, a seven-day annual celebration, held from December 26 through January 1, that reflects these principles.

Throughout the late 1960s Karenga was involved in the Black Power movement. In 1968, after a bitter argument with the **Black Panther Party**—an organization that saw social and economic struggle rather than cultural change as the key to black freedom—three US members were convicted in the shooting deaths of two Black Panthers. In 1971 Karenga was charged and later convicted of assaulting two female US members. He served three years in prison. The organization US officially ended in 1974.

In 1976 Karenga received a doctorate in leadership and human behavior from U.S. International University in San Diego, California. He received a doctorate in social ethics from the University of Southern California in 1993.

Karenga served as chairman of the Department of Black Studies at California State University at Long Beach and as the director of the African-American Cultural Center in Los Angeles in the 1990s. He is the author of several books.

In 2000 Karenga and his wife Tiamoya (she who inspires) remain supporters of Afrocentrism and have presided over hundreds of Kwanzaa celebrations all over the world. At the turn of the twenty-first century Kwanzaa is celebrated by an estimated 26 million people in the United States, Canada, Europe, the Caribbean, and **Africa.** (*See also* **Afrocentricity.**)

Kay, Ulysses Simpson

COMPOSER
January 7, 1917–May 20, 1995

Ulysses Kay is one of the twentieth century's leading African-American composers. A nephew of the pioneering **jazz** trumpeter **Joseph "King" Oliver,** Kay has composed a variety music, ranging from solo instrument and voice, and pieces for children, to band and chamber music, **opera,** and works for orchestra and chorus. He has also written extensively for **film** and **television.**

Born in Arizona, Kay earned a Bachelor of Music degree from the University of Arizona in 1938 and a Master of Music degree in 1940 from the Eastman School of Music in Rochester, New York. He studied at Yale from 1941 to 1942 before serving four years in the U.S. Navy, where he played flute, saxophone, piccolo, and piano in navy bands or jazz ensembles.

In 1948 Kay composed and arranged the score for the film *The Quiet One.* From 1949 to 1953 Kay studied at the American Academy in Rome, Italy. In 1953 he began working as a consultant for Broadcast Music Inc. (BMI). He continued composing and left BMI in 1968 to teach at Lehman College of the City University of New York. Kay retired from teaching in 1988.

**Ulysses Kay:
Selected Compositions**

Of New Horizons
(1944)

Suite for Orchestra
(1945)

A Short Overture
(1946)

Portrait Suite
(1948)

The Juggler of Our Lady
(1956)

Fantasy Variations
(1963)

Markings
(1966)

Epigrams and Hymn
(1975)

Chariots
(1978)

Festival Palms
(1983)

Frederick Douglass
(1986)

String Triptych
(1988)

Kennedy, Adrienne

PLAYWRIGHT
September 13, 1931–

Playwright Adrienne Kennedy was born in Pittsburgh, Pennsylvania, in 1931 and grew up in Cleveland, Ohio. She received her bachelor of arts degree in education from Ohio State University in 1952 and shortly thereafter moved to New York City with her husband and child. Over the next ten years she studied creative writing at various schools, including Columbia University (1954-1956) and the New School for Social Research (1957).

Kennedy's plays explore conflicts of race, gender, and identity. Her characters frequently wear masks or a single character may be played by several actors to represent a sense of racial and mental confusion.

The first of Kennedy's plays to be produced, *Funnyhouse of a Negro* (1963), was written while she was attending a workshop by noted playwright Edward Albee (1928–). *Funnyhouse*, a one-act play about a young mulatto (a person of mixed race; usually one black parent, one white) woman's efforts to come to terms with her mixed-race heritage, opened Off-Broadway in 1964. Kennedy wrote two other one-act plays in 1963, *A Rat's Mass* and *The Owl Answers*. She won an Obie Award for *Funnyhouse* in 1964.

Between 1967 and 1969, Kennedy was awarded a Guggenheim Fellowship and several writing grants from the Rockefeller Foundation. Her first full-length play, *In His Own Write*, an adaptation of John Lennon's (1940–1980) stories and poems, was written in 1967 and produced in London by the National Theatre Company. In 1971 Kennedy joined five other women playwrights in founding the Women's Theater Council, designed to promote the works of women playwrights and provide other opportunities for women in theater. In 1973 she wrote *An Evening with Dead Essex*, a one-act memorial to Mark Essex, a black New Orleans, Louisiana, youth who was killed by the police.

During the 1970s and early 1980s Kennedy taught creative writing at Yale, Princeton, and Brown universities and received grants from the National Endowment for the Arts. Her second full-length play, *A Movie Star Has to Star in Black and White*, opened in 1976. She also wrote a children's musical, *A Lancashire Lad*, about the boyhood of actor-comedian Charlie Chaplin (1889–1977), and another children's play, *Black Children's Day*.

In 1994 Kennedy received an award from the Lila Wallace-Reader's Digest Fund, which she used to establish an arts and culture program for minority children in inner-city schools in Cleveland, Ohio.

Kentucky

First African-American Settlers: African Americans were among the first settlers in Kentucky. Their numbers grew rapidly during the pioneer period, and in 1777 blacks made up about 10 percent of the inhabitants.

Slave Population: Kentucky achieved statehood in 1792. Most African-American Kentuckians were slaves and were concentrated in the central part

of the state, in the counties along the Ohio River in northwestern Kentucky, and in southwestern Kentucky. Only 28 percent of whites owned slaves, with the average owner possessing five. When an area was being settled, most slaves cleared forests and built cabins; this progressed into agricultural, domestic, or factory work.

Free Black Population: Kentucky's small free black population (about 4 percent of blacks, totaling 10,684 in 1860) moved toward cities where greater numbers made it more difficult for white authorities to monitor them. **Free blacks** provided many skilled laborers for Kentucky's economy; a few achieved enough success as entrepreneurs to purchase the freedom of loved ones.

Civil War: The **Civil War** (1861–65) offered the first viable opportunity for Kentucky slaves to openly express their opposition to **slavery.** They increasingly refused to obey orders, fled to Union (Northern) lines, and joined the federal army when black recruiting began. About twenty-four thousand Kentucky blacks served in the Union army.

Reconstruction: At the Civil War's end, the state legislature did not provide for the equal treatment of African Americans. Blacks usually found jobs at the bottom rung of the economic ladder and provided their own social services while living in a segregated society. In 1910 more than 60 percent of black men worked in agriculture, as laborers, or as servants, while fewer than 10 percent held jobs as skilled laborers or professionals; about 80 percent of black women worked as domestics. As a result, Kentucky black leaders formed the Lincoln Independent Party in the early 1900s. Challenging the white majority for jobs, education, and political positions, the party provoked changes in government hiring in the 1920s.

The Great Depression: At the outbreak of **World War II** (1939–45), positions for blacks in defense industries in Kentucky were few, and progress remained slow. In contrast, the depression effected a political revolution for Kentucky blacks. The New Deal (federal government programs aimed at creating jobs and promoting economic recovery) led to a mass exodus of blacks from the Republican Party, and a new generation of black leaders provided community leadership.

Civil Rights Movement to the Present: The integration of schools began with promise in the fall of 1955, but patterns of desegregation soon revealed a deep racial division within Kentucky society. During the 1960s Kentucky blacks won access to public accommodations, and in 1966 a bill providing for equal access to public housing and prohibiting employment discrimination became law.

Current African-American Population: According to U.S. Census Bureau estimates, the total black population in Kentucky was 284,860 (7 percent of the state population) as of July 1, 1998.

Key Figures: Josiah Henson (1789–1883), abolitionist clergyman; William J. Simmons (1849–1890), writer of the African-American biographical dictionary *Men of Mark*; civil rights leader **Asa Philip Randolph** (1889–1979); Georgia Davis Powers (1933–), the first black woman elected to the Kentucky state senate.

(SEE ALSO *UNCLE TOM'S CABIN*; **UNDERGROUND RAILROAD**.)

Killens, John Oliver

NOVELIST
January 14, 1916–October 27, 1987

Born in Macon, Georgia, in 1916, novelist John Killens was greatly influenced by his family, who taught him about cultural pride and literary values. His father encouraged him to read a weekly column by famous black writer **Langston Hughes** (1902–1967); his mother, president of a literary club, introduced him to poetry; and his great-grandmother filled his boyhood with tales of **slavery**. Such early exposure to criticism, art, and folklore is evident in his fiction, which is noted for its accurate portrayal of social classes, its engaging stories, and its blending of African-American history, legends, songs, and jokes.

Killens originally planned to be a lawyer. After attending Edward Waters College in Jacksonville, Florida, and Morris Brown College in Atlanta, Georgia, he moved to Washington, D.C., took a job with the National Labor Relations Board (a government agency that oversees activities in the workplace), and completed his bachelor's degree through evening classes at Howard University. He studied law from 1939 until 1942, when he quit to join the U.S. Army. His novel *And Then We Heard the Thunder* (1963), concerning racism in the military, was based on his service in the South Pacific. It was nominated for the prestigious Pulitzer Prize.

Killens moved to New York in 1948 and attended writing classes at Columbia and New York universities. He met other writers committed to the idea of writing as a way of social protest, and they founded the Harlem Writers Guild in the early 1950s. He also wrote regularly for the newspaper *Freedom*.

Killens's novel *Youngblood* (1954) treats the struggles of a southern black family in early-twentieth-century Georgia. Following critical praise for the book, he toured the United States speaking on African-American subjects. Killens became close friends with black religious leader and social reformer **Malcolm X** (1925–1965). Together, they founded the Organization for Afro-American Unity in 1964.

In the mid-1960s Killens was a writer-in-residence at several universities. In 1971 he was again nominated for the Pulitzer Prize for his novel, *The Cotillion; or, One Good Bull Is Half the Herd*. He was awarded a fellowship from the National Endowment for the Arts in 1980. Until his death, Killens continued to contribute articles to leading black magazines.

Kincaid, Jamaica

AUTHOR
May 25, 1949–

Born Elaine Potter Richardson in St. Johns, on the Caribbean island of Antigua, Jamaica Kincaid moved to New York at the age of sixteen. She worked various jobs and spent brief periods studying photography at New York's School for Social Research and at Franconia College in New

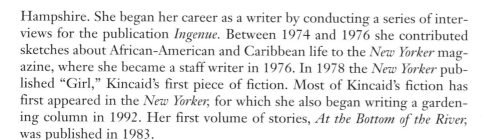
Hampshire. She began her career as a writer by conducting a series of interviews for the publication *Ingenue*. Between 1974 and 1976 she contributed sketches about African-American and Caribbean life to the *New Yorker* magazine, where she became a staff writer in 1976. In 1978 the *New Yorker* published "Girl," Kincaid's first piece of fiction. Most of Kincaid's fiction has first appeared in the *New Yorker*, for which she also began writing a gardening column in 1992. Her first volume of stories, *At the Bottom of the River*, was published in 1983.

Kincaid's work centers on her experience as an immigrant from a poor Caribbean island with a history of colonial oppression, and her straightforward language reveals a colorful personality and life history. Themes of conflict between mothers and daughters are central to Kincaid's work and can be extended to symbolic relationships, such as that between the island of Antigua and her "offspring" who move away. Kincaid's novels *Annie John* (1985), *Lucy* (1990), and *The Autobiography of My Mother* (1997) are about bold, spirited young girls from Antigua, which is also the subject of the nonfiction volume *A Small Place* (1988), an extended essay on contemporay Antigua. In 1997 Kincaid published *My Brother: A Memoir*, a story of her life and her brother's 1996 death from AIDS.

King, B. B. *See* King, Riley B.

King, Coretta Scott

CIVIL RIGHTS ACTIVIST
April 27, 1927–

Coretta Scott King is the widow of the Reverend Dr. **Martin Luther King Jr.**, the best-known leader of the **Civil Rights movement** of the 1950s and 1960s. After his assassination in 1968, she assumed much of the work that he had planned and has since promoted human and civil rights around the world.

Born in the rural Alabama, Coretta Scott studied music at Antioch College in Yellow Springs, Ohio, before entering the New England Conservatory of Music in 1952. She met King during her first year at the conservatory, while he was studying theology at Boston University.

Coretta and Martin were married on June 18, 1953, despite his father's disapproval. The following year, Coretta received a bachelor's degree, before the couple moved to Montgomery, Alabama. Coretta devoted herself to raising her children and helping her husband in his nonviolent civil rights campaigns.

Coretta endured many hardships, including Martin's frequent arrests and the bombing of their Montgomery home in 1956. Early in 1960 Martin became co-pastor of Atlanta's Ebenezer Baptist Church. Later that year, Coretta gained her husband's release from prison by asking presidential candidate John F. Kennedy for assistance.

In 1962 King became a voice instructor at Morris Brown College, but she still led marches, directed fund-raising, and gave "freedom concerts."

Coretta Scott King (center) leading the funeral procession for her husband, Martin Luther King (AP/Wide World Photos. Reproduced by permission)

She was also a delegate to the 1962 Disarmament Conference in Switzerland and was involved in anti-**Vietnam War** (1959–75) efforts during 1966 and 1967.

In 1969 Coretta King helped found the Atlanta-based Martin Luther King Jr. Center for Nonviolent Social Change. That same year, she published her **autobiography,** *My Life with Martin Luther King, Jr.*

In 1983 Coretta King led the twentieth-anniversary March on Washington (during the 1963 event, her husband gave his famous "I Have a Dream" speech). The following year, she was elected chairperson of the commission that would make King's birthday a national holiday. During the 1980s she was also active in the struggle to end apartheid (a policy of racial segregation) in South Africa.

King served as chief executive officer of the Martin Luther King Jr. Center for Nonviolent Change, after resigning the presidency to her son, Dexter Scott King, in 1989. Ten years later, King was in the news for suing the CBS television network for copyright violation, after it used footage of her husband's "I Have a Dream" speech in a documentary program.

King, Martin Luther Jr.

CIVIL RIGHTS LEADER, MINISTER
January 15, 1929–April 4, 1968

Now a figure symbolizing the **Civil Rights movement** of the 1950s and 1960s, the Reverend Dr. Martin Luther King was born Michael King Jr. Both he and his father, a Baptist minister, were renamed Martin Luther King in 1934.

King decided to become a minister after meeting religious leaders who combined theology with social activism. This happened at **Morehouse** College, where he was a student from 1944 to 1948. King also attended

"I HAVE A DREAM"

Decades after his assassination in 1968, the actions of the Reverend Dr. Martin Luther King Jr. as a courageous protestor are often overshadowed by his reputation as a well-spoken philosopher. He is perhaps most famous for his optimistic "I Have a Dream" speech (during the March on Washington, Washington, D.C., August 28, 1963), in which he said: "So I say to you, my friends, that even though we must face the difficulties of today and tomorrow, I still have a dream. It is a dream deeply rooted in the American dream that one day this nation will rise up and live out the true meaning of its creed—we hold these truths to be self-evident, that all men are created equal." However, in later years King invoked the famous speech only to emphasize how his dream had "turned into a nightmare."

Crozer Theological Seminary before beginning doctoral studies at Boston University in 1951. While in Boston, King met Coretta Scott, whom he married in 1953.

In 1955 King became pastor of Dexter Avenue Baptist Church in **Montgomery, Alabama**. When a black woman named **Rosa Parks** was jailed for refusing to give her bus seat to a white passenger, King coordinated a boycott using the support of black churches and nonviolent protest methods.

When Alabama bus-segregation laws were outlawed in 1956, King became nationally known. In 1957 he helped found the **Southern Christian Leadership Conference (SCLC)** to coordinate further civil rights activities.

In 1960 King joined his father as co-pastor of Ebenezer Baptist Church in Atlanta. He then became involved in **sit-in** protests in restaurants that would not serve blacks. He was arrested during one protest and was not released from jail until aided by future president John F. Kennedy (1917–1963).

King gained more influence after planning massive protests in **Birmingham, Alabama**, in 1963. The televised pictures of police using dogs and fire hoses against demonstrators caused a national outcry.

King showed his exceptional skill with words in a letter written in a Birmingham jail cell. It defended the protests using texts from the Bible and the Constitution. King's famous speech "I Have a Dream," given at the March on Washington in August 1963, also showed his ability to use American ideals to promote black goals.

King was named *Time* magazine's Man of the Year in 1963, and he was awarded the Nobel Peace Prize in 1964. But his success also disturbed some powerful people. FBI director J. Edgar Hoover secretly collected and leaked information about King's ties with former communists and his affairs with women in an attempt to damage King' reputation.

King's last successful campaign promoted black voting rights. On March 7, 1965, demonstrators in Selma, Alabama, were attacked by state policemen with tear gas and clubs, which only increased national support for the

Martin Luther King delivering his famous "I Have a Dream" speech (Corbis Corporation. Reproduced by permission)

campaign. President Lyndon B. Johnson soon introduced legislation that would become the Voting Rights Act of 1965.

In 1967 King began a Poor People's Campaign, which led to his involvement in a sanitation workers' strike in **Memphis, Tennessee.** On April 4, 1968, King was shot and killed as he stood on a motel balcony in Memphis. A white man named James Earl Ray was convicted of the crime.

King gained new respect after his death when many critics acknowledged his accomplishments. In 1969 his widow, **Coretta Scott King,** established the Martin Luther King Jr. Center for Nonviolent Social Change. In 1986 a national holiday was established to honor his birth. (*See also* **Montgomery Bus Boycott; National Association for the Advancement of Colored People; Student Nonviolent Coordinating Committee; Suffrage.**)

King, Riley B. "B. B."

BLUES SINGER, GUITARIST
September 16, 1925–

In a career spanning six decades, B.B. King has earned countless honors for his work as a **blues** musician, including eighteen Grammy Awards, enshrinement in the Rock and Roll Hall of Fame (1987), the Presidential Medal of the Arts (1990), and the Blues Foundation's Lifetime Achievement Award (1997).

Blues master B. B. King in performance with his signature guitar, "Lucille" ((c) Jack Vartoogian. Reproduced by permission)

Born Riley B. King in Itta Bena, Mississippi, B. B. King grew up on a plantation, working as a farmhand while teaching himself to play the guitar. He moved to **Memphis, Tennessee,** in 1947 and began singing in bars. After his first recordings, in 1949, he achieved his first national hit in 1952 with a recording of "Three O'Clock Blues." He then began his lifetime of touring as a blues singer. The focus of his music became his powerful, commanding voice and his guitar playing—so melodious it often sounds like singing of another kind.

By the mid-1960s he had become known as one of the country's greatest blues performers and a leading figure in the urban blues scene. In the early 1990s, King opened his own blues club on Beale Street in Memphis, and by 2000, at age 75, he was still known as America's "ambassador of the blues," touring an average of 250 days each year.

"Blues is meant to be shared, and the best way to do that is live and in person. I like to look out from the stage and see those smiling faces getting into the music. That's why I started playing the blues, and that's what has kept me going all these years."

(Source: B. B. King, *Down Beat* magazine, 1998.)

King, Woodie Jr.

ACTOR, DIRECTOR, WRITER, PRODUCER
July 27, 1937–

A multi-talented artist who primarily works in theater, Woodie King Jr., was born in Alabama but moved to Detroit, Michigan, when his parents separated. He attended Cass Technical High School and earned a bachelor of arts degree at the Will-O-Way Apprentice Theatre School.

King became a graduate student at Wayne State University in Detroit in 1961. Frustrated by the lack of roles for African Americans, he helped found the Concept-East Theatre in an abandoned bar, where he directed and acted in plays.

In 1964 King went to New York with a touring play and found a new artistic home. In 1965 he became cultural arts director of Mobilization for Youth, an arts training program for poor black and Puerto Rican children. In 1970 King became director of the Arts for Living Program and founded the New Federal Theatre, where he continued to work into the 1990s.

In the late-1970s King began planning the National Black Touring Circuit. Its 1980 premier was a production of **Ntozake Shange**'s *Boogie Woogie Landscapes* at the Kennedy Center for Performing Arts in Washington, D.C.

King has produced documentary films since 1968. *The Black Theatre Movement: "A Raisin in the Sun" to the Present* (1978) is perhaps his best-known film. King is also a prolific writer and has written plays, essays, short stories, and the book *Black Theater, Present Condition.* (*See also* **Drama.**)

Kitt, Eartha Mae

SINGER, ACTRESS
January 26, 1928–

Eartha Kitt is a singer and actress whose exotic looks and throaty voice made her famous. Born on a farm in the town of North, South Carolina, Kitt and her sister Pearl were raised in a foster family until 1936, when Eartha moved to New York City to live with her aunt.

In New York, Kitt attended the Metropolitan High School and at sixteen was granted a scholarship with a dance troupe. Kitt toured Europe and Mexico with the troupe, developing a stage presence and a unique singing style.

Kitt performed from the mid-1950s through the 1960s in theaters, nightclubs, and cabarets in the United States and abroad. Kitt also appeared in films, including *Anna Lucasta* (1959), which earned her an Oscar nomination. During this period she recorded two notable albums and made numerous **television** appearances, including a stint on the 1960s *Batman* series, in which she played Catwoman.

In 1968 Kitt's career took a turn when she criticized the **Vietnam War** (1959–75) at a White House luncheon hosted by the First Lady, Lady Bird Johnson. As a result she lost jobs, was criticized by the press, and was inves-

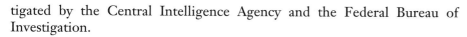

tigated by the Central Intelligence Agency and the Federal Bureau of Investigation.

In the late 1970s and 1980s Kitt continued her career as a singer and actor. She recorded an album in 1984 and published two autobiographies, *I'm Still Here* (1989) and *Confessions of a Sex Kitten* (1991). Kitt also appeared in a variety of films, including *Ernest Scared Stupid* (1991), *Boomerang* (1992), and *Fatal Instinct* (1993). A retrospective of her recordings, entitled *Eartha Quake*, was released in 1993.

Knight, Etheridge

POET
April 19, 1931–March 10, 1991

Born in Corinth, Mississippi, Etheridge Knight was raised with his six siblings in Paducah, Kentucky. A troubled youth, Knight ran away from home and enlisted in the army at age sixteen. He served as a medical technician during the **Korean War** (1950–53), only to return with a narcotics addiction. He became a drug dealer to support his habit and in 1960 was given a ten- to twenty-five-year prison sentence for robbery in Indiana.

Knight educated himself in prison and discovered poetry. After his work was brought to the attention of African-American poet **Gwendolyn Brooks,** Brooks became Knight's mentor. Knight later said: "I died in Korea of a shrapnel wound and narcotics resurrected me. I died in 1960 from a prison sentence and poetry brought me back to life."

Knight's first book of poetry, *Poems from Prison*, was published in 1968, the same year he was released from prison. Knight rapidly became one of the young African-American poets whose work had a powerful impact on the **Black Arts movement** of the late 1960s and early 1970s. Knight was particularly popular with prison audiences and spoke for nonviolence wherever he read his poetry. He spoke at the Library of Congress, served as writer-in-residence at several universities, and received numerous awards for his work, including three fellowships from the National Endowment for the Arts. His volume *Belly Song and Other Poems* (1973) was nominated for a National Book Award and a Pulitzer Prize. He won the American Book Award for *The Essential Etheridge Knight* (1986).

In 1988 Knight returned to drinking and relapsed into drug addiction. He ran out of money and eventually became a homeless person on the streets of New York. Suffering from phlebitis (a blood disorder) and lung cancer, he died in Indianapolis in 1991.

Knight, Gladys

SINGER
May 28, 1944–

Gladys Knight is a singer whose smooth voice has entertained listeners for more than fifty years. Knight, who was born and raised in Atlanta,

Georgia, made her public singing debut at age four at Mount Mariah Baptist Church. By the time she was five, Knight had performed in numerous churches. At age seven Knight won the Grand Prize on Ted Mack's nationally televised *Original Amateur Hour.*

In 1952 Knight formed a quartet with her brother Merald and her cousins William and Edward. The group, named "The Pips" after James "Pip" Woods, another cousin and the group's first manager, quickly established itself in Atlanta nightclubs. By the late 1950s, the group was a popular fixture on the national **rhythm-and-blues** (R&B) circuit. Its first recording came in 1961, when Vee Jay Records released the single "Every Beat of My Heart," which became a top ten pop and number one R&B hit. The following year Fury Records signed the group, changed its name to Gladys Knight and The Pips, and released a successful string of recordings.

In 1965 Gladys Knight and The Pips signed with **Motown** Records and was featured on the label's touring reviews. The group's 1967 Motown single, "I Heard It Through the Grapevine," reached number two on the Billboard pop chart. The late 1960s brought the group mass acclaim for its polished singing style and dance routines.

In 1973 the group switched to the Buddah record label for its top forty album, *Imagination*, which included two of the group's most lasting successes, "Midnight Train to Georgia," a number one pop single in 1973, and "I've Got to Use My Imagination." The group won two 1974 Grammy Awards.

In the late 1970s the group's popularity began to wane. It continued touring but was not able to record another chart-topping record until 1988, when "Love Overboard" reached the top twenty on the Billboard pop chart. The following year Knight left the group to establish a solo career.

Since that time, Knight has had many successful recordings and continues to perform. She and The Pips occasionally reunite for special performances. In 2000 Knight began a national tour starring in the musical play *Smokey Joe's Café: The Songs of Leiber and Stoller.*

Knight, Gwendolyn

PAINTER
May 26, 1913–

Gwendolyn Knight was born in the Caribbean island of Barbados but spent most of her childhood in New York City's **Harlem** neighborhood. As a child, Knight did portraits of her friends and relatives, and she took art classes in public school. She studied art at **Howard University** (Washington, D.C.) from 1931 to 1933. She returned to Harlem, where she became part of the community of artists working in sculptor **Augusta Savage**'s (1892–1962) studio. While studying with Savage, Knight met painter **Jacob Lawrence** (1917–2000), whom she married in 1941.

For several decades Knight pursued her career with little public attention. Beginning in the 1960s, she decided to focus intently on art and returned to school, studying in New York and Maine. Primarily a painter of

portraits and still lifes (nonmoving objects, such as a bowl of fruit), Knight used oil, charcoal, ink, and brush in her works. Her portraits were made from loose brush strokes, and while they did not present details of an individual's face, they conveyed the sitter's personality through gesture and facial expression.

Knight spent much of her career in the shadow of her husband's artistic success, and her work was not displayed in solo exhibitions until the 1970s. Her work frequently has been displayed in group exhibitions tracing the history of African-American art. Knight's paintings were included in the exhibit *Significant Others: Artist Wives of Artists* at the Kraushaar Gallery in New York City in 1993. Between 1992 and 1994 she worked on drawings and figure studies that emphasized dance as well as the form and motion of the human body.

Gwendolyn Knight: Selected Works

New Orleans, Scene I and II
(1941)

Flutist
(1981)

Portrait of the Artist
(1991)

Dancers II
(1992)

Dancer with Drapery
(1992–1994)

Korean War

The Korean War (1950–53) began when North Korea, a Communist country, invaded South Korea, a democracy, on June 25, 1950. In an effort to stop the expansion of Communism, the United States joined several other countries in offering military support and troops to help South Korea. Although President Harry S. Truman (1884–1972) had ordered the armed services to end racial segregation in 1948, the military was slow to enforce the law. By the time the war ended in 1953, U.S. military leaders understood that racial segregation was wasteful and inefficient.

The Air Force

In the 1940s, as the United States Air Force grew more dependent upon technology, several officers became concerned that African Americans, educated and trained in segregated programs, would not be able to fill the ranks if war broke out. After studying the achievements of a small group of African-American pilots, technicians, and administrators, the air force officially ended segregation in 1949. Not only did the air force integrate its ranks, it also prohibited the practice of assigning men outside their areas of expertise—employing black mechanics as laborers, for example.

The air force began its policy of integration more than a year before the Korean War began. The war demonstrated that the needs of the service, and not race, should determine assignments. The last all-black unit was broken up in June 1952.

The Navy and the Marine Corps

Although each branch of the military had plans to obey President Truman's order to integrate the forces, none had progressed as far as the air force when the Korean War began. The navy, for example, had a policy in place that allowed all enlistees to apply for any training or position without regard to race, but more than 65 percent of the African Americans in the navy served as cooks. This was because the navy heavily recruited African Americans to serve as cooks, rather than recruiting them for other positions.

In 1951 the navy began using a standardized qualification test to assign enlisted men to their positions, and this allowed African Americans to gain access to a wider variety of positions. Nevertheless, the proportion of blacks in the navy declined by about 0.2 percent between 1950 and the end of the war in 1953. Not until 1960 did black Americans account for even 4.9 percent of naval personnel, a smaller percentage than the air force had achieved ten years earlier.

Unlike the navy, the marine corps (which is a part of the navy) required large numbers of new recruits to fight the Korean War. This forced the marine corps to end the practice of racial segregation. When the war began in 1950, the only integrated marine corps units were the athletic teams. The need for many troops in a short period of time caused black and white soldiers to serve together in units that were being expanded to wartime strength, however. As the war continued, the number of African-American marines increased to more than nine times the original number.

In short, the Korean War forced the marine corps to accept large numbers of blacks, assign them where they could best help fight the war, and abandon the earlier practice of concentrating them in security and service units or employing them as cooks.

The Army

Like the navy and the marine corps, the army resisted the order to integrate its ranks. In 1950 African-American men continued to train in racially separate units. Segregated training was quickly abandoned, however, once the Korean War began. There were so many white recruits that it was impossible to keep them out of battalions reserved for blacks. As a result, by 1951, the army had abandoned segregated training.

One of the regiments sent to Korea in the summer of 1950, the 9th Infantry, had two battalions of white and one battalion of black soldiers. When casualties mounted among the white soldiers, one of the battalion commanders demanded replacements. He accepted more than two hundred African Americans, whom he assigned throughout his unit. This experience demonstrated for the army that race could not determine assignments; black soldiers had to serve wherever the army needed them, regardless of their skin color. In 1951 General Matthew Ridgway abolished segregation, which he described as "both un-American and un-Christian."

Ku Klux Klan

The Ku Klux Klan is a white supremacist (the belief that whites are superior to people of other races) organization in the United States that has acted with violence against African Americans. Klan members are often characterized by white robes and tall, pointed hoods that cover their faces and conceal their identity. The Klan is also known by its symbols, the burning cross—taken from a Scottish tradition to show obedience to God—and the letters "KKK."

The Reconstruction Klan, or First Era

The first Klan movement was organized in 1866 in Pulaski, Tennessee, with American **Civil War** (1861–65) veterans who fought on the Confederate, or Southern, side. The Ku Klux Klan—whose name comes from the Greek word for circle, *kuklos*—spread throughout the South during the **Reconstruction** period (1865–77). It fought against equal rights for freed slaves. Under the cover of hooded robes, Klansmen threatened, whipped, and killed blacks and whites who supported equal rights.

Congress passed laws in 1870 and 1871 protecting black voters and outlawing Klan activities. President Ulysses S. Grant (1822–1885) ordered mass arrests of Klansmen, and the Reconstruction Klan came to an end.

The Second Era

The second Ku Klux Klan was formed on Thanksgiving Day, 1915. William Joseph Simmons, a former preacher and the son of a Reconstruction Klansman, convinced fifteen friends to meet at the top of Stone Mountain in Georgia. They burned a cross and flew an American flag as they dedicated themselves to the revival of the Klan.

Simmons hired publicity experts to promote the organization nationwide. The Klan gained members by offering them brotherhood, mysterious rituals, and imaginative titles. The leader was called Imperial Wizard, and officers had names like Kleagle, Kludd, and Exalted Cyclops. Organizers claimed the Klan was a patriotic movement that would preserve endangered American values. They spoke in favor of white supremacy, old-time religion, and law and order.

The second Klan soon began targeting Catholics and Jews as well as blacks, by burning crosses on church lawns, getting public school teachers fired, and accusing groups of conspiracies.

Only 16 percent of members of this Klan lived in the South. Indiana, New York, Pennsylvania, and Texas had the most members, with approximately two hundred thousand each. Klan-approved candidates were elected as U.S. senators and governors, and local officials consulted with Klan leaders about government matters. By keeping men in power who shared their beliefs, the Klan controlled crime, minorities, and community improvements. But the second Klan fell by the end of the 1920s, as members became untrustworthy. In 1944 the Internal Revenue Service demanded $685,000 in back taxes from the Ku Klux Klan, putting it out of business.

The Third Era

The third Klan movement began in 1946 and had about twenty thousand members by 1949. This southern Klan used violence to keep African Americans from gaining racial and economic equality. Klan activities increased after the U.S. Supreme Court's ***Brown v. Board of Education of Topeka, Kansas*** decision in 1954 resulted in school desegregation. Three major groups formed during the 1950s, the United Klans of America, the US Klans, and the Knights of the Ku Klux Klan (founded in 1956 in

Ku Klux Klan members marching down
Pennsylvania Ave. in Washington, D.C.
(Courtesy of the Library of Congress)

Louisiana). By the 1960s the combined membership of Klan groups was about fifty thousand.

Groups used bombings, arson, and murder to stop blacks from gaining equal rights during the **Civil Rights movement** of the 1960s. The 1963 bombing of a Birmingham, Alabama, church, in which four black girls were killed, brought national attention to Klan involvement in violent crimes. The Federal Bureau of Investigation (FBI) began hiring Klan members in 1964 to cause trouble within the organization and break it down.

The Fourth and Fifth Eras

Klan membership dropped from fifty thousand to about 6,500 in the early 1970s but a splinter group rose again under the leadership of Louisiana native David Duke in 1975. However, Duke was dismissed from this position after it was learned he had offered to sell the Klan membership list for $35,000. By 1989 he was no longer a Klan member but was elected to the U.S. House of Representatives. He ran for Louisiana governor in 1991 and drew a majority of white votes but lost that election and a presidential bid as well.

Klan groups opposed busing black children to white schools, **affirmative action** programs for improving the employment and educational opportunities for minorities and women, and the illegal immigration of Mexicans to the United States. Klan members joined with neo-Nazi groups, which held the white supremacist beliefs of Nazi German leader Adolf Hitler (1889–1945). Klansmen made cruel statements against blacks, Asians, Hispanics, and Jews.

During the 1980s federal prosecutors brought Klansmen and their leaders to trial for violent acts and conspiracy to overthrow the government.

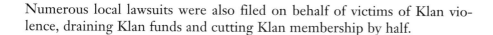

Numerous local lawsuits were also filed on behalf of victims of Klan violence, draining Klan funds and cutting Klan membership by half.

The Sixth Era

The KKK came under the leadership of Pastor Thomas Robb of the Church of Jesus Christ in Bergman, Arkansas, in the late 1980s and 1990s. His leadership marks the sixth era of the Klan. This organization favors policy that puts traditional white Christians first in all matters of U.S. government and society. It opposes programs to help minorities, like affirmative action, and supports racial discrimination in housing and business. This Klan protests setting aside **Martin Luther King Jr.** Day as a national holiday. It also opposes many dealings with foreign nations. It favors environmental protection and energy-conservation measures.

The Klan has been widely criticized for its outspoken views on AIDS, abortion, and other issues. But members say they have a right to express their opinions under the First Amendment to the Constitution, which guarantees freedom of speech. Members wear plain street clothes at public events, but otherwise many continue to wear Klan robes and hoods.

The KKK gets its message out through literature, radio and television ads, and political campaigns. Leaders speak to school and church groups and on radio and TV programs, hoping to gain new members through positive publicity. The 1990s Klan is politically active rather than violent, and its message continues to attract new members.

Kwanzaa

In 1966 African-American writer, leader, and professor **Maulana Karenga** (1941–) created a new celebration for people of African descent. Called "Kwanzaa," from the word for "first fruits" in the African language Swahili, it is based on African harvest festivals and a system of African community values called "Kawaida."

Celebrated each year from December 26 through January 1, Kwanzaa honors African heritage through seven days of ceremony and activities centered on the Seven Principles of Kawaida, created by Karenga. The Seven Principles are "umoja" (unity), "kujichagulia" (self-determination), "ujima" (collective work and responsibility), "ujamaa" (cooperative economics), "nia" (purpose), "kuumba" (creativity), and "imani" (faith).

On each evening of Kwanzaa, family and friends gather to discuss one of the Seven Principles. Each home prepares a ceremonial table covered with a Kwanzaa mat, called a "mkeka," which represents African history and tradition as the foundation of modern life. On the mat are six other Kwanzaa symbols: the "kinara," the "mishumaa saba," the "kikombe cha umoja," the "mazao," the "muhindi," and the "zawadi."

The kinara is a candleholder with seven branches, and the mishumaa saba are seven candles in black, red, and green, representing the Seven Principles. Black stands for black people, red for their struggle, and green

KAWAIDA: THE IDEAS BEHIND KWANZAA

K wanzaa is based on a system of African cultural ideas called "Kawaida," which means "tradition" or "reason" in the African language Swahili. Kawaida was created by African-American writer and professor Maulana Karenga (1941—) during the mid-1960s.

Karenga believed that black people needed to think differently before they could strengthen themselves and their community and fight racism. He believed that the African value system based on the Seven Principles of unity, self-determination, collective work and responsibility, cooperative economics, purpose, creativity, and faith would provide the foundation for a new African-American culture.

These principles guide African Americans to become one with their family, community, nation, and race; to speak for themselves and set their own goals; to work together as a community to solve problems; to establish their own shops and businesses and help all black people to prosper; to work together to build the black community and preserve its culture; to use their creativity to make the world more beautiful; and to have faith in all black people and believe in the future.

Amiri Baraka (1934—), African-American writer and activist, made Kawaida widely popular in the late 1960s. Community theaters and schools were created to focus on African cultural values. Baraka became head of the Temple of Kawaida in Newark, New Jersey, which taught African religions. He also participated in the building of Kawaida Towers, a housing project in Newark for low- and middle-income families.

Kawaida's influence continues to grow, in black America and throughout the world. It became the basis for the idea of **"Afrocentricity,"** which emerged in the late 1970s. The National Association of Kawaida Organizations (NAKO) was founded in the late 1980s under Karenga's direction. NAKO sponsors workshops and lectures to promote appreciation of African culture in the black community. But the greatest expression of Kawaida is in Kwanzaa, the African cultural celebration based on the Seven Principles.

for the promise of a good future because of the struggle. One candle is lit each evening to represent the principle being celebrated on that day.

The kikombe cha umoja is the unity cup, from which each person takes a sip of water or juice in a nightly ceremony to honor both ancient and modern ancestors. Mazao ("crops") is a bowl of fruits, nuts, and vegetables symbolizing the community work involved in the harvest, and muhindi are ears of corn representing each child in the family, symbols of the future. If the home has no children, the muhindi represent the collective work of raising children in the community. Zawadi are gifts given to children by family members on the last day of Kwanzaa.

Because Kwanzaa is not based on commercialism, all symbols are made from natural materials, even handmade by family members if possible. Zawadi are usually educational or handmade gifts that will help the child

learn about African culture and heritage. Many African Americans also give Kwanzaa greeting cards.

On December 31, the sixth day of Kwanzaa, a community celebration called the "karamu" is held. Each family prepares a dish for a feast of African, Caribbean, Latin American, and African-American foods in honor of blacks in many parts of the world. African clothing and costumes are worn, and people perform African dances and songs after discussing the Seven Principles. At the end of the karamu, a farewell statement written by Karenga is used to close the celebration, and all join in the Kwanzaa call to unity, "Harambee!" On January 1, each person spends a quiet day looking back over the past year and thinking of ways to make the family and community better in the months to come.

Kwanzaa has gained wider acceptance each year since 1966. In 1996 the U.S. Postal Service issued a special stamp to commemorate Kwanzaa's thirtieth anniversary. Some twenty million people worldwide now celebrated Kwanzaa, although it is still most popular among African Americans.

LaBelle, Patti

SINGER
October 4, 1944–

Patti LaBelle was born Patricia Louise Holt in Pennsylvania. She grew up singing in the choir of the Beaulah Baptist Church. She was sixteen years old when she joined a vocal group called the Ordettes; a year later, LaBelle and three other female singers signed on with Newton Records and named their group the BlueBelles after Newton's subsidiary label, Bluebelle records. After their song "I Sold My Heart to the Junkman" reached the top twenty in 1962, the group was renamed Patti LaBelle and the BlueBelles.

LaBelle, who is known for her fiery stage presence and outrageous attire—a mixture of leather, feathers, and glitter—received her first big break in 1968 when she and the BlueBelles opened for The Who during their U.S. tour. The following year, she married Armstead Edwards, an educator who enrolled in business courses in order to become her personal manager. In 1971 LaBelle and the BlueBelles became known as simply LaBelle. In 1974 LaBelle became the first black band to perform in New York's Metropolitan Opera House. As the lead singer, Patti LaBelle caused a sensation when she began the show by descending from the ceiling, where she hung suspended, to the stage.

LaBelle went solo in 1977 after personal and artistic differences between the singers caused the band to break up. She continued to appear live and to record albums throughout the 1980s and early 1990s. In 1985 she appeared in Pennsylvania to perform in the Live Aid Benefit Rock Concert.

LaBelle is well known for her support of numerous charitable and social organizations, including Big Sisters and the United Negro College Fund, as well as various urban renewal and homelessness projects in Philadelphia, where she lives. She has published several books, including *Don't Block the*

Patti LaBelle: Selected Works

Nightbirds
(album)

Burnin'
(album)

Your Arms Too Short to Box with God
(play, 1982)

A Soldier's Story
(film)

Beverly Hills Cop
(film)

A Different World
(television)

Out All Night
(television)

One of the more flamboyant performers, Patti LaBelle in concert (© Jack Vartoogian. Reproduced by permission)

Blessings and the cookbook *LaBelle Cuisine: Recipes to Sing About*. She and her husband separated in early 2000.

Langford, Samuel E.

BOXER
March 5, 1883–January 12, 1956

Sam Langford, the son of a farmer, was born in Nova Scotia, Canada. He immigrated to Boston, Massachusetts, and fought his first professional boxing match in 1902, picking up the nickname "the Boston Tarbaby." Although he had his most important fights in the heavyweight division, Langford's relatively slight build enabled him to box in a number of weight divisions, including lightweight, welterweight, middleweight, light heavy-

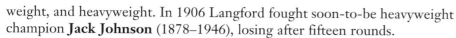

weight, and heavyweight. In 1906 Langford fought soon-to-be heavyweight champion **Jack Johnson** (1878–1946), losing after fifteen rounds.

Although most of the leading white contenders refused to meet Langford, he built an impressive record against first-rate competition. In 1909 Langford knocked out the English heavyweight champion, Ian Hagne, in four rounds, and in 1911 he defeated the reigning American light-heavyweight champion, Jack O'Brien. Langford later won the Mexican heavyweight title in 1923. During an era when boxers fought as often as three times a month and had matches that could go on for up to twenty rounds, Langford accumulated 116 knockouts (the fourth-highest record in boxing history) in a career 291 fights.

Langford's deteriorating eyesight forced him to retire from the professional boxing circuit in 1924. Unprepared for life after boxing, Langford struggled to earn a living. During the 1930s he traveled in Canada as part of a sideshow, offering to box people for small sums of money. When he returned to the United States, Langford took odd jobs in New York and the Boston area to support himself. In 1953 he was briefly confined to a mental hospital. Upon his release, he lived with his sister until her death in 1954, when he moved to a Boston rest home. Although blind and impoverished, Langford was not forgotten by the boxing world and was elected to *The Ring* magazine's Boxing Hall of Fame in 1955, shortly before his death in 1956.

Lankford, John Anderson

ARCHITECT, ENGINEER
December 4, 1874–July 1946

John Lankford was born in Missouri in 1874. In the 1880s and 1890s he attended several schools and colleges, including Shaw University in Holly Springs, Mississippi, where he received his bachelor's degree in 1898. He went on to obtain a master's degree in 1902. Even before completing his bachelor's degree, however, Lankford had opened the nation's first African-American professional architectural office in Washington, D.C., in 1897. In 1901 Lankford designed the Pythian Building in Washington, D.C., the first large office building designed by an African American.

Chiefly known for his church designs, Lankford's style reflected an appreciation for classical and European forms. His designs include the White Presbyterian Church of Potosi, Missouri; St. John's Church in Norfolk, Virginia; St. Phillips Church in Savannah, Georgia; the Allen Chapel African Methodist Episcopal (AME) Church in Franktown, Virginia; and the Haven Methodist Episcopal Church in Washington, D.C.

In 1908 the AME Church made Lankford its worldwide supervising architect. He went on to design additional churches in South America and in West and South Africa, such as the AME Church of Cape Town, South Africa. In 1916 Lankford published a pamphlet entitled *Christian Art*, which explained his approach to designing churches.

Lankford also designed a number of buildings other than churches. One was Palmer Hall at the State Agricultural and Mechanical College for Negroes (now Alabama A&M University) in Normal, Alabama. Another was

Allen University's English colonial style Chappelle Administration Building in Columbia, South Carolina.

Larsen, Nella

NOVELIST
April 13, 1891–c. March 30, 1964

Born in Chicago, Illinois, in 1891, novelist Nella Larsen was a mixed-race child of Danish and West Indian parents. Brought up in a visibly "white" family, she was a lonely child who was confused about her racial identity because of her darker skin color. Because she spent so much time alone, she became an avid reader of novels and travel books and a keen observer of life around her.

Larsen moved to New York City and completed nurse's training at the Lincoln Hospital School of Nursing in 1915. In 1919 she married Elmer S. Imes, a research scientist, and became part of the upwardly mobile African-American middle class. She left nursing in 1922 to work at the New York Public Library.

Larsen's novel *Quicksand*, published in 1928, follows the exploits of an educated mulatto (of mixed white and black ancestry), Helga Crane, as she struggles to understand herself, her psychological and physical needs, and her relationships with other people. Larsen's novel *Passing* is the story of two light-skinned African-American women who attempt to "pass"; "passing" is when light-skinned blacks pretend to be white. Larsen received a Guggenheim Fellowship in creative writing in 1930.

Larsen stopped publishing during the 1930s after several public humiliations. She was accused of copying another writer's work, and her divorce in 1933 was considered a scandal for the times and was featured in many of the African-American newspapers. She returned to the nursing profession, working in New York hospitals until her death in March 1964.

Lateef, Yusef

SAXOPHONIST AND FLUTIST, COMPOSER
October 9, 1920–

Yusef Lateef: Selected Works

Eastern Sounds
(1961)

A flat G flat and C
(1966)

Suite
(1970)

Yusef Lateef's Little Symphony
(1987)

Concerto for Yusef Lateef
(1988)

Nocturnes
(1988)

Born William Evans in Tennessee, musician Lateef combined the music of swing and bebop with the instruments and performance traditions of Africa, the Middle East, and Asia. He became a well-known figure in **jazz,** both as a sideman (member) and as a leader of his own small groups.

Lateef studied alto and tenor saxophone while growing up in Detroit, Michigan, eventually playing in New York in the 1940s. In 1949 he converted to **Islam,** adopting the name Yusef Lateef, and toured with bandleader **Dizzy Gillespie** (1917–1993). He returned to Detroit in 1950 to study composition at Wayne State University, mastering flute, oboe, and bassoon, as well as double-reed instruments from Asia and Africa and homemade instruments. In 1955 he resumed performing and recording, both as leader and sideman. During the 1960s he continued performing and recording and also received bachelor's and master's degrees from the Manhattan School of Music.

Yusef Lateef in concert (Archive Photos. Reproduced by permission)

From 1971 to 1975, when he received a Ph.D. in education from the University of Massachusetts at Amherst, Lateef taught music at the Borough of Manhattan Community College. Since the mid-1970s he has continued to perform, teach, and record in the United States, Europe, and Africa, gaining recognition for his virtuosity on the tenor saxophone as well as for his compositions. During the 1980s he ceased performing in places that sold alcohol. Lateef objected to the classification of his music as "jazz," preferring to describe it as "auto-physio-psychic" music.

Latimer, Lewis Howard

INVENTOR
September 4, 1848–December 11, 1928

Lewis Latimer was born in Massachusetts, the son of runaway slaves. In his youth Latimer worked at a variety of odd jobs, including selling copies of William Lloyd Garrison's *The Liberator*, sweeping up in his father's barbershop, hanging wallpaper, and waiting tables. In 1863 he joined the Union navy. Latimer served on the James River in Virginia until the end of the Civil War in 1865.

After the war Latimer returned to Boston, where in 1871 he was hired by patent lawyers Crosby and Gould. Although hired as an office boy, he became an expert mechanical drafter. He also tried his hand at inventing, and in 1874 he patented a pivot bottom for a water closet (toilet) for railroad cars. Latimer helped sketch the drawings for Alexander Graham Bell's 1876 patent on the telephone.

In 1880 Latimer was hired by inventor Hiram Maxim's United States Electric Lighting Company in Connecticut. Maxim was a competitor of Thomas A. Edison's, who had patented the incandescent light bulb in 1879. In 1881 Latimer and a colleague shared a patent for an electric lamp. Latimer's most important invention, patented (protected by license) in 1882, was a carbon filament that increased the brightness and longevity of the lightbulb. Because of its decreased costs, the resulting product made electric lighting more accessible.

From 1880 to 1882 Latimer oversaw the establishment of factories for U.S. Electric's production of the filaments and the installation of electric-light systems in New York City and Philadelphia and later in London. After his return from Britain, he worked for firms in the New York area until he joined the Edison Electric Light Company in 1884. There, he served as engineer and chief draftsman. Latimer wrote *Incandescent Electric Lighting* (1896), one of the first textbooks on electric lighting. When General Electric and Westinghouse decided that year to share patents, they created the Board of Patent Control to monitor patent disputes and appointed Latimer to the board. He used his drafting techniques and knowledge of patent law in this capacity until 1911. He then did patent law consulting with the New York firm of Hammer & Schwarz.

Latimer moved to New York in the late 1800s and was active in New York City politics and civil rights issues. In 1902 he circulated a petition expressing concern about the lack of African-American representation on the school board. He also taught English and mechanical drawing to immigrants in 1906. Latimer's booklet *Poems of Love and Life* was privately published by his friends on his seventy-fifth birthday in 1925. Latimer died in 1928. On May 10, 1968, a public school in Brooklyn, New York, was named in his honor.

Lawrence, Jacob Armstead

PAINTER, DRAFTSMAN
September 7, 1917–June 9, 2000

Painter Jacob Lawrence was influenced artistically as a child in **Harlem, New York.** Around 1930 his mother enrolled her three children in a Harlem day-care program that offered after-school arts and crafts activities at low cost. The arts program was run by painter Charles Alston

(1907–1977), who encouraged the young Jacob Lawrence. Lawrence's mother was often on welfare, so Jake, as he was called, took on several jobs as a teenager. But in the evenings he continued to attend art classes, and he committed himself to painting.

Between 1932 and 1937 Lawrence received training at several schools. He was still a student when he had his first one-person exhibition in 1938. Lawrence drew upon Harlem scenes and black history for his subjects, portraying the lives and aspirations of African Americans.

By 1936 Lawrence had work space in the studio of Charles Alston. He worked there for several years, meeting and learning from such African-American intellectuals as the philosopher **Alain Locke** (1885–1954) and the painter **Aaron Douglas** (1899–1979).

Lawrence's earliest works are scenes of Harlem activity. He was primarily influenced by other community artists, such as Alston and sculptor **Augusta Savage** (1892–1962), who believed in him and inspired him by their interest in ethnic origin and social injustice. Lawrence's general awareness of art came from his teachers as well as from books, local exhibitions, and frequent trips to the Metropolitan Museum. When he was a youth, he met painter **Gwendolyn Knight** (1913–), and they were married in 1941.

Lawrence's art remained remarkably consistent throughout the decades. He painted scenes of everyday life as well as historical events or people. He used water-based media applied in vivid color. He received almost overnight acclaim when his *Migration of the Negro* series was shown at New York's prestigious Downtown Gallery in 1941. With this exhibition, he became the first African-American artist to be represented by a major New York gallery. By the time he was thirty, he had become widely known as the foremost African-American artist in the country.

For more than forty years, Lawrence also taught drawing, painting, and design at several schools and colleges. During **World War II** he served in the U.S. Coast Guard. After serving, he received a Guggenheim Fellowship to paint a series about his war experiences.

During the 1960s Lawrence produced powerfully strident works in response to the civil rights conflicts in America. When he was appointed professor of art at the University of Washington in 1971, he and his wife moved to Seattle. He retired from teaching in 1987. After the mid-1960s Lawrence concentrated on works emphasizing humanity's aspirations and constructive potential. Lawrence died in Seattle, Washington, in June 2000 after a long illness.

Lawrence's work is full of humor, compassion, and intensity. His central theme is human struggle. Lawrence's greatest contribution to the history of art may be his reassertion of painting's ability to tell a story. His art speaks to the often neglected episodes of African-American history and the black experience.

Ledbetter, Hudson William "Leadbelly"

BLUES SINGER, GUITARIST
January 15, c. 1888–December 6, 1949

Born Hudson William Ledbetter on an uncertain date (some time around 1888) and raised near Mooringsport, Louisiana, Leadbelly, as he was known later in life, worked as a child in the cotton fields of his sharecropper parents. Ledbetter learned to play twelve-string guitar—as well as to shoot a revolver—in his early teens and began to perform in Shreveport, Louisiana, nightclubs. By the time he left home for good in 1906, Ledbetter had a reputation for hard work, womanizing, violence, and musical talent.

In 1908 Ledbetter, who had already fathered two children with another woman, married Aletta Henderson and settled down briefly in rural Texas. In 1910 he and his family moved to Dallas, where he began playing professionally with **Blind Lemon Jefferson.** The two were inseparable for five years.

Ledbetter was sentenced to a chain gang in 1915 for possessing a weapon. He escaped, but in 1917 he shot and killed a man in a fight. He served time at a state prison from 1918 to 1925—the year Texas governor Pat Neff visited the prison and Ledbetter made up a song on the spot asking to be released. Apparently convinced, Neff later pardoned him and set him free. By this time Ledbetter was known as "Leadbelly," a variation of his last name that also referred to his physical toughness. In 1930 Leadbelly was again jailed, this time for attempted homicide. He had served three years when John Lomax, a music historian, came to the penitentiary to record music by the prisoners. Lomax, impressed by Leadbelly's gifts, argued for his release, which came in 1934.

It was not until 1935 that Leadbelly made his first commercial recordings. From then on, aside from another brief prison term for assault, he enjoyed huge success. In the late 1930s and throughout the 1940s he appeared all over the country, as well as on radio and film, and was a key influence in American folk and blues music.

Leadbelly was best known for his songs about prison and rural life in the South. Among his most popular songs, some of which were recorded by

Lomax for the Library of Congress, are "Goodnight Irene" (1934), "The Midnight Special" (1934), and "Rock Island Line" (1937). He died in New York City at the age of sixty-one from amyotrophic lateral sclerosis (Lou Gehrig's disease). In 1988 Leadbelly was inducted into the Rock and Roll Hall of Fame. (*See also*: **Blues**)

Lee, Canada

ATHLETE, ACTOR
May 3, 1907–May 9, 1952

Born in New York City, Canada Lee (who also used the name Leonard Lionel Cornelius Canegata) began studying violin at age seven and made his first concert appearance four years later. At age fourteen he ran away from home and went to Saratoga, New York, where he became a horse-race jockey. Opportunities for African-American jockeys were few, and he returned home to New York after two years. He soon turned to boxing, winning ninety of one hundred amateur bouts. In 1926 he turned professional and adopted the name Canada Lee. However, a 1933 eye injury ended his career in the boxing ring.

Lee returned to New York and tried to make a career as a dance bandleader, supporting himself by working at New York's shipping docks. He won an acting role in a musical, and two years later he was cast as Banquo in the film and theater director-producer Orson Welles's famous "voodoo" production of *Macbeth*, set in the Caribbean island nation of Haiti.

During the 1940s Lee played lead roles in theater, produced a play, and had a radio show. He also made three films. By the late 1940s, however, Lee's career was stalled by accusations that he was a communist. He was fired from his radio show in 1948. Although he was outspoken about racial matters and participated in demonstrations for civil rights causes, Lee denied that he was a communist. Nevertheless, under the pressure of criticism and unemployment, his health began to fail.

In 1951 Lee was cast in the drama *Cry, the Beloved Country*, which was filmed in South Africa. After completing the film, Lee returned to the United States, but he was unable to find work. He traveled to England, where he collapsed and died shortly thereafter of a heart attack. While his career was cut too short for his fame to last, the Canada Lee Foundation, which he set up and which provides scholarships to black drama students, remains a lasting legacy.

Canada Lee: Selected Plays

Brother Mose
(1934)

Haiti
(1937)

Mamba's Daughters
(1939)

Across the Board Tomorrow Morning
(1942)

South Pacific
(1943)

On Whitman Avenue
(1944)

The Dutchess of Malfi
(1946)

Anna Lucasta
(1944)

The Tempest
(1945)

Lee, Shelton Jackson "Spike"

FILMMAKER
March 20, 1957–

Filmmaker Spike Lee was born in Atlanta, Georgia, and grew up in Brooklyn, New York. He received a bachelor's degree from **Morehouse College** in Atlanta in 1979, then enrolled at New York University, where he

Filmmaker Spike Lee addresses the media (AP/Wide World Photos. Reproduced by permission)

Spike Lee: Selected Films

She's Gotta Have It
(1986)

Do The Right Thing
(1989)

Malcolm X
(1992)

Clockers
(1995)

Girl 6
(1996)

Summer of Sam
(1999)

The Original Kings of Comedy
(documentary; 2000)

Bamboozled
(2000)

received a master's degree in film production in 1983. Among his several student films, *Joe's Bed-Stuy Barbershop: We Cut Heads* was awarded a Student Academy Award in 1982.

Lee has since produced many feature films. In most films he has served as director, writer, actor, and producer. Lee's first film was the highly acclaimed low-budget comedy *She's Gotta Have It* (1986), about a young black woman who is having affairs with three men.

Lee's second film, *School Daze* (1988), was financed by Columbia Pictures for $6.5 million and grossed more than $15 million. It deals with the conflict at a southern black college between light-skinned and dark-skinned students.

In 1989 Lee produced the highly successful film *Do the Right Thing*, which focuses on a pizza place run by an Italian-American family in a black Brooklyn neighborhood. During the course of one hot day, racial tensions climax in a riot in which one black youth is killed and the pizzeria is destroyed.

In *Mo' Better Blues* (1990), Lee tells a story of the personal growth and professional development of a jazz musician in New York City. In *Jungle Fever* (1991) Lee explores interracial relationships.

One of Lee's most ambitious films was *Malcolm X* (1992). A traditional Hollywood epic biography of the slain civil rights leader, the film is three hours long and cost $34 million. **Denzel Washington,** who portrayed Malcolm X, was nominated for an Academy Award as best actor.

Lee has since produced several films. *Crooklyn* (1994) is the story of a working-class black family in Brooklyn. *Get on the Bus* (1996) celebrated the the Million Man March. *4 Little Girls* (1997) is a documentary about four girls murdered in a church bombing in Birmingham in 1963. *He Got Game* (1998) explores the relationship between a teenage basketball star and his estranged, formerly imprisoned father.

Lee has also become a familiar face in a series of television commercials for such products as Nike athletic gear and Pizza Hut.

Lee, Spike. *See* Lee, Shelton Jackson

Leonard, Ray Charles "Sugar Ray"

BOXER
May 17, 1956–

Ray Charles "Sugar Ray" Leonard was a middleweight champion who threw one of the quickest punches in **boxing** history. Leonard was known for his lightning-fast jabs and electric personality.

Born in Wilmington, North Carolina, Leonard took his boxing name from "Sugar Ray" Robinson, a former middleweight champion. By the time he was twenty years old, Leonard had already proved himself as a first-class boxer. In 1974 he fought in Moscow with the U.S. National Boxing Team. In a unique display of sportsmanship, Leonard's Russian opponent immediately gave Leonard the trophy after the judges declared the Russian the winner. Leonard was virtually unbeatable as an amateur, winning 145 matches and a gold medal in the 1976 Olympics.

Leonard then turned professional and defeated several top-ranked boxers. In 1979, two years after turning professional, Leonard claimed the North American Boxing Federation and World Boxing Council titles. Leonard's two most famous fights came against Roberto Duran. In 1980 Duran defeated Leonard, and Leonard then defeated Duran in a rematch the same year. The fight became known as the "no mas" fight because Duran declared *no mas* (Spanish for "no more") after the eighth round. In 1981 Leonard won the World Boxing Association championship by defeating **Thomas Hearns** in fourteen rounds. That same year, *Sports Illustrated* named Leonard "Sportsman of the Year." Leonard retired for three years because of an eye injury, returning to the ring in 1987 to defeat **Marvelous Marvin Hagler** for the World Boxing Council title. Leonard was the first boxer to win titles in five different weight classes. He ended his career with thirty-five wins (twenty-five by knockout) and two losses. After boxing,

Boxer Sugar Ray Leonard strikes a pose for the camera (AP/Wide World Photos. Reproduced by permission)

Leonard began a television-announcing career. He returned to the ring in 1997 at the age of forty-one, but he lost in a brutal match against Hector Camacho.

Lester, Julius

WRITER, PROFESSOR
January 27, 1939–

The son of a Methodist minister, Julius Lester was born in St. Louis, Missouri. In 1960 he received his bachelor's degree from **Fisk University**

(Nashville, Tennessee). From 1968 to 1970 he was a lecturer at the New School for Social Research in New York City, and he also hosted radio and television shows in New York until 1975. Lester was a professor at the University of Massachusetts at Amherst for seventeen years (1971–88) and then became a professor of Near Eastern and Judaic studies.

Throughout his career, Lester has written or collaborated on dozens of works for both adults and children, usually focusing on African-American history or folklore. His diverse works include *The 12-String Guitar as Played by Leadbelly* (with Pete Seeger) (1965); *Look Out Whitey! Black Power's Gon' Get Your Mama!* (1968); and *The Tales of Uncle Remus* (four volumes collected in one, 2000). One of his best-known children's books, *To Be a Slave* (1969), was nominated for the prestigious Newbery Award, and *The Long Journey Home: Stories from Black History* (1972) was a National Book Award finalist. Lester's retelling of the American folk legend **John Henry** won the 1995 Caldecott Medal for children's literature.

Lester has had a long and controversial public record, perhaps best illustrated by the events following the 1988 publication of *Lovesong: Becoming a Jew*—an account of Lester's conversion to Judaism in which he accuses the late author **James Baldwin** of anti-Semitism (hostility toward Jews). The accusation led to furious debates on the University of Massachusetts campus, and while Lester did not flinch from igniting such a conflict, he remains deeply concerned about the tensions between African Americans and American Jews.

Lewis, Carl

TRACK-AND-FIELD ATHLETE
July 1, 1961–

Carl Lewis was one of the most athletically gifted people the world has ever seen. He is known for winning a record-tying nine gold medals in four consecutive Olympic Games (1984, 1988, 1992, and 1996). His specialty was the long jump.

Born in Birmingham, Alabama, Lewis was raised in Willingboro, New Jersey. He was brought up surrounded by sports. His parents were both athletes who started and ran a track club. Although Lewis showed athletic promise as a youngster, his talent was overshadowed by those of his siblings. In the 1980s, however, Lewis began to demonstrate his remarkable athletic gift. He attended the University of Houston in Texas, where he won consecutive national championships in the long jump and the 100-meter dash. In the 1984 Olympics Lewis won gold medals for the long jump, the 100- and 200-meter dashes, and a relay event. In the 1988 Olympics he repeated the performance, winning a gold medal for the long jump and the 100-meter dash. (He won the 100-meter dash when Ben Johnson was disqualified because of steroid use.) In 1992 Lewis again won an Olympic gold medal for the long jump and a relay event in which the United States set a world record.

At the age of thirty Lewis set a world record for the 100-meter dash at 9.86 seconds (1991). He capped off his stunning Olympic career by

Carl Lewis launches into the air in the long jump competition at the 1992 Olympics (AP/Wide World Photos. Reproduced by permission)

winning a ninth gold medal in the 1996 Olympics. In 1997 Lewis retired from competition.

Lewis, Edmonia

SCULPTOR
c. 1844–1909

Edmonia Lewis was the first African American to gain an international reputation as a sculptor. She was born in upstate New York in 1844 to a Chippewa Indian mother and a black father. Lewis, who was given the Indian name Wildfire, and her older brother, Sunrise, were orphaned when she was five years old. Raised by aunts, she was able to study at a school near Albany.

With financial help from her older brother, Lewis attended Oberlin College in Ohio, where her studies included drawing and painting. She ended her studies and moved to Boston, Massachusettes, to pursue a career in the arts. There, she found encouragement and support from a community of friends and patrons of the arts, many of whom were active in the abolitionist movement. Her Bust of Robert Gould Shaw (1864), a Civil War hero who died leading black troops into battle, was a great success. Sales of copies of that work enabled her to finance a trip to Europe, where, following travels in England, France, and Italy, she settled in Rome, Italy. Lewis's studio was a popular stop for Americans touring Europe. Many of them ordered sculptures of family members or of literary and historical figures to adorn their mantels and front parlors.

Lewis created over sixty items, not all of which have been located. Her early work in Boston included portrait medallions and busts of major abolitionists. While it is known that she was living in Rome as late as 1909, it is not certain where and when she died. (*See also*: **Painting and Sculpture**)

Lewis, John

CIVIL RIGHTS ACTIVIST, POLITICIAN
February 21, 1940–

John Lewis was one of the most influential black leaders of the **Civil Rights movement.** Known for his energetic speech-making and strong leadership abilities, Lewis calls on black and white Americans to put an end to racial injustice.

Born in Pike County, Alabama, Lewis grew up in a large family on a small sharecropping farm (sharecroppers rented the land they farmed, giving part of their crop as the rent). As a young boy, Lewis dreamed of entering the ministry. He fulfilled his dream in 1957 when he received a bachelor's degree from the American Baptist Seminary. While in college, Lewis became active in organizations committed to social equality.

In 1960 Lewis fought for desegregation and helped found the **Student Nonviolent Coordinating Committee (SNCC).** In 1960 he led "**freedom rides**" with the **Congress of Racial Equality (CORE),** trips through the South to determine whether public transportation facilities, such as bus terminals, were desegregated. Along with other black and white protesters, Lewis was violently attacked by southern whites during the rides.

Lewis's strong leadership skills earned him the position of national chairman of the SNCC (1963-66). As chairman he gave a controversial speech during the 1963 March on Washington in which he criticized the federal government for failing to do what was necessary to stop racism. Lewis participated in a protest with **Martin Luther King Jr.** in Alabama that was designed to strengthen blacks' voting rights. Although blacks were given the right to vote by the Fifteenth Amendment, unfair tactics such as poll taxes and literacy tests kept them from voting. Lewis was one of many who were severely beaten during the protest in what became known as "Bloody Sunday."

In 1976 President Jimmy Carter (1977–81) appointed Lewis to serve on ACTION, a government agency designed to promote volunteer activities. In 1986 Lewis won a hard-fought battle for a seat in the United States Congress. As a member of the House of Representatives, Lewis has served on the influential House Ways and Means Committee (which is in charge of funding projects with tax money) and has continued working for racial equality. In July 2000 Lewis indicated a desire to serve in the U.S. Senate.

Lewis, Reginald F.

ATTORNEY, FINANCIER
December 7, 1942–January 19, 1993

Reginald Lewis was a successful businessman and an African-American legal pioneer. Born in Baltimore, Maryland, Lewis received a law degree in 1968 from Harvard Law School (Cambridge, Massachusetts). After graduating, he accepted a position at a New York law firm. In 1973 he founded the first black law firm on Wall Street, Lewis & Clarkson, concentrating on corporate law and venture capital business.

In 1983 Lewis established a successful investment firm, the TLC Group. TLC (The Lewis Company) made headlines in 1984 when it bought the 117-year-old McCall Pattern Company, which it sold three years later. In 1987 TLC bought Beatrice International Foods, a collection of sixty-four companies in thirty-one countries. This was a very large acquisition, and it made TLC the largest black-owned company in the United States.

In 1992 Lewis was inducted into the National Sales Hall of Fame. That same year, he was named to the Municipal Assistance Corporation of New York City.

At the time of his death from brain cancer, Lewis's personal fortune was estimated at $400 million. Through his charitable organization, The Lewis Foundation, Lewis donated approximately $10 million in four years to various institutions, charities, and artistic organizations, including the Abyssinian Baptist Church in Harlem, New York, **Howard University** (Washington, D.C.), and Virginia State University. His $3 million donation to Harvard Law School, establishing the Reginald F. Lewis Fund for International Study and Research, was the largest the school ever received from a single donor. The Lewis Center at Harvard was the first such facility there named in honor of an African American.

Liberator, The

The *Liberator* was an antislavery newspaper begun in 1831 by **William Lloyd Garrison** (1805-1879) and Isaac Knapp (1804-1843) in Boston. From the start, the *Liberator*, which was published weekly, received substantial African-American support. Of its 450 initial subscribers, roughly 400 were black.

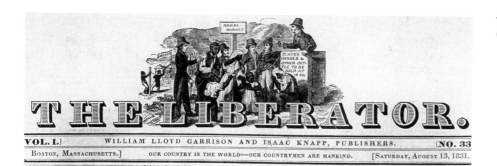

The masthead of *The Liberator* newspaper
(Courtesy of the Library of Congress)

The publication of the *Liberator* brought furious reaction from politicians in the South, who passed legislation banning its circulation. Columbia, South Carolina, offered a reward of $5,000 for the arrest and conviction of Garrison or Knapp. In October 1831 the corporation of Georgetown, D.C., forbade any free black to take the *Liberator* out of the post office. Offenders were to be punished by fine and imprisonment, and if they did not pay, they were to be sold into **slavery** for four months. Despite the *Liberator's* appeal, its circulation remained relatively small, particularly among the white population. In its fourth year, nearly three-quarters of the two thousand subscribers were African Americans.

The *Liberator* contained some of the most important writings on the abolitionist (antislavery) cause. Aside from Garrison's fiery editorials, it published the writings of John Rankin, Oliver Johnson, Wendell Phillips, and English abolitionist George Thompson. As the **Civil War** (1861–65) progressed, Garrison used the *Liberator* to pressure President Abraham Lincoln (1809–65) for **abolition.**

Garrison cheered the issuance of the **Emancipation** Proclamation, which freed slaves in the Southern states, but he kept working, hoping to secure the freedom of slaves in all of the states. With the passing of the Thirteenth Amendment, which ended slavery throughout the United States, Garrison believed the mission of the paper had been accomplished. On December 29, 1865, the *Liberator,* the most influential and important abolitionist newspaper, ceased publication.

Lincoln University

Founded: Lincoln University was founded in 1854 by John Miller Dickey, a pastor of the Oxford Presbyterian Church.

History Highlights:

- 1852: Pastor John Dickey unsuccessfully attempts to enroll James Ralston Amos into Princeton Seminary and several other "white" religious schools. Amos is an African American who is treasurer of the "Negro Church" established by minister and black leader **Richard Allen** in 1794.

- 1854: Frustrated by his failed attempts, Dickey establishes an institution for "colored" men. It is originally called Ashmun Institute, named after Jehudi Ashmun, the first governor of Liberia. After the Civil War (1861–65), it is renamed Lincoln University in honor of President Abraham Lincoln.
- 1945: Dr. **Horace Mann Bond** is the first African-American president of Lincoln; he serves until 1957.
- 1953: Women are first allowed to attend Lincoln.
- 1987: Dr. Niara Sudarkasa becomes the first African-American woman to be president of Lincoln University.

Location: Lincoln University, Pennsylvania

Known For: Lincoln is the oldest existing black college in the United States. It is known for academic excellence and for its distinguished alumni, many of whom are leaders in both the United States and Africa.

Number of Students (1999–2000): 2,084

Grade Average of Incoming Freshman: 3.0

Admission Requirements: SAT or ACT scores; minimum 2.5 GPA; four years of English, three years of math, three years of science, three years of social studies; personal essay; letter of recommendation from a teacher.

Mailing Address:
Lincoln University
Office of Admission
Lincoln Hall
Lincoln University, Pennsylvania 19352

Telephone: (800) 790-0191

E-mail: admiss@lu.lincoln.edu

URL: http://www.lincoln.edu

Campus: Lincoln's 422-acre campus is located in southern Chester County, forty-five miles southwest of Philadelphia. Buildings include an African museum, a fine arts center, and a learning resource center. The library contains over 170,000 documents and houses the personal library of the poet **Langston Hughes** and an African-American literature collection.

Special Programs: Courses offered in Swahili, Zulu, and Yoruba; Center for Public Policy and Diplomacy; Center for the Study of Critical Languages; minority aging program.

Extracurricular Activities: Student government; student newspaper, the *Lincolnian*; radio station; four fraternities and four sororities; over ninety organizations, including honor societies, Militants for Christ, a gospel choir, a drama group, and a law society; athletics (men's baseball, basketball, bowling, cross-country, soccer, tennis, track-and-field; women's basketball, bowling, cheerleading, cross-country, track-and-field, volleyball).

Lincoln Alumni: Thurgood Marshall (1908–1993), former Supreme Court justice; Kwame Nkrumah (1909–1972), Ghana's first prime minister; poet Langston Hughes (1902—1967).

Liston, Charles "Sonny"

BOXER
May 8, 1932–December 30, 1970

Charles "Sonny" Liston had one of the most ferocious left hooks in the history of boxing. He is known for his intimidating appearance and rugged street-fighting style.

Born on a poor cotton farm in Arkansas, Liston moved with his mother to St. Louis, Missouri, in 1945. He had a troubled childhood; he could not read or write, got into fights, and participated in armed robbery. In 1950 he was arrested for robbing a gas station and served nine months in prison. While in prison, a priest helped him channel his rage into the sport of boxing.

Boxing proved to be a perfect fit for Liston; in 1953 he won the national Golden Gloves championship. After turning professional, Liston began his career with fourteen wins and one loss. He returned to prison in 1953 for assaulting a police officer. When he returned to the ring, he picked up where he had left off, winning his next nineteen fights. In 1962 he won the championship with a first-round knockout. However, just when the world was beginning to believe that Liston was unbeatable, **Muhammad Ali** knocked him out in the first round in 1965. Liston ended his career with fifty wins and four losses.

Little Richard

SINGER
December 25, 1935–

Born to a devout Seventh-Day Adventist family, Richard Penniman began singing and playing piano in the church. He left home at thirteen to start a musical career. In 1951 he made some recordings with various blues bands but with little success. Shortly after, he began recording and had six hits (including "Tutti Frutti," 1954) that outlined the style that became rock and roll.

In 1957 he left his music career behind, received a degree, and became a minister in the Seventh-Day Adventist Church. He returned to rock and roll in 1964, but he was unable to recapture his early success. During the 1970s he took his flamboyant act to Las Vegas, Nevada, billing himself as "the bronze Liberace," after the flamboyant white entertainer. He returned to the church in the early 1980s, but his influence on rock and roll was not forgotten. In 1986 he was among the first artists inducted into the newly established Rock and Roll Hall of Fame.

Little Richard's style featured shrieking vocals, suggestive lyrics, and boogie-woogie-style piano performed at a remarkably fast tempo. His flamboyant stage personality and extravagant costumes also became a significant part of his act. He continued to perform at the beginning of the twenty-first century.

Locke, Alain Leroy

PHILOSOPHER
September 13, 1885–June 9, 1954

Best known for his literary contribution to the **Harlem Renaissance** of the 1920s (an exciting time of artistic and cultural development in New York City's Harlem section), Alain Locke was a leading spokesman for African-American values from 1925 to 1950. Born into Philadelphia, Pennsylvania's black middle class, Locke became the first African-American Rhodes scholar, taught at **Howard University** (Washington, D.C.) for over forty years, encouraged black artists and writers and served as a role model for them, and wrote books, essays, and reviews.

Locke's parents provided their only child with an extraordinarily cultivated environment. He entered Harvard College in 1904 and graduated with high honors. Locke studied philosophy and Greek at Oxford University in England and in Berlin, Germany, from 1907 to 1911. In Europe he developed his interests in the creative and performing arts and also formed close relationships with African and West Indian students that gave him an international perspective on racial issues. He returned to the United States in 1912 to begin his career at Howard University. He helped foster the school's development as a training center for Negro intellectuals and as a center for research on worldwide racial and cultural issues.

In the 1920s Locke was dismissed from Howard because of his allegiances with student protesters. He took advantage of the three-year break in his career to assume a leadership role in the emerging Harlem Renaissance. Locke edited the anthology the *New Negro*, which established him as an important figure in the **New Negro** movement (a movement that celebrated African Americans' increasing distance from slavery). More than just an interpreter of the New Negro movement, Locke became its leading thinker. Over the following fifteen years he created a "New Negro formulation" of racial values, charting what he thought was a unifying strategy for freedom in art and in American life.

Locke applied the methods of philosophy to the problems of race. He attempted to turn the fascination with the art and culture of **Africa** to political advantage. In the course of developing his ideas, Alain Locke became a leading American collector and critic of African art. He organized a series of African-American art exhibitions, and he played a role in the developing national black theater movement.

Locke's early interest in the scientific study of global race relations was revived when he coedited *When Peoples Meet: A Study in Race and Culture Contacts* (1942). During a year as an exchange professor in the Caribbean nation of Haiti, Locke studied the cultural contributions of African Americans. This occupied the last ten years of his life. His reputation and the lessening of segregation (enforced separation of blacks and whites) in American higher education kept him in demand as a visiting professor and lecturer around the world. The effects of lifelong heart ailments led to Locke's death in June 1954.

Lorde, Audre Geraldine

POET, NOVELIST, TEACHER
February 18, 1934–November 17, 1992

Born in **Harlem, New York**, to West Indian parents, Audre Lorde did not speak until she was nearly five years old and also suffered from impaired vision, which may have helped form her passion for both words and images. She described herself as "a black lesbian feminist mother lover poet," and her writing explores personal and political pain, rage, and love.

Lorde published her first poem while in high school, in *Seventeen* magazine. She studied for a year at the National University of Mexico before returning to the United States to earn a degree from Hunter College in New York in 1959. She went on to receive a master's degree from the Columbia School of Library Science (New York) in 1960, and during this time she married attorney Edward Ashley Rollins and had two children. Lorde and Rollins divorced in 1970, and Lorde, now a member of the Harlem Writers Guild, became actively involved in causes for social justice.

In 1968 Lorde published her first collection of poetry, *The First Cities* (1968), and from then on she was a full-time writer and teacher. In 1973 her third book, *From a Land Where Other People Live*, was nominated for the National Book Award for poetry; her best-known and most highly praised work, *The Black Unicorn*, was published in 1978.

Lorde's devotion to honesty and outspokenness is evident in the works she produced in the 1980s. She published her first nonpoetry work, *The Cancer Journals* (1980), so she could share the experience of her cancer diagnosis and treatment with as wide an audience as possible. Her first work of fiction, *Zami: A New Spelling of My Name*, appeared in 1982, and she went on to publish various essays and poetry throughout the decade. In 1991 she became New York State's poet laureate (an honor recognizing the leading or most representative poet). She died in St. Croix, U.S. Virgin Islands.

Los Angeles, California

The experiences of African Americans in Los Angeles have differed from those of black people in most other large American cities. Los Angeles has always been characterized by cultural diversity. This diversity has shaped the history of African Americans in Los Angeles: African Americans have frequently compared themselves to Latinos and Asian Americans, and patterns of cooperation and competition among these groups have left indelible marks on the city's politics and culture.

Los Angeles's Beginnings

The U.S. conquest of northern Mexico and the Gold Rush of 1848-1849 scarcely affected Los Angeles, which remained a small, largely Mexican town. In the 1850s and '60s, Southern California's remoteness attracted some **Fugitive Slaves**. Reports of some of these escaped slaves' success helped Southern California to develop a reputation as a land of economic opportunity for African Americans.

The completion of railroad lines and harbor improvements in the 1870s and '80s sparked explosive growth in Southern California. Among the new residents were small but significant numbers of African Americans.

New black residents moved into a segregated city. The first black neighborhood, labeled "Nigger Alley" by white residents, developed in the 1870s on Alameda Street, near Chinatown. By 1910 a ghetto had formed around the Central Avenue Hotel in downtown Los Angeles. This ghetto expanded south along Central Avenue toward Watts, a community that attracted African Americans from the rural South. By 1930, some 70 percent of the city's black residents lived in the Central Avenue neighborhood. Significant numbers of African Americans also settled in the West Adams district, west of downtown.

The Growth of Community and Culture

The Central Avenue district became the center of African-American culture. Businesses, entertainment houses, restaurants, and churches served the expanding community. Notable musicians such as tenor saxophonist Dexter Gordon emerged from the **jazz** clubs of Central Avenue. The district's theaters regularly drew celebrated black performers such as **Nat King Cole**, **Duke Ellington**, and **Paul Robeson** to Los Angeles in the 1930s and '40s.

Prior to **World War II**, black residents were routinely denied access to public swimming pools and parks. They were also excluded from many theaters and restaurants. Employers refused to hire black people for clerical or white-collar jobs, and skilled black workers found few openings in the city's small industrial sector. Most black men worked as manual laborers, and most black women worked as domestic servants.

Despite the pervasive housing and employment discrimination, the city's African Americans were able to exercise some political power. Frederick Roberts, a black Republican, represented the "East Side" in the State Assembly from 1919 until 1933. Democrat Augustus Hawkins defeated Roberts in the 1932 election and served in the Assembly from 1933 until his election to Congress in 1962.

World War II

World War II offered African-American leaders the opportunity to test multicultural cooperation. Federal propaganda fueled the desire of African and Mexican Americans to destroy racial discrimination in the United States. The federal government's decision to incarcerate Japanese Americans also haunted minority community leaders. Thousands of African Americans moved into the houses and storefronts of vacated by the interred Japanese.

During the war years, black and Mexican-American civil rights organizations cooperated in their efforts to combat discrimination. Peaceful demonstrations and formal complaints to the President's Fair Employment Practices Committee (FEPC), which Franklin Roosevelt had created in 1941, succeeded in placing many black and Mexican-American workers in high-paying jobs in war industries. By 1945 black workers held 14 percent of the shipyard jobs in Los Angeles, even though African Americans comprised only 6.5 percent of the city's population.

After the war ended, however, civil rights activists found it difficult to reform local institutions. Many African Americans lost their jobs, and financial support for the organizations such as the **National Association for the Advancement of Colored People (NAACP)** and the National Urban League diminished. Politicians and newspaper publishers attached the "communist" label on all civil rights activism. The fears of white residents dominated the 1946 election: two-thirds of Los Angeles's voters rejected an initiative that would have outlawed employment discrimination in California.

The Postwar Era and the Watts Riots

Southern California's mild climate and its image as a land of opportunity continued to attract black people from the East and the South after World War II. The population growth promised greater political power. **Tom Bradley**, a retired police officer, put together a coalition of African Americans and liberal white voters—many of them Jews—and won a seat on the City Council in 1963.

Bradley's election lifted the hopes of many of Los Angeles's black residents, but conditions in the ghetto did not improve in the 1960s. Unemployment was higher in African-American districts than in the rest of the city, and police officers routinely harassed black people, often using excessive force in arresting black suspects.

An arrest on August 11, 1965, turned into a confrontation between police and residents of the Watts community and ignited a six-day rebellion. As many as 30,000 African Americans looted and burned hundreds of businesses. State officials mobilized more than 15,000 National Guard troops and police officers to quell the rebellion. The violence left thirty-four people—thirty-one of whom were black—dead and hundreds injured. The police arrested more than 4,000 people.

After the rebellion, government officials and community leaders called for sweeping reforms, including programs to train and employ the thousands of unemployed African Americans in south central Los Angeles. Local, state, and federal agencies, however, never fully implemented these reforms.

Power through Art and Education

While unemployment and other social problems continued to fester in the ghetto, changes within U.S society helped to open new opportunities for some African Americans. Access to good schools and colleges led to the emergence of a new black middle class in Los Angeles. Pressure from the NAACP and other civil rights organizations created new opportunities for black performers in **film** and **television**. Black superstars such as **Eddie Murphy** and **Michael Jackson** began to wield power within the entertainment industry in the 1980s. The wealth and power of these stars, however, put them out of touch with the hundreds of thousands of people trapped by poverty and discrimination in South Central Los Angeles.

In the mid- to late-1980s, some young African Americans began to address ghetto conditions in their art and music. South Central Los Angeles and the surrounding black suburbs produced a number of influential filmmakers and musical artists. Motion picture director John Singleton received an Oscar nomination for *Boyz N the Hood* (1991), which explored life in the ghetto. Musicians such as NWA and Ice Cube sold millions of copies of their releases. Many of these artists succeeded in appealing to a large, diverse audience while retaining their base in Los Angeles's black community.

L.A. at the End of the Twentieth Century

Los Angeles became a sharply divided city in the minds of many of its African-American residents in the 1990s. The divide between African Americans and other residents of the Los Angeles area had already been underscored by the 1991 police beating of black motorist Rodney King and by the riots that followed a partial acquittal of the four white officers involved. On June 12, 1994, Nicole Brown Simpson the estranged wife of former professional football star **O. J. Simpson**, was murdered in a California suburb along with a male companion, Ronald Goldman. Considerable circumstantial evidence linked Simpson with the crime, but his defense team argued that Simpson had been framed by Los Angeles police officers for racial reasons. The racial divide opened once again when a predominantly black jury acquitted Simpson in 1995, but a predominantly white panel in the suburb of Santa Monica found him responsible for the murders two years later in a wrongful-death lawsuit brought by Brown's family. A *Los Angeles Times* opinion poll conducted before the second trial found that 71 percent of white residents believed that Simpson was guilty, but only 10 percent of blacks agreed. Part of the alienation blacks experienced came from what many perceived as a reduction in the opportunities available to them: attacks on affirmative action policies at the state government level were coupled with a decline in black political power in the Los Angeles basin itself. The percentage of blacks in the population of Los Angeles County dropped from 17 percent in the 1970s to about 10 percent at the century's end as the area's Hispanic and Asian populations exploded.

Latino groups challenged blacks' hard-won share of political patronage jobs (positions created as the result of politicians' efforts to return the favor of minority votes), and relations between blacks and Koreans, whose retail establishments bore the brunt of the 1991 riots, remained poor. The bleak social conditions of southern California's inner cities found expression in the new "gangsta rap" music genre, whose texts reproduced the violence endemic to those communities.

(SEE ALSO **CALIFORNIA**; **RODNEY KING RIOTS**; **RAP**; **O. J. SIMPSON**)

Louisiana

First African-American Settlers: The first two blacks came to the French colony of Louisiana in 1709 as slaves of the governor, Jean Baptiste, Sieur de Bienville. In 1712 King Louis XIV granted the privilege of sending one ship to Africa to transport blacks to the Louisiana colony, and the next year twenty slaves were imported.

Slave Population: Between 1719 and 1731 twenty-seven slave ships arrived from **Africa.** Many slaves resided in New Orleans, where they worked for the colonial government or private masters to build the city, were trained in skilled trades, or were forced into agricultural work. The treatment of blacks was made less harsh by the presence of **American Indians** in the colony and by a *code noir* (black code) that provided for slave marriage, property ownership, and religious worship. Under the Louisiana Purchase of 1803, President Thomas Jefferson (1743–1826; president 1801–09) bought the territory for the United States, and Louisiana achieved statehood nine years later. By 1860 there were four hundred thousand slaves in the state, working mostly at planting and harvesting sugar.

Free Black Population: Antebellum (pre–Civil War) Louisiana was notable for the presence of a large free black population, especially in the capital of New Orleans. The population of **free blacks** swelled with the entry of four thousand *gens de couleur libres* (free people of color), who arrived in exile from Haiti. By 1860 **Creoles** owned $15 million worth of property in New Orleans, including enslaved blacks.

Civil War: In the spring of 1862 Union (Northern) troops occupied New Orleans. Slaves in the city were freed, and others in the surrounding countryside fled to freedom behind Union lines. Louisiana provided more black troops for the Union cause—over twenty-four thousand—than any other Southern state, and in 1863 blacks fought bravely under fire at the battle for Port Hudson, a Confederate (Southern) fortress north of Baton Rouge, Louisiana.

Reconstruction: After a group of black marchers supporting a **suffrage** convention was attacked in the New Orleans Riot of 1866, Congress dissolved the Louisiana government and enfranchised (extended voting rights to) the state's black majority; blacks comprised 65 percent of registered voters. When **Reconstruction** ended, however, a white supremacist (superiority) sentiment prevailed and blacks were subjected to intimidation, violence, and economic hardship.

The Great Depression: The first government efforts to improve black life came in the 1930s under the regime of Governor Huey Long, who made quiet efforts to include black citizens in his "Share-the-Wealth" efforts, offering free school textbooks and homestead tax exemptions on a nonracial basis.

Civil Rights Movement: The first major efforts toward the **Civil Rights movement** came in May 1960 when a two-year campaign of **sit-ins** against segregation was begun by Southern University (Baton Rouge) students. The Louisiana Summer Projects of 1963 and 1964 organized volunteers who built community organizations, marched against segregated facilities, and promoted voter education.

Current African-American Population: According to U.S. Census Bureau estimates, the total black population in Louisiana was 1,407,201 (32 percent of the state population) as of July 1, 1998.

Key Figures: Norbert Rillieux (1806–1894), inventor of the vacuum sugar-refining process; former Louisiana lieutenant governor P. B. S. Pinchback (1837–1921).

(SEE ALSO CIVIL WAR; CONGRESS OF RACIAL EQUALITY (CORE); JAZZ; ZYDECO.)

GETTING LOUIS IN THE RING

Louis faced racist obstacles early in his career because he wanted to fight in the heavyweight division. At the time, there was an unwritten agreement that no blacks could contend for the heavyweight title. This was because **Jack Johnson,** the first black to win the heavyweight title, led a lifestyle that was displeasing to whites. However, fight promoters knew they had a winner on their hands with Louis and found a way to get him in the ring as a heavyweight. First, they told Louis to avoid all public scandal and to behave respectfully in the ring. Second, they set up a rival to the existing boxing establishment: the Twentieth Century Sporting Club was created and allowed blacks to fight for the heavyweight title.

Louis, Joe

BOXER
May 13, 1914–April 12, 1981

Joe Louis was a heavyweight boxing champion and one of the greatest boxers of all time. He is known for being a symbolic figure in the fight against racism and a beloved American patriot.

Born in Chambers County, Alabama, Louis had a difficult childhood. Louis lost his father to mental illness, and his mother remarried, moving the family to Detroit, Michigan, to seek financial stability. At the beginning of the Great Depression (a period of severe economic hardship in the 1930s), Louis's stepfather was laid off from his job and Louis left school to work. Like many young men at the time, Louis picked up **boxing** out of necessity; it provided money as well as a way to release stress.

Although he lost his first amateur fight badly, Louis later went on a rampage, winning fifty fights (fory-three by knockout). In 1934 he won the Amateur Athletic Union's light-heavyweight title and turned professional. At the time, racism prevented blacks from participating in all professional sports except boxing. Louis's presence in the ring with whites made him an instant hero within the African-American community.

Standing six feet one inch and weighing two hundred pounds, Louis was instantly successful. He won thirty out of his first thirty-one fights, including the heavyweight title in 1937. In 1936 Louis was defeated by Max Schmeling. Up until that fight, Louis had been described as unbeatable by sportswriters and had been given the nickname "the Brown Bomber." After defeating Schmeling in a rematch in 1938, Louis went on to successfully defend his title numerous times. However, few of his opponents presented much competition.

After World War II (1939–1945) Louis's career as a boxer began to decline. He retired in 1949 with sixty-six wins and only three losses. He was elected to the Boxing Hall of Fame in 1954. Louis's life declined after boxing, and he turned to drugs and suffered several nervous breakdowns. In 1993 a postage stamp was released in his honor.

Joe Louis, the "Brown Bomber" of Detroit (AP/Wide World Photos. Reproduced by permission)

LOUIS MAKES A POLITICAL STATEMENT

In 1938 a rematch was staged between Joe Louis and the German Max Schmeling. The fight meant more than the title for heavyweight boxing champion of the world. At the time, the German dictator Adolf Hitler was invading territories in Europe and threatening world peace. Hitler believed that Germans were racially superior human beings. In effect, the fight between Louis and Schmeling had political impact because it represented a symbolic standoff between democracy and Nazism (Hitler's political program). With the world watching, and on the brink of global conflict, Louis demolished Schmeling, knocking him out two minutes into the first round. Louis became a national hero and went on to fight in World War II (1939–1945). He continued to fight during the war and donated his proceeds to the war effort. He became a symbol of patriotism. At one point during the war, he gave a speech at a Navy Relief Society dinner in which he inspired the country by saying, "We're going to do our part, and we will win, because we're on God's side."

Cowboy Nat "Deadwood Dick" Love

Love, Nat "Deadwood Dick"

COWBOY
June 1854–1921

Born into **slavery**, Nat Love was the child of a slave foreman and a cook on a Tennessee plantation. After the **Civil War** (1861–65), Nat's father farmed twenty acres he rented from his former master. At age fifteen, Nat became responsible for the family's meager finances after his father and brother-in-law died and his older brother left home.

Love began supplementing his income by breaking horses for a neighbor. He also proved to be clever and lucky. In early 1869 Love won a horse in a raffle, sold it back to the owner for fifty dollars, and then rewon the horse when the owner raffled it off again. Love sold the horse again for fifty dollars, split his winnings with his mother, and like one of thousands of African Americans seeking opportunity, set off for the West.

Love's horse-breaking skills won him a job with cowboys in the Texas panhandle. Love described himself in those days as "wild, reckless and free, afraid of nothing." In 1876 Love was in Deadwood, South Dakota, delivering three thousand head of three-year-old steers. The cowboys' route had taken them past Little Bighorn, Wyoming, only two days behind Gen. George Armstrong Custer; they arrived in Deadwood on July 3, 1876, eight days after the Battle of Little Bighorn. The next day, Love won the annual cowboy competition in Deadwood by roping, throwing, tying, bridling, saddling, and mounting an untamed bronco in nine minutes flat. This feat, along with his marksmanship, earned him the name "Deadwood Dick." With his long hair, he cut a striking figure as a rough-and-tumble cowboy.

In 1890 Love left the range. He believed that the railroads had made his job obsolete, and he saw them as the wave of the future. Love became one of the first Pullman porters, working the Denver and Rio Grande Western Railroad. He published his autobiography, *The Life and Adventures of Nat Love, Better Known in Cattle Country as Deadwood Dick*, in 1907. By that time, he had left the railroad and moved to Los Angeles, California. Love died in Los Angeles in 1921.

Loving, Alvin

ARTIST
September 19, 1935–

Artist Al Loving was born in Detroit, Michigan. His father was an associate dean at the University of Michigan and an important figure in international education. When Loving traveled to India in 1955 with his father, he observed an artist working on large-scale murals and decided to become a painter.

From 1958 to 1960 Loving served in the U.S. Army as a propaganda (the spreading of ideas, facts, or rumors to gain support for the army) illustrator. He graduated from the University of Illinois in 1963 and taught at Eastern Michigan University while pursuing a master's degree at the University of Michigan.

Loving's interest in geometry, illusions of space, and the organization of color was evident in his painting style by the 1970s. Geometric shapes, particularly the square, became the central subjects of his paintings.

Loving presented his first solo exhibition in 1969 at the Gertrude Kasle Gallery in Detroit. Kasle also helped him establish connections at the Whitney Museum of American Art, where Loving was invited to organize a solo show.

In 1972 Loving was commissioned to paint a seventeen-story mural for the First National Bank Building in Detroit. After a worker was seriously injured during the construction, Loving shifted away from large-scale geometric painting and began to create smaller pieces using strips of cut, dyed, and sewn material.

In the mid-1970s Loving created large-scale paper and cardboard collages. From 1981 to 1985 he made monoprints and experimented with works of handmade paper, including the production of paper pulp.

Loving has received grants from the National Endowment for the Arts and a Guggenheim Fellowship. He has been associate professor of art at City College, City University of New York, since 1988.

Lynching

Lynching is believed to have begun during the **American Revolution** (1775–83) when Colonel Charles Lynch and other Virginia frontiersmen formed groups to hunt down and punish outlaws. But it usually refers to the killing of black men and women in the South by white mobs—by hanging, shooting, or burning—from the end of the American **Civil War** (1861–65) through the mid-twentieth century. Approximately 4,745 people died at the hands of lynch mobs between 1882 and about 1960.

"Lynch law" came to mean the supposed right of a band of angry citizens to take the law into their own hands when they thought judges and lawmen acted too slowly. Early lynch mobs used whippings, tarring and feathering, and sometimes hanging or shooting to punish horse thieves and outlaws; but they also used these methods on Catholics, immigrants, and abolitionists (people working to end **slavery**).

During the **Reconstruction** period at the end of the Civil War, mobs in the South used lynching to restore white control over freed slaves. Most lynchings occurred during the late 1880s and in the 1890s, when more than 150 lynchings took place each year. After 1882 about 72 percent of the victims were African Americans, and by the 1920s blacks accounted for 90 percent of the victims. About 95 percent of the lynchings occurred in isolated rural communities in southern states.

Lynch mobs gave a variety of reasons for their actions. An African American might be lynched for murder, assault, rape, theft, or arson, or for something as simple as failing to move off the sidewalk to let whites pass. Black men were lynched most often on charges of raping a white woman.

Lynchings could be secret hangings or shootings by a small group or carried out by a posse after a manhunt. But they were often large public affairs that were advertised and drew crowds, including women and children. Victims were tortured and mutilated before they were killed. People sometimes took "souvenirs" of the lynching, like body pieces or bone fragments, and some took photographs of the victims.

Police could rarely stop a lynching, even when they tried, and mob members were almost never caught. Most records show lynchings were done by "persons unknown." Investigators in the early twentieth century found that many types of events could trigger a lynching, from the number of blacks in the community to the price of cotton. Because lynchings usually occurred in the poorest southern counties, historians think they might have been a way for white men to vent their frustration at economic failure onto blacks.

A few people spoke out against lynching in the late 1800s. The most well known was **Ida Bell Wells-Barnett** (1862–1931), a black woman activist

Depiction of spectators viewing a lynching
(Courtesy of the Library of Congress)

from Memphis, Tennessee, who wrote articles and gave lectures to let the public know about the horrors of lynching. In the early 1900s the **National Association for the Advancement of Colored People (NAACP)** investigated and publicized lynchings and tried to get laws passed to stop them. A few states passed laws banning lynchings, but they were difficult to enforce. No federal laws against lynching were ever passed.

When new roads, electricity, telephones, and automobiles brought progress to isolated areas in the twentieth century, the number of lynchings decreased. Business leaders wanted to change the violent image of small southern towns, and law enforcement officers became better at preventing lynching. Other forms of black oppression, such as segregation, disfranchisement (taking away legal rights such as voting), and tenant farming, began to take its place.

During the **Civil Rights movement** of the 1960s violence against blacks increased, but the old form of lynching stopped. The last known true lynching victims were **Emmett Louis Till,** in 1955, and Mack Charles Parker, in 1959.

Mabley, Jackie "Moms"

COMEDIENNE
March 19, 1897–May 23, 1975

Jackie Mabley became famous as her hilarious comedy character, "Moms." Born Loretta Mary Aiken in Brevard, North Carolina, Jackie "Moms" Mabley was one of twelve children of mixed African-American, Cherokee, and Irish ancestry. Mabley, who borrowed her name from Jack Mabley, an early boyfriend, began performing as a teenager. In the mid-1920s, she was brought to New York by the dance team of Butterbeans and Suzie. After making her debut at Connie's Inn, Mabley became a favorite at **Harlem, New York**'s **Cotton Club** and at the Club Harlem in Atlantic City, New Jersey. It was during this time that she began creating the badly dressed, granny-like stage personality for which she became famous. Shuffling onto the stage in a housedress with a frilly nightcap, sagging stockings, and outsized shoes, "Moms"—as she was later known—would begin her stand-up comedy routine.

Mabley appeared in small parts in two motion pictures, *Jazz Heaven* (also distributed as *Boarding House Blues*, 1929) and *Emperor Jones* (1933). She collaborated with **Zora Neale Hurston** in the Broadway play *Fast and Furious: A Colored Revue in 37 Scenes* (1931) before she started performing regularly at the **Apollo Theater** in Harlem. By the time she made the film *Killer Diller* (1948), she had cultivated a considerable following among black audiences, as well as among fellow performers; however, it was not until 1960, when she cut her first album for Chess Records, that she became known to white audiences. *Moms Mabley at the U.N.*, which sold over a million copies, was followed by several albums, including *Moms Mabley at the Geneva Conference; Moms Mabley: The Funniest Woman in the World; Moms Live at Sing Sing;* and *Now Hear This.*

Mabley made her television debut in 1967 in an all-black comedy special, *A Time for Laughter*, produced by **Harry Belafonte.** Throughout the late 1960s and early 1970s, she was featured in frequent guest spots on television comedy and variety shows. Mabley had a heart attack while starring in *Amazing Grace* (1974), a successful feature film, and died the following year.

Mabley, Moms. *See* Mabley, Jackie

Mackey, John

FOOTBALL PLAYER
September 24, 1941–

Football player John Mackey was born in New York and went on to Syracuse College, where he received a bachelor's degree in history and political science. He joined the football team as a halfback and played for three seasons. In 1963 Mackey joined the Baltimore Colts of the National Football League (NFL), playing tight end. A fine receiver and a speedy rusher, Mackey was the first great modern tight end. He made the All-Pro team from 1966 to 1968 and played in five Pro Bowls. In Super Bowl V, he scored a touchdown on a 75-yard pass play. In 1970 the NFL named him the greatest tight end in history, but a knee operation in 1970 and an elbow operation in 1971 limited his effectiveness. In 1972 Mackey was traded to the San Diego Chargers and finished his career that season, with a record lifetime average of 15.8 yards per reception.

In 1970 Mackey was named head of the new NFL Players Association. Mackey gained respect for the association by leading players in a short strike. In 1972 he filed suit in federal court to overturn the (Pete) Rozelle Rule, which made it difficult for players to change teams as free agents. In 1975 the case was decided in Mackey's favor, revolutionizing NFL labor relations. In 1992 Mackey was elected to the Pro Football Hall of Fame, having been previously excluded, most likely because of his labor activism. Mackey serves as the CEO of Whole Foods Market. A strong supporter of labor unions, he makes a point of staffing none of his stores with union staff. He has also worked in California programs to benefit inner-city youth.

Madhubuti, Haki R.

POET, ESSAYIST

1942–

Born Don L. Lee in Little Rock, Arkansas, Haki Madhubuti was raised in Detroit, Michigan. His father deserted the family when Madhubuti was very young, and his mother died when he was sixteen, forcing Madhubuti to seek employment and become self-reliant at an early age. In the late 1950s, he attended a vocational high school in Chicago, Illinois, and he joined the U.S. Army for three years beginning in 1960.

With the publication of his first volumes, *Think Black!* (1967), *Black Pride* (1968), and *Don't Cry, Scream* (1969), Madhubuti established himself as a leading poet among his generation of American black artists. He was especially praised among critics associated with the **Black Arts movement** of the 1960s and early 1970s. In his poems Madhubuti makes use of black cultural forms, such as street talk and **jazz** music. His early literary criticism, included in *Dynamite Voices* (1971), constituted one of the first overviews of the new black poetry of the sixties.

In 1973 the poet rejected his "slave name," Don L. Lee, to become Haki R. Madhubuti (Swahili for "precise justice"). In the same year, he published two collections, *From Plan to Planet* and *Book of Life*, both of which illustrate his commitment to **black nationalism**—a philosophy that promotes black unity and self-reliance. In 1978 Madhubuti published *Enemies: The Clash of the Races*—a stinging criticism of white racism. As founding editor of Third World Press and the Organization of Black American Culture (OBAC) Writers Workshop, Madhubuti continues to be active in in both local and national politics. He edited the 1992 book *Why L.A. Happened: Implications of the 1992 Los Angeles Rebellion*, a collection of essays and poems by writers such as **Gwendolyn Brooks** and Bell Hooks commenting on the 1992 Los Angeles riots.

In 1990 Madhubuti published *Black Men: Obsolete, Single, Dangerous? (The Afrikan American Family in Transition)*, a collection of essays speaking specifically to black men and offering analyses and guidance on topics ranging from fatherhood to AIDS. In 1998 he published the volume *GroundWork: New and Selected Poems of Don L. Lee/Haki R. Madhubuti from 1966–1996.*

Magazines. *See* **The Crisis; Ebony; Jet Magazine**

Maine

First African-American Settlers: African Americans have lived in Maine for over three hundred years. Slavery existed in the state as early as 1663, but it was confined to the well-to-do and produced a slave population that never exceeded five hundred.

Slave Population: **Slavery** in seventeenth- and eighteenth-century Maine was not an integral part of the economic system, which instead depended on family labor and working for a salary. Nonetheless, until 1820 the state had just as complex a legal system of slave codes as Southern states. Slavery ended after the Massachusetts Supreme Court ruled in 1793 that the "free and equal" clause of the state constitution made the practice of slavery illegal (Maine was part of Massachusetts until 1820).

Free Black Population: With the end of slavery, Maine's black population began to grow as free African Americans from other states were attracted to the state. Although limited to certain occupations, African Americans played important roles in Maine's economy as farmers, fishermen, and seamen.

Reconstruction: From 1870 to the end of the nineteenth century, African Americans withdrew from the direct production of food as farmers or fisherman and turned to service occupations. Many held personal-service occupations as gardeners, cooks, waiters, and barbers. The population of African Americans reached 1,606 in 1870.

The Great Depression: The black population slowly declined in Maine in the early years of the twentieth century. With the opening of Loring Air Force Base in the 1950s, however, a new generation of African-American service personnel flocked to Maine. The black population jumped from 1,221 in 1950 to 3,318 in 1960 with the influx of African-American families and individuals into towns near military installations.

Civil Rights Movement: The 1960s saw the growth of a more assertive spirit among Portland's African-American community, with a revitalized **National Association for the Advancement of Colored People (NAACP)** participating in the 1963 march on Washington. The basic economic status for many African Americans had not changed much, however. A survey of Portland in the early 1960s showed that, in general, African Americans outside the military held the same types of jobs as in 1870: common laborers, porters, janitors, custodians, clerks, seamstresses, and domestics. Only a handful owned their own business.

Current African-American Population: According to U.S. Census Bureau estimates, the total black population in Maine was 6,321 (0.5 percent of the state population) as of July 1, 1998.

Key Figures: John Brown Russwurm (1799–1851), abolitionist and government official; Charles Lenox Remond (1810–1873), former slave who toured Maine to lecture about slavery.

(SEE ALSO *UNCLE TOM'S CABIN.*)

Major, Clarence

WRITER
December 31, 1936–

Born in Atlanta, Georgia, and raised in Chicago, Illinois, Clarence Major decided early in life to become a painter, but a brief stay at the School of the Art Institute of Chicago in 1953 convinced him to set his sights on a writing career instead. After a stint in the U.S. Air Force (1955–1957), Major returned to Chicago, where he worked as an editor and composed the poems that made up his first two volumes, *Love Poems of a Black Man* (1965) and *Human Juices* (1966).

In 1966 Major relocated to New York, and three years later his first novel, *All-Night Visitors*, was published; also in 1969, *Major's New Black Poetry*, an anthology that included the work of **Amiri Baraka, Nikki Giovanni,** and **Sonia Sanchez,** appeared. In 1970 he released his *Dictionary of Afro-American Slang* and his *Swallow the Lake*, a poetry collection. Major continued to publish poetry, fiction, and criticism at a remarkable rate over the next three decades.

In 1977 Major joined the faculty of the University of Colorado, and he taught briefly at the University of Nice, in France 1981–82. His later work includes the editing of two important collections of African-American literature, *Calling the Wind: Twentieth Century African-American Short Stories* (1993) and *The Garden Thrives: Twentieth-Century African American Poetry* (1999). In 1994 he published both an expanded and updated version of his dictionary, *Juba to Jive: A Dictionary of African American Slang*, as well as a collection of his artwork.

Makeba, Miriam Zenzi

SINGER, DIPLOMAT
1932–

Miriam Makeba was born in Prospect, South Africa, and spent the first six months of her life in prison with her mother, who had been arrested for illegally selling homemade beer. As a child, she sang in school choruses, performing traditional and popular southern African songs. She attended the Kimerton Training Institute in Pretoria and was a domestic worker before touring southern Africa in 1954–57 with the Black Mountain Brothers, a singing troupe.

Miriam Makeba, "Mama Africa," places her vote in a ballot box (AP/Wide World Photos. Reproduced by permission)

In 1959 Makeba performed in the African opera *King Kong* in London, and with the encouragement of **Harry Belafonte** traveled to New York. That year, she appeared in the anti-apartheid film *Come Back, Africa*. In New York, Makeba began performing and recording the music of South Africa, in particular songs in her native Xhosa language, which features a distinctive clicking sound.

Makeba, who struggled against cervical cancer in the early 1960s, came to national prominence as a political figure after she addressed a United Nations Special Committee on Apartheid in 1962. As a result, from 1962 until 1990, her music was banned in South Africa. The 1965 album she made with her mentor (guide; teacher), *An Evening with Belafonte/Makeba*, won a Grammy Award.

Makeba, who became known as "Mama Africa" and "the click-click girl," was married from 1964 to 1966 to the South African jazz trumpeter Hugh Masekela before marrying the radical African-American activist **Stokely Carmichael** (later known as Kwame Toure) in 1968. Because of Carmichael's politics, Makeba found herself shunned by the entertainment industry in the United States. Makeba and Carmichael moved to Guinea, West Africa, where she continued to live after their 1978 divorce.

Although her popularity had declined, Makeba continued to record and perform and remained politically active. She served a term as United Nations delegate from Guinea starting in 1975, and in 1986 won the Dag Hammarskjold Peace Prize. The next year, she performed alongside Masekela in Paul Simon's *Graceland* tour. In 1990, after the ban on her music was lifted, she traveled to South Africa for the first time in three decades. In

1991 she recorded *Eyes on Tomorrow*, and the next year starred in the film version of the Broadway hit *Sarafina!* She toured in the United States in 1994 with Masekela before returning permanently to South Africa later that year. (*See also*: **Africa**)

X, Malcolm

NATIONALIST LEADER
May 19, 1925–February 21, 1965

Malcolm Little, better known as Malcolm X, was one of the most controversial and influential black leaders of the **Civil Rights movement.** He is known for taking a radical stance in the fight against racism, encouraging blacks to separate from whites and develop their own brand of pride (a movement called **black nationalism**).

Born in Omaha, Nebraska, Malcolm X had a difficult childhood. He moved with his family to Lansing, Michigan, where his father was killed by a group of white supremacists, whites who believe the white race is superior to the black race. After his father's death, Malcolm was sent to live with his aunt in Boston, Massachusetts, where he began using drugs and got into trouble with the law. He was sentenced to serve six years in prison for armed robbery.

In prison Malcolm learned about a group called the **Nation of Islam (NOI),** whose members practiced the Muslim faith. The Nation of Islam was led by **Elijah Muhammad,** who believed that African Americans must reject white society and create their own wealth and prosperity. Malcolm X found a new home with the NOI and began turning his life around through reading and self-discipline. When he was released from prison, Malcolm X began working for the Nation of Islam. He soon became the most effective speech maker and recruiter in the organization. In 1954 he was appointed head minister of a temple in New York and spread the message of the NOI throughout the city and in many parts of the United States. Malcolm X grew very powerful in the NOI. He preached a message of "by any means necessary," which meant that the fight for racial equality had to be achieved at all costs, even if it meant using violence. This was in direct contrast to the peaceful efforts of other civil rights activists like **Martin Luther King Jr.**

However, Malcolm X began to grow apart from the NOI. He wanted to reveal the truth about racism in America, and he wanted to "wake up" those blacks he called "dead Negroes," those who chose to ignore the racial injustices in America.

Malcolm X left the NOI in 1964 and went on a spiritual journey. He discovered that racism is a global problem and that the best way to fight it is through education and understanding, with different racial groups living together in peace. He formed a new group called the Organization of Afro-American Unity, which petitioned the United Nations for an investigation into human rights violations in the United States. However, Malcom X's plans came to a tragic end when he was assassinated in 1965.

Markham, Dewey "Pigmeat"

COMEDIAN
April 18, 1906–December 13, 1981

Comedian Dewey Markham was born in Durham, North Carolina, in 1906. At age thirteen he ran away from home to join a traveling circus. Markham left the carnival circuit to become the star comic of Gonzelle White's Minstrel Show. It was then that he acquired the nickname "Pigmeat" from a song used in his act entitled "Sweet Papa Pigmeat."

From 1925 through 1938 Markham toured with A. D. Price's "Sugar Cane" revue and appeared at the Alhambra Theatre and at the fledgling **Apollo Theater.**

Markham moved to Hollywood in 1938, where he was featured in such all-black films as *Mr. Smith Goes Ghost* (1940), *Am I Guilty?* (1940), and *That's My Baby* (1944). He also appeared in the feature studio production *Moonlight and Cactus* (1944) with the Andrews Sisters. He worked with the singers again on their radio show, *Eight to the Bar*, playing Alamo, the chief cook. A talented vocal performer, Markham made sixteen records of blues and comedy, including an album with Jackie "Moms" Mabley, *The Best of Moms and Pigmeat*.

Markham made numerous television appearances in the 1950s and 1960s, performing on talk shows. He was a guest on *The Ed Sullivan Show* more than thirty times during its twenty-three-year run. Markham was also a regular performer on the television show *Laugh-In* during its run from 1968 through 1973. Markham was famed for his comedy sketch "Here Come de Judge."

Markham continued to perform in New York City through the early 1970s until illness forced him to retire. He died in New York City of cancer in 1981.

Marsalis, Wynton

JAZZ TRUMPETER, COMPOSER
October 18, 1961–

Showing his talent from an early age, Wynton Marsalis in 1984 became the first musician to win Grammy Awards for both **jazz** and classical recordings. He has won praise for his great technical skill, his musical sensitivity, and his gift for improvisation (creating new musical sections as a piece is played). Marsalis is a spokesperson for the preservation of "mainstream" jazz through his performances and writings, and, beginning in 1991, as artistic director of the classical jazz program at Lincoln Center in New York.

Marsalis was born into a musical family in New Orleans, Louisiana. His father, Ellis, a pianist, and his brothers Branford (tenor and soprano saxophonist), Delfeayo (trombonist), and Jason (drummer) are all well-known jazz artists. As a child, Wynton took private music lessons and played in a children's marching band directed by New Orleans musician and scholar Danny Barker. At age fourteen he performed with the New Orleans Philharmonic Orchestra.

Marsalis enrolled at the prestigious Juilliard School of Music, New York, New York, in 1980. While a student there, he joined drummer and bandleader **Art Blakey**'s (1919–1990) Jazz Messengers and toured in a quartet with musicians **Herbie Hancock** (1940–), **Ron Carter** (1937–), and Tony Williams (1945–), who had formerly worked with trumpeter and composer **Miles Davis** (1926–1991). Marsalis recorded his first album as the title artist, *Wynton Marsalis*, in 1981. After leaving Blakey in 1982, Marsalis formed his own group.

Since the late 1980s, he has concentrated on jazz performance with new groups, made up of saxophonists and clarinetists Wes Anderson, Todd Williams, and Victor Goines; bassist Reginald Veal; trombonist Wycliffe Gordon; drummer Herlin Riley; pianists Eric Reed and Marcus Roberts, and others.

During the 1990s Marsalis built the jazz program at Lincoln Center into the most prestigious center for jazz in the United States. Some musicians complain, however, that he concentrates on a small group of jazz greats and ignores the contribution of white jazz musicians.

Marsalis has composed several pieces, including *In My Father's House* (1995) and *Blood on the Fields* (1996), for which he was awarded the Pulitzer Prize in 1997. He has also written several adaptations of the music of his hero, composer and bandleader **Duke Ellington** (1899–1974), including *Harlem* (1999).

Wynton Marsalis: Selected Recordings

Marciac Suite
(2000)

Selections from the Village Vanguard
(2000)

Reeltime
(1999)

Big Train
(1999)

Jump Start & Jazz
(1996)

Blood on the Fields
(1996)

Joe Cool's Blues
(1994)

In This House on This Morning
(1992)

Crescent City Christmas Card
(1989)

Live at Blues Alley
(1986)

Black Codes
(1985)

Hot House Flowers
(1984)

Think of One
(1983)

Wynton Marsalis
(1981)

Marshall, Paule

NOVELIST
April 9, 1929–

Novelist Paule Marshall was born in Brooklyn, New York, in 1929 to emigrants from the Caribbean island of Barbados. She graduated from Brooklyn College with high honors in 1953. While attending New York's Hunter College in the mid-1950s, she began her first novel—*Brown Girl, Brownstones*. Its publication in 1959 was followed by a Guggenheim Fellowship (1960). Later honors include an award from the National Institute for Arts and Letters (1962) for *Soul Clap Hands and Sing*, a Ford Foundation grant (1964-65), and a National Endowment for the Arts grant (1967-68).

During the 1950s Marshall was a writer for a small magazine, *Our World*, which sent her on assignments to Brazil and the Caribbean. Since 1959 Marshall has been a full-time writer and a part-time teacher. She has taught African-American literature and creative writing at Yale and Columbia universities and the University of Iowa, and, since 1987, at Virginia Commonwealth University in Richmond, Virginia.

Marshall's writing explores the differences between the money-based values of modern-day white America and the spiritual and community values of African-American culture. The characters in her works are African-American and Caribbean women who do not fit into or accept modern society. *The Chosen Place, The Timeless People* (1969), is about a woman struggling to understand herself and how she fits into the world around her. *Praisesong for the Widow* (1983), features a middle-class black American woman who realizes the depth of her spiritual emptiness and embarks on a quest to rediscover her spirituality. *Daughters* (1991) is the complex story of how an only child comes to grips with her conflicting feelings about her relationship with her politician father.

Marshall, Thurgood

CIVIL RIGHTS LAWYER, ASSOCIATE JUSTICE OF THE SUPREME COURT
July 2, 1908–January 24, 1993

Thurgood Marshall was one of the most well respected and influential people to serve on the U.S. Supreme Court. He is known for his firm commitment to equality and justice and for overseeing the most dramatic period of legal and social reform in American history.

Born in Baltimore, Maryland, Marshall earned a bachelor's degree from **Lincoln University** and attempted to enroll in law school at the University of Maryland. However, he was prohibited from attending because of racial segregation policies that called for separate schools and other public facilities for blacks and whites. Instead, Marshall attended **Howard University** School of Law, where he finished first in his class (1933). From 1938 to 1961 Marshall worked as the leading attorney for the **National Association for the Advancement of Colored People (NAACP)**. During his legal career with the NAACP, he argued thirty-two cases before the Supreme Court, winning twenty-nine of them. His triumphs include convincing the Court to overturn laws that prevented blacks from voting in elections and helping eliminate segregation policies. However, his greatest achievements with the NAACP came in the 1950s when he helped put a stop to racial discrimination in the area of education. In 1954 he helped argue the landmark case **Brown v. Board of Education of Topeka, Kansas,** in which the Supreme Court ruled that school segregation violated the U.S. Constitution.

U.S. Supreme Court Justice Thurgood Marshall with his wife Cecilia (Corbis Corporation. Reproduced by permission)

In 1961 Marshall was nominated by President John F. Kennedy (1917–1963) to serve on the U.S. Court of Appeals. President Lyndon Johnson nominated Marshall to become the first black to serve as solicitor general (assistant to the attorney general, the chief law officer of the United States) in 1965 and then as an associate justice of the Supreme Court. While Marshall served on the Supreme Court, his decisions were consistently liberal, often favoring individual liberties. He was heavily in favor of abortion rights and opposed to the death penalty. Marshall retired from the bench in 1991 and died in 1993. After his death a controversy emerged when his confidential papers were reviewed. It was discovered that he had secretly passed papers to the director of the Federal Bureau of Investigation (FBI) while working for the NAACP. Despite the discovery, Marshall remains a highly respected man of integrity in the eyes of legal experts and political observers. In 1999 President Bill Clinton (1993–2001) honored Marshall's legal legacy by opening an exhibit at the federal Thurgood Marshall Building, which displays some items related to Marshall's career. President Clinton also named Marshall's son, Thurgood Marshall Jr., to a cabinet department.

Maryland

First African American Settlers: Mathias de Sousa, who arrived in 1634 with the first colonists on the *Ark* (a ship sent by Lord Baltimore), was the first black in Maryland. He was an indentured servant (a person who works for another for a specified period of time, often in payment of travel expenses and upkeep) of a Jesuit priest and worked as a boat captain after his term of service was completed.

Slave Population: In 1663 Maryland became the first colony to rule that all Africans brought into the colony, as well as their children, were to be slaves for life. In 1704 only four thousand blacks lived in Maryland; by 1775 that number reached forty-five, with about one-half of white Maryland families owning slaves. During the antebellum (pre–Civil War) years, many slaves were freed when farmers switched from tobacco to wheat cultivation, for which slave labor was inefficient. In 1860, however, the state still had ninety thousand slaves. Maryland achieved statehood in 1788.

Free Black Population: In the 1700s approximately 1 percent of blacks of pure African ancestry and 40 percent of those of mixed descent were free. **Free blacks** often worked as field hands or servants; some were craftsmen; others were land-owning farmers. When the **American Revolution** (1775–83) began some African Americans joined the forces when the governor of neighboring Virginia offered freedom as an incentive to join. By 1860, 45 percent of the state's African-American population was free, with many freed blacks living in integrated areas.

Civil War: During the **Civil War** (1861–65) the federal government began massive recruitment of African Americans into the Union (Northern) army—first free blacks, then the slaves of consenting owners. Eventually, at least one-third of Maryland's enslaved black men fought in the military. By the end of the war, approximately 25 percent of the state's population was black.

Reconstruction: A significant migration of African Americans began after the Civil War and continued through the mid-1880s. African-American men gained the right to vote with the passage of the **Fifteenth Amendment** in 1870. Increasing racial tension due to segregation and discrimination led to violence in the 1920s and 1930s.

The Great Depression: The **Great Depression** of the 1930s hit African-American Marylanders especially hard. New Deal programs (government programs intended to promote economic recovery from the depression) gave jobs to many unemployed blacks, and the Baltimore chapter of the **National Association for the Advancement of Colored People (NAACP)** led protests against employment discrimination. During **World War II** (1939–45) many black Marylanders moved to the cities to take advantage of industrial jobs. Many Maryland blacks served in the military and subsequently took advantage of the G.I. Bill of Rights to obtain education and training.

Civil Rights Movement: During the 1960s **sit-ins** were inaugurated in many Maryland towns in response to rampant segregation. Demonstrations protesting the slow pace of integration were met with increasing violence, while law after law intending to rectify inequities failed.

Current African-American Population: According to U.S. Census Bureau estimates, the total black population in Maryland was 1,428,207 (28 percent of the state population) as of July 1, 1998.

Key Figures: Abolitionists **Frederick Douglass** (1818–1895) and **Harriet Ross Tubman** (c. 1820–1913); religious cult leader **Father Divine** (c. 1880–1965); **Thurgood Marshall** (1908–1993), former U.S. Supreme Court justice; boxer **Sugar Ray Leonard** (1956–).

(SEE ALSO **ABOLITION; EMANCIPATION; FIFTEENTH AMENDMENT.**)

Massachusetts

First African-American Settlers: The first blacks in Massachusetts arrived as slaves in 1638 at a Puritan colony on Noodles Island, or what is now East Boston.

Slave Population: The number of black slaves in the colony would never be large, as the rocky soil was not suited to large-scale agriculture. Most blacks became house servants or farm laborers. Although they never made up for more than 2 percent of the population, by 1720 there were 2,000 blacks in the colony, the vast majority slaves; by 1776 that number had increased to 5,249.

Free Black Population: Public opinion began to form solidly against **slavery** in the late eighteenth century, and by 1790, two years after Massachusetts became a state, there were 5,369 blacks—all free—in the state. In the early eighteenth century Boston became a center for the abolitionist movement.

Civil War: When the **Civil War** (1861–65) broke out, Massachusetts blacks raised money for the Union (Northern) cause. In 1863 blacks were recruited as soldiers for the Union army, and African Americans from across the state volunteered for service. The **54th Massachusetts Regiment** was one of the first black units formed, and it distinguished itself by a courageous charge at Fort Wagner in Charleston, South Carolina, in November 1863.

Reconstruction: In the decades following the Civil War, Massachusetts's black population seemed to form two distinct groups: the native-born "colored elite," college graduates who worked in prestigious professions; and the masses who migrated north escaping the hardships of the South, most of whom were poor and uneducated. Although class tensions existed among the two groups, they did unite for common objectives, such as the 1915 boycott of the film *The Birth of a Nation.*

Civil Rights Movement: During the 1960s and 1970s demands by Boston's black community for quality education led to court-ordered school integration and forced busing of schoolchildren, resulting in rioting by whites.

Current African-American Population: According to U.S. Census Bureau estimates, the total black population in Massachusetts was 394,645 (6 percent of the state population) as of July 1, 1998.

Key Figures: Early civic leader **Prince Hall** (c. 1735–1807); **Crispus Attucks** (c. 1723–1770), acclaimed to be the first martyr of the American Revolution; historian and novelist **W. E. B. Du Bois** (1868–1963).

(SEE ALSO **ABOLITION; NIAGARA MOVEMENT.**)

Massey, Walter

PHYSICIST, SCIENTIFIC ADMINISTRATOR
1938–

Physicist Walter Massey was born in Mississippi and received a bachelor's degree in physics and mathematics from **Morehouse College** (Atlanta, Georgia) in 1958. He later earned both a master's and a Ph.D. degree. Following seven years of research at the Argonne National Laboratory, he was professor of physics and later a college dean at Brown University in Providence, Rhode Island. His research has focused on examining the behavior of various substances at very low temperatures.

Upon his return to the Argonne National Laboratory as its director in 1979, Massey was responsible for overseeing a wide array of research projects involving nuclear fission, solar energy, fossil fuels, and the effects of energy production on the environment. He managed a staff of five thousand, including two thousand scientists and engineers, with an annual budget of $233 million.

Massey has lectured and written widely on the teaching of science and mathematics in the nation's public schools and colleges and on the role of science and technology in society. He is an ardent advocate of African-American involvement in science.

In 1974 Massey received the Outstanding Educator in America award. In 1991 he began a six-year term as director of the National Science Foundation (NSF). In 1996 Massey was appointed president of Morehouse College. (*See also*: **Science**)

Mayfield, Curtis

SINGER, SONGWRITER
June 3, 1942–December 26, 1999

Curtis Mayfield was an influential singer and songwriter. Born and raised in Chicago, Illinois, he sang with the Northern Jubilees gospel choir as a child. In 1956 Mayfield and some childhood friends formed a group called The Impressions. The Impressions recorded the hit "For Your Precious Love," which sold 150,000 copies during a two-week period in 1958. In 1961 the group recorded the top twenty hit "Gypsy Woman." The Impressions' next big hit came in 1963 when "It's All Right" reached number one on the **rhythm-and-blues** (R&B) charts and number four on the pop charts.

Through the 1960s the group recorded numerous hit singles and became one of the most successful non-**Motown** R&B acts. Mayfield was also one of the first songwriters to merge music with political lyrics, and the **Civil Rights movement** served as inspiration for many of the Impressions' most popular singles, such as "Keep on Pushing" and "Amen" in 1964, "People Get Ready" in 1965, and "We're a Winner" in 1968.

In 1970 Mayfield left the group to pursue a solo career. Although he made numerous albums on the Custom label, Mayfield is best remembered for the soundtrack of the film *Superfly*, which was the number-one-selling album in the United States for four weeks in 1972. The *Superfly* soundtrack, which is often considered one of the finest examples of soul music, included the hit singles "Freddie's Dead," "Superfly," and "Pusherman."

After *Superfly* Mayfield wrote a number of successful film scores and hits for other groups. In 1981 he signed with the Boardwalk label, for which he recorded the album *Honesty*. In 1983 he was reunited with The Impressions for a concert tour.

In 1990 Mayfield was paralyzed from the neck down when sudden winds knocked over a lighting rig just before his performance at a free outdoor concert in Brooklyn, New York. In 1994 he was honored at the Grammy Awards show with a Grammy Legend Award. Though unable to perform, Mayfield continued to write music and to record new songs, even though he had to record lying on his back. Mayfield released his album *New World Order* in 1996. He died on December 26, 1999.

Mayfield, Julian H.

ACTOR, WRITER, ACTIVIST
June 6, 1928–October 20, 1984

The writer and actor Julian Mayfield grew up in Washington, D.C., served in the army, and eventually moved to New York City in 1949. In New York he held many jobs to make ends meet—from washing dishes to writing for the leftist black newspaper *Freedom*. At the newspaper, he met **Paul Robeson** (1898–1976) and other black leftists who deeply influenced him. Mayfield soon became an actor, debuting on Broadway as the juvenile lead in *Lost in the Stars* (1949). While in New York, he became a member of the Harlem Writers Guild, a cooperative enterprise whose members critiqued each other's work.

In 1954 Mayfield married Ana Livia Cordero, and the couple moved to Puerto Rico. Mayfield helped establish the first English-language radio station on the island and, in 1956, founded the *Puerto Rico World Journal*, a magazine about international affairs. While in Puerto Rico, Mayfield wrote his first novel. By the time his third novel was published, Mayfield had become a radical black nationalist. This was reflected in the novel, which focused on the efforts to integrate a school in a "nowhere" city situated between the northern and southern United States. The novel's vision was deeply pessimistic.

In 1960 Mayfield visited Cuba after Fidel Castro's revolution. He published many magazine articles on African-American affairs and was active in black nationalist circles. Mayfield arrrived in the West African country of Ghana in 1962, where he served as a speechwriter and aide to President Kwame Nkrumah and founded and edited the *African Review*. He was in Spain in 1966 when Nkrumah was overthrown in a coup. Mayfield moved to England for a while, then returned to the United States in 1968.

In 1968 Mayfield was given a fellowship at New York University. During this time he edited publications and wrote several screenplays. In 1971 he

Julian Mayfield: Selected Works

The Hit
(novel, 1957)

The Long Night
(novel, 1958)

The Grand Parade
(novel, 1961)

Uptight
(screenplay, 1968)

The Hitch
(screenplay, 1969)

Children of Anger
(screenplay, 1971)

The Long Night
(screenplay, 1976)

moved to Guyana in South America as an adviser to the minister of information and later functioned as an assistant to Prime Minister Forbes Burnham. Mayfield returned to the United States in 1974 and taught for two years at the University of Maryland in College Park. He later taught in Europe and Tunisia. In 1977 he relocated to the University of Maryland, and the next year he accepted an appointment as writer-in-residence at **Howard University,** a position he maintained until his death of a heart ailment in 1984.

Maynor, Dorothy Leigh

CONCERT SINGER
September 3, 1910–February 19, 1996

Dorothy Leigh Maynor's twenty-five-year singing career was launched in 1939 when she sang for Russian-born American orchestra conductor Serge Koussevitzky (1874–1951), who said, "Her voice is a miracle, a musical revelation that the world must hear." He immediately arranged concerts for her and a recording with the Boston Symphony.

Maynor was born in Norfolk, Virginia, and graduated from **Hampton Institute** (now University), Hampton, Virginia, in 1933. She received a second degree in 1935 from Westminster Choir School in Princeton, New Jersey.

After her 1939 debut at New York Town Hall, Maynor's career included tours and recordings, radio and television shows, and appearances with major orchestras. The gifted soprano (highest singing voice) was especially famous for her performance of "Depuis le Jour," from French composer Gustave Charpentier's (1860–1956) opera *Louise* (1900).

Maynor became the director of Bennett College in Greensboro, North Carolina, in 1945 and received an honorary doctor of music degree from **Howard University,** Washington, D.C., in 1959.

After her retirement from professional singing in 1965, she started a music-education program for children at Saint James Presbyterian Church in Harlem, New York, where her husband, Shelby Rooks, was minister. This program expanded into the Harlem School for the Arts, which she directed from 1964 to 1979. She retired to Pennsylvania in 1992. (*See also*: **Opera**)

Mays, Benjamin Elijah

EDUCATOR, CLERGYMAN
August 1, 1894–March 28, 1984

Educator Benjamin Mays was born in Ninety-Six, South Carolina, where his father was a sharecropper. After a year at Virginia Union University, Mays went on to earn a degree at Bates College in Maine. At the Divinity School of the University of Chicago, he earned a master's degree in 1925 and later a Ph.D.

Benjamin Mays (center) meets with President John F. Kennedy and other advisors

In the early 1920s, Mays was active in the Urban League of Tampa, Florida, exposing police brutality and attacking discrimination in public places. Between 1921 and 1926 Mays taught at **Morehouse College** in Atlanta, Georgia, and South Carolina State College in Orangeburg as an instructor in mathematics, psychology, religious education, and English.

In 1934, with his Ph.D. nearly finished, Mays went to **Howard University** in Washington, D.C., as dean of the School of Religion. During his six years there, graduate enrollment increased, the quality of the faculty improved, and the library was expanded.

Mays was president of Morehouse College from 1940 to 1967. During his presidency, the percentage of faculty with Ph.Ds increased from 8.7 percent to 54 percent and the campus underwent many improvements. One of Mays's students at Morehouse was civil rights activist **Martin Luther King Jr.** (1929–1968)

During his career in higher education, Mays remained involved in religious affairs. Although he was a pastor for only a few years, he was active in several religious organizations. In 1944 he became vice president of the Federal Council of Churches of Christ. In 1948 Mays helped to organize the World Council of Churches (WCC) in Amsterdam, the Netherlands, where he successfully promoted an official statement acknowledging racism as a divisive force among Christians.

Mays also did research work on the black church and black religion. In 1930 he surveyed black churches in twelve cities and four rural areas to create the study *The Negro's Church* (1933) with Joseph W. Nicholson. The authors found that there were too many black churches, often with untrained clergy and too much debt.

In 1938 Mays produced *The Negro's God as Reflected in His Literature.* Mays argued that many blacks believed God to be involved in and aware of their condition as an oppressed group. In later years Mays wrote an autobiography, *Born to Rebel* (1971; abridged in 1981 as *Lord, the People Have Driven Me On*). (*See also*: **Education**)

Willie Mays's history-making, over-the-shoulder catch during the 1954 World Series (AP/Wide World Photos. Reproduced by permission)

Mays, Willie Howard

BASEBALL PLAYER
May 6, 1931–

Willie Howard Mays was one of the greatest **baseball** players of all time. He is known for his consistent all-around play and making one of the most remarkable catches in baseball history. In the 1954 World Series, Mays ran down a 440-feet hit to center field, caught it, and made a perfect throw to the infield, thus preventing the runner from scoring.

Born in Westfield, Alabama, Mays was raised by his aunt because his parents divorced shortly after he was born. Mays was a diverse athlete in high school, playing football, basketball, and baseball. By the time he was seventeen, he was playing for the Negro National League. In 1950 he was signed by the major league's New York Giants. Mays won Rookie of the Year his first full year with the Giants, during which he earned the nickname "the 'Say Hey' kid." The name caught on when Mays used the phase to get the attention of a teammate whose name he had forgotten.

After serving in the U.S. Army, Mays returned to baseball in 1954, recording one of his best seasons ever. Mays led the National League with a batting average of .345, hit 41 home runs, and helped carry the Giants to the world championship. Mays's well-rounded game earned him several awards, including twelve consecutive Gold Glove awards for fielding (1957–1968) and trips to every All Star Game from 1954 to 1973. He was inducted into the Baseball Hall of Fame in 1979.

Mays's consistently brilliant play made him the target of racist attacks, including "bean balls," which is when a pitcher "accidentally" hits the batter with a pitch. Politically, Mays held a soft-spoken neutrality toward the **Civil Rights movement**. He retired from baseball in 1973 and began coaching with the New York Mets. Mays became the focus of controversy when the commissioner of baseball ordered him to make a choice between coaching or honoring a public relations contract with the Bally's Casino Hotel. Because Mays chose to honor his contract with the casino, he was banned from baseball. In 1985 a new commissioner, Peter Ueberroth, lifted the ban.

McCoy, Elijah J.

INVENTOR
May 2, 1843–October 10, 1929

Elijah McCoy was born in Canada to former slaves who had fled Kentucky. After attending grammar school, McCoy moved to Scotland, where as an engineer's apprentice he acquired technical training that was hard for blacks to obtain in North America. Moving to Michigan after the **Civil War** (1861–65), he found work as a locomotive fireman. His duties led him to consider the limitations in existing lubrication technology. Railroad engines were lubricated only periodically, so they tended to overheat and cause the entire train to stop. Relubrication was awkward and wasted oil, labor, and time.

After two years of experimenting, McCoy developed a "lubricating cup" for steam engines. His next three patents were for improvements on the lubricator. To finance a machine shop to advance his research, McCoy assigned his patents to various companies and individuals. While this enabled him to work continuously on his own inventions and ensured him due credit, it meant that almost all of the profits made from his machines went to others. McCoy was only a minor stockholder in the Elijah McCoy Manufacturing Company of Detroit.

In 1883 McCoy designed a lubricating device to be used with air pump brakes. Previously, oil had been depleted in the brakes whenever the steam was cut off. McCoy placed an additional lubricator on top of the brake cylinder, ensuring a continuous flow of oil into the system. In 1892 McCoy introduced a system that soon lubricated most locomotive engines in the West and those on steam ships of the Great Lakes. He also experimented with solid lubricants, such as graphite, which, when applied to machine gears, enabled them to glide smoothly over one another.

By the time of his death in 1929, McCoy held over fifty-eight patents, including a folding iron table and an automatic sprinkler and was known as "the father of lubrication." Many believe that his reputation for quality and authenticity was the source for the phrase "the real McCoy."

Hattie McDaniel's career reached its high point in 1939 when she won an Academy Award, the first ever given to a black performer, for her portrayal of "Mammy" in Gone With the Wind. *Praised by some and put down by others for the image she portrayed, McDaniel in her Oscar Award (given for achievement in movies) acceptance speech announced that she hoped always to be a credit to her race and to her industry. Ironically, McDaniel (along with the other black cast members) had been excluded from the Atlanta, Georgia, first showing of the film, and her picture was removed from the promotional programs that the studio distributed in the South.*

McDaniel, Hattie

SINGER, ACTRESS
June 10, 1895–October 26, 1952

Hattie McDaniel was a singer and actress whose career spanned more than forty years. McDaniel was born in Wichita, Kansas, one of thirteen children. She became famous for her role as "Mammy" in the movie *Gone With the Wind.*

Soon after her birth the family moved to Denver, Colorado. In 1910, at the age of fifteen, she was awarded a gold medal by a local group for excellence in "the dramatic art" for her recital of "Convict Joe," which reportedly "moved the house to tears." On the strength of this success, McDaniel persuaded her family to allow her to leave school and to join her brothers in her father's newly formed traveling company, the Henry McDaniel Minstrel Show. Over the next decade she traveled and performed with her father's company, and she began at this time to develop her abilities as a songwriter and singer.

Around 1920 McDaniel came to the notice of George Morrison, one of Denver's notable popular musicians. Taken on as a singer with Morrison's orchestra, McDaniel became increasingly well known throughout the West. She also appeared with the orchestra on Denver radio during this time, and she is reputed to have been the first black woman soloist to sing on the radio.

Encouraged by her success, McDaniel moved to Hollywood, California, in 1931 and soon began working regularly in radio and film. Over the course of the next two decades she appeared in more than three hundred films, though mostly in minor roles. The first film for which she received screen credit was *Blonde Venus* (1932), in which she played the affectionate, loyal, but willful domestic, the only role available at the time to large black women in Hollywood. McDaniel successfully established herself in this role, gaining substantial, credited parts in over fifty films, including *Alice Adams* (1935), *The Mad Miss Manton* (1935), *Show Boat* (1936), *Affectionately Yours* (1941), *Since You Went Away* (1944), and Walt Disney's animated *Song of the South* (1946). McDaniel's most well known role was in *Gone With the Wind.*

McDaniel continued to play similar roles throughout the 1940s, despite increased criticism that she and other black actors who played servant stereotypes (the same types of characters, with the same traits and in the same roles) were helping to continue those stereotypes. In 1947 McDaniel signed her first contract for the radio show *Beulah*, in which she once again

Bobby McFerrin in performance (© Jack Vartoogian. Reproduced by permission)

played a southern maid. In the contract McDaniel demanded the right to alter any script that did not meet her approval.

McDaniel died in Los Angeles in 1952 after completing the first six episodes of the television version of *Beulah*. (*See also*: **film**)

McFerrin, Bobby Jr.

JAZZ SINGER
March 11, 1950–

Jazz singer Bobby McFerrin was born in New York City, the son of two distinguished opera singers. He began his musical studies on piano at the preparatory division of the Juilliard School of Music, in New York City, and later studied at California State University. Before attending college, he played piano in several local bands in California. Beginning in 1977, McFerrin concentrated on singing. His repertory is eclectic, ranging from the top ten hit "Don't Worry, Be Happy" (1988) to jazz classics.

McFerrin's ability to emulate jazz giants like **Miles Davis** and **Wayne Shorter** in his vocal improvisations was the most important factor contributing to his winning a 1984 and 1985 *Downbeat* best male vocalist poll. Since 1983, McFerrin's vocal improvisations have included classical, jazz, and popular types of music. He has a vocal range that extends over three octaves. In addition, he likes to involve his audience in improvised performance, and he uses a variety of vocal and body-percussion sounds in his recordings and live performances. In unaccompanied songs, McFerrin performs all the musical parts, in a multilayered texture.

McFerrin has organized a vocal group named Voicestra that ranges from eight to fourteen voices. The group generates its musical ideas from melodies, harmonies, and rhythms that are fed to it by McFerrin. McFerrin made his conducting debut in 1990 with the San Francisco Symphony, and he recorded *Hush* with classical cellist Yo-Yo Ma in 1992. During the 1990s, he also devoted progressively more time to conducting ensembles such as the New York Philharmonic. He signed a contract to conduct the St. Paul Chamber Orchestra (in Minnesota), beginning in 1995. (*See also*: **concert music**)

McGhee, Walter Brown "Brownie"

BLUES GUITARIST, SINGER
November 30, 1925–February 16, 1996

A self-taught guitarist from a musical family, Brownie McGhee was born in Knoxville, Tennessee, and left home at eighteen, lame from a childhood struggle with polio. He wandered about and played his country blues in juke joints (southern rural bars) for six years and made his first recording in 1939. Moving to New York in the early 1940s, McGhee began to collaborate with **Sonny Terry,** and in 1948 he founded a **blues** guitar school in **Harlem.**

McGhee and Sonny Terry were important in a blues and folk music revival of the 1960s, touring widely in the United States and in Europe. In June 1982 McGhee was one of the fifteen artists named to receive the first National Heritage Fellowships awarded by the National Endowment for the Arts. McGhee died in Oakland, California, of stomach cancer in 1996.

McKay, Claude

POET, NOVELIST
September 15, 1889–May 22, 1948

Claude McKay was the child of farmers in the Caribbean island of Jamaica. He left Jamaica in 1912 to study agriculture in the United States, and in that year he published two volumes of Jamaican dialect poetry, *Songs of Jamaica* and *Constab Ballads*, which reflect the British influences of his youth and the rebellion that came to characterize most of his poetry.

In 1914 McKay moved to New York City and later achieved fame among black Americans for his sonnet "If We Must Die," which urged African Americans to fight against the violence directed against them in the aftermath of **World War I**. McKay's poetry expressed modern black feelings of anger and rebellion, and he quickly became an important—and disturbing—voice in the **Harlem Renaissance** of the 1920s. He became a communist briefly, from 1919 to 1922, but later criticized communism because of the anti-democratic way in which the Soviet Union practiced it.

From 1923 until 1934 McKay lived in western Europe and northern Africa. While abroad, he published three novels and a collection of stories. Each of these books dealt in some way with poor blacks in the United States or Jamaica, struggling against the dominance of white society. In 1934 the **Great Depression** forced McKay back to the United States, and for the rest of his life he wrote primarily as a journalist critical of international communism, black integration, and white American racial and political hypocrisy.

Although best known as a poet and novelist of the Harlem Renaissance, McKay was also an important social critic in the 1930s and 1940s. As a native Jamaican, he believed that blacks in their various American ethnic origins had much to contribute to the collective American life, and that accepting and celebrating cultural differences was the best way to strengthen and unite the American population. In his essays he continued to champion working-class African Americans, who he believed best understood the need for community development. He published a memoir, *A Long Way from Home* (1937), and in 1944—ill, broke, and isolated—he joined the Roman Catholic Church and spent the last years of his life in Chicago working for the Catholic Youth Organization.

McKissick, Floyd B.

CIVIL RIGHTS ACTIVIST
March 9, 1922–April 28, 1991

Floyd McKissick was a dedicated leader and activist. After serving in the U.S. Army during **World War II**, McKissick graduated from college with a bachelor of arts degree in 1951. He became the first African-American student to attend the University of North Carolina Law School at Chapel Hill after **National Association for the Advancement of Colored People (NAACP)** lawyer **Thurgood Marshall** filed suit on his behalf. McKissick challenged segregation laws by filing suits on behalf of his five children to gain admission to all-white schools.

McKissick took part in civil rights activism as early as 1947, when he chal-lenged segregated travel laws. In 1960 he became a key legal adviser for the **Congress of Racial Equality (CORE)**, an interracial civil rights organization. McKissick often defended CORE activists who had been arrested for civil disobedience.

McKissick and other black activists in CORE, who had faced southern white violence, began to question the goals of the movement. McKissick's disillusionment was fueled by the harassment that his children had faced in their "integrated" school setting. Subsequently, McKissick called for black economic empowerment and black control over black institutions within CORE. By 1966 McKissick had become an advocate of the Black Power movement and steered CORE toward black economic development.

After leaving CORE in 1968, McKissick established a consulting firm to promote black capitalism. In 1969 he wrote a book that suggested strategies to assist African Americans economically.

McKissick also founded the Soul City Corporation in 1974. His aim was to create a community in which African Americans would have political and economic control. Funding was cut, however, and the city was unable to attract enough business to become self-sufficient. By 1980 the corporation was taken over by the federal government.

McKissick remained active in public life, and in 1990 he was appointed district court judge for North Carolina's ninth district. The following year, McKissick, who had been suffering from lung cancer, died in his Soul City home. (*See also*: **Black Nationalism**)

McLean, John Lenwood Jr. "Jackie"

TENOR SAXOPHONIST
May 17, 1932–

Born in New York City, Jackie McLean grew up in Harlem. He began to play alto saxophone at the age of fifteen. He was influenced by the tenor saxophone of **Lester Young** (1909–1959) and was considered a child prodigy, studying and practicing with many of the rising giants of bebop. McLean made his first recordings in 1951 with **Miles Davis** (1926–1991) and eventually recorded as a leader in 1955. By this time he had gained renown as a fluent, aggressive hard-bop soloist who also possessed a sensitive, lyrical side. From 1955 to 1958 he played for short periods with other musicians including **Art Blakey** (1919–1990) and the Jazz Messengers and **Charles Mingus** (1922–1979).

In the late 1940s McLean became a heroin addict. He was arrested in 1957 and was denied the cabaret card required in order to perform in New York City nightclubs. Nonetheless, in the late 1950s he began developing a more exploratory style. In 1959–60 McLean was player and actor in an Off-Broadway drama about drug use, and he later appeared in the film version, as well as recorded the sound track. From 1960 to 1963 McLean toured Germany and Belgium with his own group and recorded albums.

A turning point in McLean's life came in 1967 when he kicked his drug habit. He became a drug counselor for the New York State Department of Corrections and began teaching at the University of Hartford in Connecticut. In 1971 he joined the faculty of the university's Hartt School of Music and helped found its African-American Music Department; he also started the Artists' Collective, a cultural center in Hartford's inner city. During this time McLean settled into a more conventional playing style, though he retained his commanding tone. McLean continues to teach at Hartford and frequently performs at jazz festivals in Europe and Japan. (*See also*: **Jazz**)

Jackie McLean: Selected Albums

Jackie's Bag
(1959)

Bluesnik
(1961)

Let Freedom Ring
(1962)

One Step Beyond
(1963)

Destination Out
(1963)

Antiquity
(1974)

New Wine in Old Bottles
(1978)

It's About Time
(with McCoy Tyner, 1985)

Rhythm of the Earth
(1992)

Fire and Love
(1998)

Nature Boy
(2000)

McMillan, Terry

NOVELIST
October 18, 1951–

The eldest of five children, Terry McMillan was born in Point Huron, Michigan, and left for California at the age of seventeen. She received a bachelor's degree in journalism from the University of California at Berkeley in 1978. After a brief stay at Columbia University's film school in New York City, McMillan left in 1979 and joined the Harlem Writers Guild.

The first story McMillan read aloud to the guild became the opening chapter of her first novel, *Mama* (1987), about a single mother's struggle to raise a family during the 1960s and 1970s. The book was well-received and followed by the popular *Disappearing Acts* in 1989, but it was her third novel, *Waiting to Exhale* (1992), that became a best-seller within the first week of its release and made McMillan a national celebrity. The novel centers on the friendships among four African-American women in Phoenix, Arizona, and how each of them looks for and hides from love.

McMillan's next book, *How Stella Got Her Groove Back* (1996) also quickly became a best-seller. During the 1990s both *Waiting to Exhale* and *How Stella Got Her Groove Back* were adapted to film and became hit movies whose success at the box office demonstrated both strong appeal to black (especially female) viewers and a substantial crossover appeal to white audiences.

McMillan, who lives in the San Francisco Bay area, hopes her success will open doors for other African-American writers. To this end, in 1991 McMillan edited *Breaking Ice: An Anthology of Contemporary African-American Fiction*, which includes short stories and book excerpts by fifty-seven African-American writers.

Terry McMillan, one of the most influential and highly regarded authors of the late 20th century (AP/Wide World Photos. Reproduced by permission)

McNeil, Claudia

ACTRESS
August 13, 1917–1993

Born in Baltimore, Maryland, actress Claudia McNeil was best known for her role as Lena Younger in the play and film versions of **Lorraine Hansberry**'s *A Raisin in the Sun* (1959, 1961). While a teenager, McNeil began a singing career at the Black Cat, a New York City nightclub. She later toured as a vocalist in "Hot from Harlem" and in **Katherine Dunham**'s dance troupe.

McNeil's acting break came when writer **Langston Hughes** (1902-1967) invited her to audition for *Simply Heavenly* (1957), in which she became a Broadway star. Her other credits include *Winesburg, Ohio* (1958), *Tiger, Tiger Burning Bright* (1962; Tony Award nomination), *To Be Young, Gifted, and Black* (1972), and the musical *Raisin* (1981). (*See also*: **Drama**)

Butterfly McQueen, best known for her role as Prissy in *Gone with the Wind* (AP/Wide World Photos. Reproduced by permission)

McQueen, Thelma "Butterfly"

ACTRESS
1911–December 22, 1995

Thelma McQueen grew up in New York City and Augusta, Georgia. She began her acting career in New York as part of Venezuela Jones's Theater Group for Negro Youth, appearing as part of the Butterfly Ballet in *A Midsummer Night's Dream*. From this ballet she earned the nickname "Butterfly." In 1937 she made her Broadway debut, then went on to appear in other shows.

McQueen was best known for her Hollywood debut as the silly maid "Prissy" in the movie *Gone With the Wind* (1939). McQueen was aware of the stereotypical nature of the role (its "sameness," with blacks often cast in that role) of Prissy and worked successfully to lessen the offensive nature of the role, refusing, for example, to eat watermelon on camera. McQueen played a variety of similar roles during the following years, in such films as *Duel in the Sun* (1945) and *Mildred Pierce* (1946). She also acted in radio and television roles. However, McQueen was so frustrated by being typecast in stereotypical black servant roles that in 1947 she quit acting for a year, and in the 1950s gave up acting entirely. Eventually she opened her own restaurant, and she also ran a radio talk show.

In 1968 McQueen made a well-publicized and well-received return to acting when she appeared in the play *Curly McDimple*. In 1972 she returned to school, and in 1976, at the age of sixty-four, McQueen received her bachelor's degree from the City College of New York. Beginning in 1978, she toured in a one-woman nightclub act. She also wrote, produced, and starred in a bilingual (in two different languages) play tribute to educator **Mary McLeod Bethune.** McQueen was deeply involved in teaching drama to African-American and Latino children in projects at the **Marcus Garvey** Mount Morris Welfare Center and Public School 153 in the Bronx, New York. Thelma McQueen died in a fire in 1995. (*See also*: **Film**)

Meek, Carrie P.

CONGRESSWOMAN
April 29, 1926–

Congresswoman Carrie Meek is the granddaughter of a slave and the daughter of a sharecropper. She was born in Tallahassee, Florida, and graduated from Florida A&M University (Tallahassee) with a bachelor of science degree in 1956. In 1948 Meek received her master's degree from the University of Michigan (Ann Arbor) and later studied at Florida Atlantic University in Boca Raton.

Meek began her teaching career at **Bethune-Cookman College** (Daytona Beach, Florida) in 1949, remaining there until 1958. She then taught at Florida A&M University for three years, from 1958 to 1961. She was women's basketball coach at both institutions. After teaching at Miami-Dade Community College (Miami, Florida) from 1961 to 1968, Meek moved into administrative posts, serving as associate dean for community services and assistant to the president (1968–79).

Aware that programs for blacks in Dade County were not fairly funded by the federal government, Meek decided to run for a seat in the Florida House of Representatives in 1979. Meek was so popular in her district that she decided to run for Congress in 1992; she won by a staggering margin. With her victory, Meek, a sixty-seven-year-old grandmother, became the first African-American woman since **Reconstruction** to be elected to Congress from Florida.

Meek's record in Congress is impressive. She served on the powerful House Appropriations Committee, drafted a bill to ease restrictions on Haitian refugees, and advised President Bill Clinton as he worked to reduce the budget deficit without cutting social welfare programs.

Memphis, Tennessee

Beginnings

Memphis, Tennessee, located on a bluff overlooking the Mississippi River, received its first African-American settler shortly after its founding in 1819. Its early black population was largely free, and Shelby County's state representatives opposed **slavery.** African Americans worked as domestics, blacksmiths, haulers, and craftsmen. As the town grew into a major port city, racial attitudes began to change. In 1834 Tennessee enacted a new state constitution, which stripped blacks of citizenship rights. The town's African-American population lost its voting rights and was forced to observe a curfew. Black clergymen were not allowed to preach. In the 1840s Tennessee repealed its ban on the domestic **slave trade.** Memphis, with its large port, became a center for slave trading. Nevertheless, Memphis was more cosmopolitan than most southern cities in that a large number of European immigrants had settled there. By 1860 the city's population was 17 percent black and more than 36 percent foreign born.

The Civil War Years

As the American **Civil War** (1861–65) threatened, Memphis initially was opposed to secession. Local support for the Confederacy built once the war began, but the city fell to advancing Union troops in 1862 and remained occupied and largely undamaged throughout the war. The Union army established a large freedmen's camp near Memphis, and many blacks migrated there, remaining after the end of the war. **Emancipation** (1863) created economic competition between blacks and white immigrants, especially the Irish, who lived in many of the same neighborhoods as blacks. In 1866 struggling Irish residents turned their frustrations on their newly arrived black neighbors in a riot that left forty-six blacks dead, nearly twice that many injured, and black homes, churches, and schools destroyed.

Once the U.S. Congress passed the Civil Rights Act (1866), the political situation of the city's African Americans improved. By 1875 a group of blacks, Irish and Italians dominated Memphis politics. African Americans were elected to the city council and the school board, and others were appointed to positions such as wharf master and coal inspector. But with the coming of **Jim Crow** laws, no African American held elective office from 1888 until 1960. Due to black migration as well as yellow-fever epidemics that took a heavy toll on the white population of Memphis, blacks remained a significant group of voters. Although prohibited from holding public office, black **suffrage** was never formally restricted except by selective enforcement of a poll tax. Thus, even after Southern Democrats regained political control of Tennessee during the late 1870s, they had to seek the black vote. Furthermore, black Republican leaders continued to influence policy and the awarding of city and federal jobs.

Despite this limited political power, the social conditions of blacks in Memphis grew steadily worse as the nineteenth century drew to a close. Many well-to-do whites had fled the yellow fever epidemics of the 1880s and had been replaced by poorer whites from surrounding rural Tennessee, Mississippi, and Arkansas. Blacks' civil and property rights were violated, and the city became increasingly segregated. **Lynching** of blacks by white mobs became widespread. When **Ida B. Wells-Barnett** denounced the lynching in her newspaper, the *Memphis Free Speech*, a mob burned her press and forced her to flee the city.

The Early Twentieth Century

Memphis blacks resisted Jim Crow laws in the early twentieth century. When Mary Morrison was arrested for resisting street car segregation in 1905, a huge rally followed in Church Park, and several thousand dollars were raised for her legal defense. There were also forms of even more direct resistance. A white trolley conductor was stabbed when he tried to collect extra fare from a black rider. Shootings and arson took place on occasion, and lower-class blacks used a variety of physical means to resist white police officers. Meanwhile, Beale Street became known as the "Main Street of Negro America." The size and segregation of the black community had created a need for a number of black professionals and businesspersons. Black doctors, lawyers, and teachers provided essential services. Black entrepreneurs owned many of the groceries, barber shops, hair salons, funeral parlors, and even banks, open to blacks. Beale Street, the black commercial center in Jim Crow years, was lined with offices, stores, theaters, saloons, gambling joints, and small shops. Bert Roddy founded the city's first black grocery chain and subsequently organized the Supreme Liberty Life Insurance Company. Included in his effort was an attempt to build on **W. E. B. Du Bois**'s socialist notion of developing community cooperative businesses.

Thomas H. Hayes started the T. H. Hayes and Sons Funeral Home, the longest continuously running black business in Memphis. Robert Church Sr., however, was the best known businessman. A former slave, he arrived in Memphis in 1863; by the time of his death in 1912, he had amassed more than a million dollars worth of real estate and other holdings. He was most likely the United States's first black millionaire. His Solvent Savings Bank was the first black-owned bank in the city's history. Memphis gradually became an African-American cultural center. The city boasted several black theaters. The Theater Owners' Booking Association was later founded in Memphis, and concerts were held in the Church auditorium.

Memphis also contained the Julia Hooks Music School, a black-owned, interracial institution. Beale Street's saloons and gambling clubs were known for their **blues** music. Blues musician **W. C. Handy,** wrote down much of this music and introduced it to the rest of the United States. His "Memphis Blues," originally written as a campaign song, became the city's unofficial anthem. In more recent years, Beale Street has fostered many leading blues musicians such as **B. B. King** and Memphis Slim.

Mississippi-born Irishman Edward H. "Boss" Crump first won city office in 1905. Although an avowed segregationist, he successfully registered sizable numbers of black voters, and he turned them out to vote with the help of prominent blacks such as Handy. By the late 1920s, Crump had consolidated his political power. Thereafter, although no longer actually holding the mayor's office, he dominated Memphis **politics** until his death in 1954. Crump's base of support was an odd mix of blacks and Irish; and like most bosses of the day, he held his coalition together with selective patronage. Blacks, then, although not allowed to rise to positions of authority within the party structure or the bureaucracy, went to the polls and in return received a share of the city's generosity for voting. Black leaders, although many were Republicans, were able to work effectively with Crump.

In 1951, Dr. J. E. Walker challenged the political machine by running for a position on the school board. In the course of the campaign, the first of many aggressive voter registration drives was launched within the black community. Although Walker was defeated, he was the first black candidate in decades, and black voter registration nearly tripled in 1951 alone. By 1963, as blacks struggled for the right to vote across the South, black Memphians were already registered at the same rate as white Memphians.

The Civil Rights Movement

Businessman Bert Roddy headed the first Memphis branch of the NAACP. Roddy and others were at the forefront of much resistance during the **Civil Rights movement** of the 1960s. In 1960, for example, a sizable number of student **sit-ins** appeared and a boycott was launched against downtown retailers. A major sanitation workers' strike occurred in 1968, shortly before the Reverend Dr. **Martin Luther King Jr.** was assassinated in Memphis. Police, firefighters and teachers would walk the picket lines ten years later. Meanwhile, public protests against police brutality began in the nineteenth century and continue in 2000.

Throughout the 1950s, black candidates ran unsuccessfully for citywide and statewide office. In 1960, Jesse Turner became the first African American since the Reconstruction Era to win an elective post, winning a seat on the democratic Executive Committee.

Memphis Today

In 1974 Harold Ford became the first black Tennessean ever elected to the United States Congress. Ford and a group of loyalists continue to regularly compose and distribute a sample ballot endorsing a variety of candidates. In 1996 they appeared to help his son, Harold Ford Jr., succeed his father as the district's congressperson. Despite political victories, the city's commerce and service-oriented economy has offered African Americans far more low-wage positions than higher paying ones. This has left Memphis with arguably the poorest black underclass of any large U.S. city. As the twentieth century drew to a close, despite the federal War on Poverty, more than a third of that population was still poor.

Mercer, Mabel Alice Wadham

CABARET SINGER
February 3, 1900–April 20, 1984

Singer Mabel Mercer was born in Burton-on-Trent, England, to an African-American jazz musician and a British singer. At age fourteen, she went on tour with a group of musicians in her family.

After World War I (1914–18) Mercer became a popular cabaret (nightclub) performer in Paris, France. From 1931 to 1938 she performed at Bricktop's, an African American-owned club, gaining a large following because of her careful yet emotional renditions of **jazz** and pop standards.

In 1938 Mercer moved to the United States, where, despite her singing talent, she never gained a large following. However, she was a favorite of pop and jazz singers such as **Billie Holiday,** Frank Sinatra, and **Nat "King" Cole."** Her recordings from this time include *Mabel Mercer Sings Cole Porter* (1955) and *At Town Hall* (with **Bobby Short,** 1968).

New interest in Mercer's music during the early 1970s led to a 1972 television special, *An Evening with Mabel Mercer and Bobby Short and Friends.* In 1982 she sang songs by Alec Wilder at the Kool Jazz Festival in New York, and in 1983 she was awarded the Presidential Medal of Freedom at the White House.

Mabel Mercer: Selected Recordings

Sings Cole Porter
(1955)

Midnight at Mabel Mercer's
(1956)

Once in a Blue Moon,
(1958)

Merely Marvelous,
(1960)

At Town Hall
(live concert, 1968)

Meredith, James H.

CIVIL RIGHTS ACTIVIST
June 25, 1933–

Born in Koscuisko, Mississippi, James H. Meredith was a hero of the **Civil Rights movement** of the mid-twentieth century. He is especially known for his involvement in two events that have come to symbolize the adversity that blacks faced during their long fight for equality in America.

Previously a student at Jackson State University, in 1962 Meredith attempted to enroll at the segregated (whites only) University of Mississippi. A court order removed the racial barrier, paving the way for Meredith and other black students to attend the university. The governor of Mississippi, Ross Barnett, led an opposition group to Meredith's enrollment and personally stood in the way at the enrollment office to keep Meredith out. With the help of President John F. Kennedy (1917–1963), Meredith was able to attend classes. U.S. troops policed the campus while Meredith attended the University of Mississippi.

In the summer of 1966, Meredith became involved in another major civil rights event. Frustrated by the history of violence against blacks, Meredith took a "walk against fear" from Memphis, Tennessee, to Jackson, Mississippi. The walk was to symbolize a stand against racial crimes that prevented blacks from living peaceful lives. On the second day of the walk, Meredith was shot and wounded. Black leaders organized another march to continue Meredith's mission, and Meredith joined them when he regained his health.

Meredith then wrote a book called *Three Years in Mississippi* and earned a law degree from Columbia University (New York) in 1968. In 1989 he joined the staff of conservative senator Jesse Helms of North Carolina as domestic policy adviser. This came as a shock to political observers because Helms was known for being unsympathetic to the **Civil Rights movement.** Meredith has written at least twenty-five books since graduating from the University of Mississippi. He claims that reading his books is the only way to get a true picture of racism in the United States.

James Meredith (Courtesy of the Library of Congress)

Meriwether, Louise

AUTHOR
May 8, 1923–

Louise Meriwether was born in New York. During her childhood in Brooklyn and Harlem, she experienced the despair of the ghetto. The effects of prejudice formed the basis of her fiction, nonfiction, teaching, and social activism.

Educated at New York University and the University of California at Los Angeles (UCLA), Meriwether has taught at Sarah Lawrence College (Bronxville, New York) and the University of Houston (Texas), among others. During the 1950s and early 1960s, she worked in various legal and reporting jobs. In 1965 she became the first African-American story analyst at Universal Studios. She also began writing book reviews but found that she often had to initialize her first name to get her work past sexist editors.

Meriwether joined the Watts Writers' Workshop in Los Angeles, organized in the wake of rights in 1965, and in 1967 published a short story that she would later develop into a novel. Critics credited Meriwether for her vivid and painful portrayal of desperate people who have almost no chance for secure and fulfilling lives.

Louise Meriwether: Selected Publications

Daddy Was a Number Runner
(1970)

The Freedom Ship of Robert Smalls
(1971)

The Heart Man: Dr. Daniel Hale Williams
(1972)

Don't Ride the Bus on Monday: The Rosa Parks Story
(1973)

Fragments of the Ark
1994

> *"The deliberate omission of Blacks from American history has been damaging to the children of both races. It reinforces in one a feeling of inferiority and in the other a myth of superiority."*

Louise Meriwether

In addition to stories and essays published in periodicals, Meriwether has written three biographies of pioneering African Americans for young readers. Meriwether has frequently taken time from writing to devote herself to causes, including civil rights. In the early 1970s, angered by African-American entertainers who were performing in South Africa, she worked to publicize the appalling conditions that minorities suffered under apartheid (racial segregation). She has also actively opposed American interventions abroad, from the **Vietnam War** (1959–75) to the 1991 Persian Gulf War.

Meriwether strives to give her readers a broad sense of the role of African Americans in American history. In 1994 she published a long-awaited historical novel based on the life of **Civil War** (1861–65) hero Robert Smalls (1839–1915), a slave who captured a Confederate gunboat for the Union navy. During the 1990s she continued to teach at Sarah Lawrence College.

Mexican War

The Mexican War was fought between the United States and Mexico from 1846 to 1848. Even though black soldiers had served in the military during the **American Revolution** (1775–83) and the War of 1812, they were not allowed to serve during the Mexican War. Despite this, African Americans made an important contribution to the war as servants to white army officers. As servants, blacks were part of every contingent of American troops involved in the war. They cooked, tended to the wounded, drove wagons, and otherwise assisted their masters on the battlefield.

Black servants in the Mexican War were placed in an especially difficult position, however. Mexico had already abolished **slavery**, and many African-American leaders and abolitionists opposed the war. They believed the U.S. government was only trying to win land so that it could expand slavery throughout the western states. After the American victory, one congressman proposed that slavery be banned in any land that the United States won in the war. However, his proposal was quickly defeated. The Compromise of 1850 admitted California as a free state and allowed Utah and New Mexico to decide for themselves whether to allow slavery. These territories, acquired by the war, sparked the debates about slavery that would eventually lead to the **Civil War**.

Mfume, Kweisi (Gray, Frizzell)

CONGRESSMAN, CIVIL RIGHTS LEADER
October 24, 1948–

Born Frizzell Gray in Turner's Station, Maryland, the eldest of four children, Kweisi Mfume grew up in a poor community just outside of Baltimore, Maryland. His mother, Mary Willis, worked on an assembly line at an airplane parts manufacturer. His stepfather, Clifton Gray, abandoned the family when Mfume was twelve years old. Four years later, his mother was diagnosed with cancer and literally died in Mfume's arms.

Mfume was devastated by his mother's death. He dropped out of high school and began working at odd jobs to make ends meet while he and his three sisters lived with relatives. Mfume found that he could make more money hustling on the streets than shining shoes or pushing bread through a slicer. By age twenty-two, he had already fathered five children from four different women. Gang life on the streets had became deadly, and a number of his closest friends had been killed in the **Vietnam War** (1959–75).

Despite these personal difficulties, Mfume resolved to turn his life around. He began taking night courses to complete his high school equivalency degree and then enrolled at Baltimore Community College. He developed a keen interest in **politics** in the early 1970s while working as a disc jockey on local **radio** stations. He changed his name from Frizzell Gray to the African name Kweisi Mfume ("conquering son of kings").

In 1976 Mfume graduated magna cum laude with a degree in urban planning from Morgan State University. Two years later he used his popularity as a talk-radio host to win a seat as a Democratic Party member of the Baltimore City Council. Mfume served two terms on the city council and then went on to graduate school at Johns Hopkins University. He received an M.A. in political science and briefly taught political science and communications at Morgan State University.

In 1986 he won the seat in the U.S. Congress left vacant by his political mentor, the legendary black politician Parren J. Mitchell. Mfume went on to serve five terms in Congress, rising to the position of chairman of the Congressional Black Caucus (CBC).

By the early 1990s Mfume's relentless campaign to end apartheid (a system of racial segregation) in South Africa earned him the respect and friendship of South African leader Nelson Mandela. Although he helped sponsor laws favoring the development of independent parties in the early 1990s, Mfume remained committed to the Democratic Party as a vehicle for the advancement of African Americans.

In 1996 he left Congress to accept the position of president and chief executive officer of the **National Association for the Advancement of Colored People (NAACP).** As president of the NAACP, Mfume has pursued corporate donations to retire the organization's debt and has worked to recruit younger African Americans to the nation's oldest civil rights organization. His target areas for the NAACP include: the scarcity of African Americans in television programming, the Confederate battle flag's longtime perch over the South Carolina Statehouse, the hotel industry's treatment of black guests, and the costs of gun violence.

Mfume's autobiography, *No Free Ride: From the Mean Streets to the Mainstream* (1996), details his rich life.

Micheaux, Oscar

NOVELIST, FILMMAKER
January 2, 1884–March 25, 1951

Largely ignored during his lifetime, novelist and filmmaker Oscar Micheaux was born in Metropolis, Illinois, in 1884, one of thirteen children of former slaves. He apparently worked as a porter, acquiring enough money to buy two very large plots of land in South Dakota. His first novel, *The Conquest: The Story of a Negro Pioneer* (1913), is about his experiences settling this land. To publicize the book Micheaux created the Western Book Supply Company and toured the Midwest. He sold most of the books and stock in his first company to white farmers, although his later ventures were financed by African-American businessmen.

His travels as a bookseller formed the basis for his second novel, *The Forged Note: A Romance of the Darker Races* (1915). Micheaux's third novel, *The Homesteader* (1917), attracted the attention of black filmmaker George P. Johnson, who, with his Hollywood actor brother Noble, owned the Lincoln Film Company. Fascinated by the new medium of film, Micheaux offered to sell the Johnson Brothers the film rights to his novel, on the condition that he direct the motion picture. When they refused, Micheaux decided to produce and direct the film himself, financing it through what became the Micheaux Book and Film Company.

The film version of *The Homesteader* (1918) was the first of about fifty films Micheaux directed. He distributed the films himself, carrying the prints from town to town; the films usually played for only one night. His films were shown mostly in white-owned (but often black-managed) black theaters throughout the country. Although the black press sometimes criticized Micheaux for projecting a rich black fantasy world and ignoring real African American problems, he dealt frankly with such social themes as interracial relationships, "passing" (light-skinned blacks' pretending to be white), racial prejudice, and the threat posed to African Americans by hate groups, such as the **Ku Klux Klan.**

About twelve of Micheaux's films still exist. His interior scenes are often dimly lit, but his location scenes of urban streets are usually crisp and clear, providing a realistic glimpse of the period. Micheaux featured some of the most talented African-American actors of his time, including Andrew Bishop and **Paul Robeson** (1898–1976).

Film scholars rediscovered his work in the early 1970s, and since then critics have hailed him as an original filmmaker who was a true film pioneer. The Black Filmmakers Hall of Fame began giving an annual Oscar Micheaux Award in 1974. In 1987 he received a star on the Hollywood Walk of Fame. (*See also*: **Film**)

Michigan

First African-American Settlers: Black men accompanied French explorers to the part of the Great Lakes region that would become Michigan as early as 1679.

Slave Population: Slaves were documented in Michigan as early as 1731, when sixteen slaves were recorded by parish priests at the Church of Saint Anne on the Upper Peninsula. Slaves generally worked as lumberjacks, dockworkers, carriage drivers, or farmhands, although a few ran away and formed colonies. In the latter part of the eighteenth century, slaves began escaping through Michigan into Canada via the **Underground Railroad.**

Free Black Population: When the Michigan Territory was established in 1805, there were relatively few African-American residents; the first census taken in 1810 counted only 24 slaves and 120 **free blacks.** The free population slowly increased, and in 1837, the year Michigan became a state, the legislature formally abolished **slavery.**

Civil War: Michigan's black residents vigorously endorsed the Union (Northern) cause during the **Civil War** (1861–65), and nearly fourteen hundred African-American men served in Union armies.

Reconstruction: Suffrage (voting rights) was granted to black Michiganders in 1870 after five years of intense lobbying. The first blacks were admitted into the University of Michigan in 1869, and public schools were desegregated in 1869. Beginning in 1880, African Americans were elected to local offices, and in 1899 the first black was elected to a county board of supervisors. The Great Migration of the 1910s and 1920s brought an enormous number of blacks to Michigan, most of whom settled in the Detroit area in response to the expanding auto industry.

The Great Depression: During the **Great Depression** large numbers of African-American laborers were laid off and many black landowners became impoverished. White supremacist groups such as the **Ku Klux Klan** grew in numbers as racial tensions increased. The coming of **World War II** (1939–45), however, brought war contracts and prosperity to Detroit's industries and renewed the migration of blacks to the area. Race relations worsened, and in 1943 a two-day riot erupted, leaving thirty-four people dead and over six hundred injured.

Civil Rights Movement: The **Civil Rights movement** became a powerful force in Michigan black life during the 1960s as demonstrations were organized protesting housing discrimination. A major race rebellion stemming from racist oppression in 1967 left forty-three people dead in Detroit. Michigan's African Americans have suffered from chronic unemployment since 1950, and the jobless rate rose sharply after 1970.

Current African-American Population: According to U.S. Census Bureau estimates, the total black population in Michigan was 1,404,748 (14 percent of the state population) as of July 1, 1998.

Key Figures: Black nationalist leader **Malcolm X** (1925–1965); **Charles C. Diggs** (1922–), Michigan's first African American in Congress; actor **James Earl Jones** (1931–); singers **Diana Ross** (1944–) and **Stevie Wonder** (1950–); basketball star **Earvin "Magic" Johnson** (1959–).

(See also **Detroit, Michigan.**)

Middle Passage. *See* Slave Trade

Military

Throughout history, serving in the military has provided African Americans with financial, social, and political opportunities. During emergencies, the British colonies would admit both free blacks and slaves to the fighting ranks. The United States has also relied heavily on African Americans in nearly every war, from the **Civil War** (1861–65), to the **Vietnam War** (1959–75), to the Persian Gulf War (1991).

Colonial Wars and the American Revolution

In colonial times, black slaves accompanied their white masters to war, serving as cooks, soldiers, and sailors. Trusted slaves were allowed to serve as soldiers and were promised freedom for exceptional service. **Free blacks** also benefited from helping to defend their colonies—for example, George Gire, a free black man from Massachusetts, earned a pension for his service during the French and Indian War (1754–1763).

When the American colonies rebelled against Great Britain in 1775, blacks fought in the Massachusetts militia and in General George Washington's (1732–99; first U.S. president 1789–97) Continental army. Southern colonies, however, refused to employ blacks except as military labor. Even South Carolina, which had allowed slaves to serve in the military in 1760, refused them weapons during the **American Revolution** out of fear that the slaves would rebel. Despite southern resistance, Washington not only allowed black veterans to reenlist in his army but also admitted more African Americans to the ranks.

The New Nation's Armed Forces

Although five thousand blacks fought during the Revolutionary War, the United States excluded them from military service almost as soon as the war was won. Not until 1798 were blacks again allowed to fight for the United States, this time for the navy. During a period of naval battles with France and Britain, the navy discovered that white Americans disliked the harsh discipline of military life at sea and were reluctant to enlist. As a result, the navy became the first branch of the military to admit free blacks to its ranks, in 1818. Slaves were still banned from all naval service, however. By 1839 so many African Americans had applied to enlist that the navy placed a limit on the number that could be accepted.

The army's policy toward African-American servicemen continued to be inconsistent. Barred from service during peacetime, free blacks were again allowed to enlist during the War of 1812 (1812–15). African Americans formed two battalions and helped win a series of important battles. Black volunteers received the same pay and bonuses as whites, but the equality did not last. By 1834 African Americans were once again banned from the army.

Unlike the navy and the army, the Marine Corps, which relied on fewer men, did not suffer a shortage of white recruits. As a result, the marines barred African Americans from service until 1942.

The Civil War

Although the navy continued to recruit blacks, no other branch of the military allowed them to serve until the Civil War (1861–65). When the war began in 1861, the Union (the Northern states) resisted the idea of allowing African Americans to fight in the war. **Frederick Douglass**, a former slave and prominent political leader, predicted that the first side to use black soldiers would win the war. By 1862 a shortage of white manpower, combined with a huge number of newly freed slaves, forced a change in military policy. At first, Union officers employed the slaves they had freed as servants. But in the spring of 1862, several Union commanders began training the former slaves to fight.

After President Abraham Lincoln's **Emancipation Proclamation** (which declared that all slaves in the South were free) in 1863, the Union began creating all-black regiments, which helped win several key battles. By the time the war ended in 1865, 186,000 African Americans had enlisted in the Union army, and 30,000 had enlisted in the navy.

Of the Union army's black soldiers, fewer than a hundred became officers. No African Americans were made officers in the navy. Although willing to accept free blacks and liberated slaves as sailors, the navy refused to appoint black officers until World War II (1939–45). Both the army and the navy paid African-American enlisted men less than white enlisted men throughout the Civil War. Despite unequal treatment, African-American soldiers and sailors benefited from Civil War service, helping to defeat the South, end **slavery,** and finally gain full citizenship and voting rights for all African Americans.

The Segregated Military

Despite the victory of the Civil War, African Americans still suffered from widespread racism. A policy of "separate but equal" was enforced throughout the armed forces. This policy, sometimes referred to as "Jim Crow," kept white and black soldiers and sailors segregated (assigned to different military units and living quarters).

During **World War I** (1914–18), which the United States entered in 1917, black soldiers saw little action. Of 380,000 African-American soldiers, only 11 percent were called upon to fight. The remaining soldiers were used as manual laborers. After the end of the war in 1918, the U.S. War Department concluded that black soldiers would be used primarily as laborers in future wars.

During **World War II** (1939–45), however, the United States once again found itself calling upon its African-American soldiers. President Franklin Roosevelt (1882–1945; president 1933–45) expanded opportunities for blacks in the armed forces, allowing black pilots to train in the Army Air Corps—although they had to train separately from whites. But once the war started, the army could no longer afford the cost of keeping black and white soldiers separate. As a result, for the first time in U.S. history, black and white soldiers began to fight and train side by side. Likewise, the navy discovered that keeping African Americans out of combat undermined the morale of both black and white soldiers. White soldiers often had to spend more time at sea because black soldiers were not allowed to replace them. The navy soon integrated the races on board a number of its ships. Only the Marine Corps, after accepting its first black recruits since the American Revolution, maintained racial segregation.

After the war ended in August 1945, all the armed forces returned to their peacetime policy of segregation. The army and the navy once again set limits on the number of blacks who could enlist.

THE FIRST AMERICAN SLAVES TO FIGHT FOR FREEDOM

In 1777 Connecticut adopted a policy of buying slaves to serve in the Contintental army and then setting them free for life when their service was complete. Rhode Island soon followed, raising a whole battalion who then earned their freedom in battle.

Integration

By the late 1940s several U.S. courts had begun to challenge the practice of segregation, both inside the military and out. In 1948 President Harry S. Truman faced a very difficult reelection campaign. To win, he would need the help of black voters. On July 26, 1948, he issued an executive order requiring the armed forces to end segregation and provide equal treatment and opportunity to all men, regardless of race. His stand against racism contributed to his victory in the election.

The air force was the first branch of the armed forces to embrace this new policy. Even before Truman's decision, it had abolished segregated units and forced all personnel, regardless of race, to compete for technical training solely on the basis of their abilities. The other services lagged behind the air force. Not until the United States became involved in the **Korean War** (1950–53) and the army and the navy were confronted with the need to use their manpower more efficiently, did they abolish their race-based policies. By the end of the war in 1953, African Americans were eligible for most specialties and could expect a meaningful assignment when they completed training. Despite the racism that survived into the late 1950s and early 1960s, blacks still enjoyed greater opportunity in the military than in civilian (nonmilitary) jobs.

Many African Americans served throughout the Vietnam War (1959–75), in which the United States became involved in 1965, in military units that were totally integrated. At this time, the military relied on a method of enlisting soldiers called the Selective Service System, or the "draft," in which eligible men were selected randomly from the entire U.S. population by each of the armed forces and were required to serve.

The Modern Military

When the Vietnam War ended in 1975, the national draft was suspended, and the military relied entirely on volunteers. Since 1975, African Americans have made up a large percentage of enlisted personnel. In 1983 African Americans made up 20 percent of military personnel, which was almost twice their percentage in society as a whole; the army also had a large proportion of African Americans in the officer corps, almost 10 percent.

In 1991 a coalition led by the United States went to war against the Middle Eastern country of Iraq, which had invaded the small neighboring state of Kuwait. During the ensuing Persian Gulf War, 30 percent of the

American force in the Middle East consisted of African Americans. In the years that followed, African Americans in the military experienced new levels of success. General **Colin Powell,** the first African American to chair the Joint Chiefs of Staff, became a national hero and best-selling author. Military service continues to present black Americans with an opportunity to assume responsibility, learn skills, and earn respect.

Million Man March

The Million Man March was an event held on October 16, 1995, in which at least four hundred thousand black men gathered to show their intention to take responsibility for their lives and communities, to vow to stop mistreating black women, and to unite African Americans against racial inequality.

The march was organized by Minister **Louis Farrakhan** of the **Nation of Islam,** an African-American branch of the Islamic faith. Many blacks and whites spoke out against the march. African-American feminist scholar **Angela Davis** and black leader and writer **Amiri Baraka** led those who criticized the march because it did not include black women. Journalist Carl Rowan and scholar Roger Wilkins said the idea was racially discriminatory. Many blacks supported the ideas behind the march but did not want to be associated with Farrakhan and his anti-Jewish message.

Father and son participants in the 1995
Million Man March (AP/Wide World
Photos. Reproduced by permission)

The march gathered at the Lincoln Memorial in Washington, D.C., the site of the largest civil rights demonstration in American history, the 1963 March on Washington. Numerous speakers addressed the crowd. Farrakhan closed the gathering by reminding the marchers, "We are in progress toward a more perfect union."

Although the Million Man March caused more blacks to register to vote and become politically active, its long-term effect is uncertain.

EXCERPT FROM FARRAKHAN'S MILLION MAN PLEDGE

I, [say your name], pledge from this day forward I will never abuse my wife by striking her, disrespecting her for she is the mother of my children and the producer of my future. I, [say your name], pledge that from this day forward I will never engage in the abuse of children, little boys, or little girls for sexual gratification. But I will let them grow in peace to be strong men and women for the future of our people. I, [say your name], will never again use the "B" word to describe my female, but particularly my own Black sister.

I, [say your name], pledge from this day forward that I will not poison my body with drugs or that which is destructive to my health and my well-being. I, [say your name], pledge from this day forward, I will support Black newspapers, Black radio, Black television. I will support Black artists, who clean up their acts to show respect for themselves and respect for their people, and respect for the ears of the human family.

I, [say your name], will do all of this so help me God....

From Minister Louis Farrakhan's remarks at the Million Man March, October 16, 1995.

Mills Brothers, The

POPULAR MUSIC GROUP

The Mills Brothers were among the earliest African-American popular music groups to achieve a national following. The main members of the group were brothers Herbert (1912-1989), Harry (1913-1982), and Donald Mills (1915-1999), all born in Piqua, Ohio. Another brother, John (1910-1936), played guitar and sang with the group until his death, when he was replaced by his father, John Sr. (1882-1967), who performed with The Mills Brothers until 1957.

The brothers began their career singing in small-town shows. A ten-month stint during the late 1920s on radio station WLW in Cincinnati, Ohio, provided them with their first big break; in 1929 they became the first black group to be sponsored on a national network, CBS. By 1930 the brothers were in New York performing in theaters, clubs, and on radio as well as recording and appearing in films. They also played with orchestras and big bands.

The brothers' signature style was a smooth harmony that pleased both blacks and whites. Among their many hit songs in the 1930s and 1940s were "Tiger Rag" (1930), which sold one million copies; "Paper Doll" (1943), which sold six million copies; and "You Always Hurt the One You Love" (1944), another million-seller. Their last hit was "The Glow Worm" in 1952. The group continued to perform as a threesome until 1982, making more than 1,200 recordings in all.

Mills, Florence

SINGER, DANCER
January 25, 1896–November 1, 1927

Florence Mills was born in Washington, D.C., the daughter of emigrants from Virginia's depressed tobacco industry. A talented singer and dancer, she appeared at age six in the Washington production of *Sons of Ham* singing "Miss Hannah from Savannah." She traveled with the white vaudeville team of Bonita and Hearn, and then at age fourteen organized a vaudeville (traveling variety show) act with her sisters. Around 1915 she worked at Chicago's notorious Panama Café as part of the Panama Trio. When the police closed the Panama, she joined the Tennessee Ten on the vaudeville circuit, where she met and married the acrobatic dancer Ulysses "Slow Kid" Thompson.

Mills came to national attention when she replaced Gertrude Saunders in the trendsetting all-black 1921 musical *Shuffle Along*. Taken up by producer Lew Leslie, she starred in his *Dover Street to Dixie* (1923). She was offered a major role by theatrical producer Florenz Ziegfeld in his famous Follies but turned him down to create more all-black revues. In 1924 *From Dixie to Broadway* opened in the heart of Broadway with Mills singing "I'm a Little Blackbird."

Mills died unexpectedly in New York on November 1, 1927. She was beloved in Harlem; over 150,000 people lined the streets for her funeral.

Mingus, Charles Jr.

JAZZ MUSICIAN
April 22, 1922–January 5, 1979

Although he was a superb bass guitar player early in his career, Charles Mingus's main contribution to **jazz** was as a composer and bandleader. For more than thirty years he created works comparable to those of great jazz composers **Duke Ellington** (1899–1974) and **Thelonious Monk** (1917–1982).

Mingus was an emotional, independent artist whose compositions ranged from somber but gritty tributes to the musicians he worked with—including saxophonists **Lester Young** (1909–1959), **Charlie Parker** (1920–1955), and Eric Dolphy (1928–1964)—to roaring pieces that recalled African-American gospel prayer meetings. He was known for yelling at audiences and musicians from the bandstand and for firing and rehiring musicians during performances. However, his "workshops" (in-concert rehearsals where his compositions were developed) achieved a musical passion unmatched in the history of jazz, as Mingus conducted and shouted instructions from the piano or bass, or, late in life, from a wheelchair.

Mingus was born in Nogales, Arizona, and grew up in the Watts section of Los Angeles, California. He studied the trombone and the cello as a boy, then switched to the bass at age sixteen and began performing while still a teenager. During the 1940s he played in the rhythm sections of the bands of top jazz musicians like trumpeter and singer **Louis Armstrong** (1901–1971) and vibraphonist **Lionel Hampton** (1908–). He made his first recordings with Hampton in 1947, a session that included Mingus's first recorded composition, "Mingus Fingers."

Mingus settled in New York in 1951 and played with Ellington, pianist **Art Tatum** (1909–1956), white jazz saxophonist Stan Getz (1927–1991), and others. His most important work during this time was a concert he recorded for his own company, Debut Records, in Toronto, Canada, in 1953. The group featured Mingus, pianist Bud Powell (1924–1966), drummer **Max Roach** (1924–), Parker, and trumpeter **Dizzy Gillespie**—the perfect group to play the jazz style known as "bebop."

Mingus formed his own music workshop in 1955 and began his mature style, in which concerts often became long, brooding performances, building to aggressive, even savage, endings. His compositions used elements of African-American folk music, like blues shouts, field hollers, call-and-response, and gospel-style musical phrases. This period lasted until 1966, and Mingus worked with notable musicians to produce numerous albums that are considered classics, including *Tijuana Moods* (1957) and *Mingus, Mingus, Mingus* (1963), as well as important compositions like "Percussion Discussion" (1955), "Reincarnation of a Lovebird" (1957), and "The Black Saint and the Sinner Lady" (1963).

Beginning in the 1950s, Mingus combined politics and music, writing musical attacks against segregation and racism, like "Meditations on

Jazz bassist and composer Charles Mingus
(© Jack Vartoogian. Reproduced by
permission)

Integration" (1964), which addresses the mistreatment of black prisoners in the southern United States. Mingus encouraged black jazz musicians to take their careers out of the hands of club owners and recording executives. He twice organized his own record companies—Debut Records in 1952 and Charles Mingus Records in 1963.

Mingus stopped performing in 1966 because of psychological problems that had bothered him for years. By 1969, however—in spite of his worsening physical condition due to a disease of the nervous system known as Lou Gehrig's disease—money problems forced him out of retirement. He experienced a new burst of creativity; he published his fictionalized autobiography, *Beneath the Underdog,* and was awarded a Guggenheim Fellowship in 1971. The fellowship provided financial assistance so he could continue his creative work. He worked until 1977, when he became ill after recording *Three or Four Shades of Blue.* He released his last albums, *Me, Myself an Eye* and *Something Like a Bird* in 1978. His last appearance on record was on *Mingus,* an album by the singer Joni Mitchell (1943–), in 1978. He died in Cuernavaca, Mexico.

Minnesota

First African-American Settlers: African Americans in Minnesota predate the state's territorial status. They often accompanied French fur trappers and acted as interpreters between Europeans and **American Indians.** The earliest record of blacks in Minnesota dates to the end of the eighteenth century.

Slave Population: Although Minnesota, as part of the Wisconsin Territory, forbade **slavery** under the Northwest Ordinance of 1787, African-American slaves arrived in the area as early as 1825. They worked as servants to officers stationed at Fort Snelling and as domestics to the wealthy Southern slave owners who frequently vacationed in Minnesota. In 1848 Minnesota slave Dred Scott sued for his freedom in a Missouri court, leading to the U.S. Supreme Court's 1857 decision in *Dred Scott v. Sandford.*

Free Black Population: By the time Minnesota achieved territorial status in 1849, approximately forty free persons of African descent were recorded as territorial residents. During the 1850s more **free blacks** entered the territory, many as laborers or cooks. By 1860, two years after Minnesota became the thirty-second state, some 259 blacks resided in twenty-two of the state's eighty-seven counties.

Civil War: Although black men were not initially allowed to become members of the state's militia, 104 black men from Minnesota ultimately served in the Union (Northern) army during the **Civil War** (1861–65).

Reconstruction: The black population in Minnesota grew after the Civil War. African Americans migrated to the state to homestead land (claim and settle it), to improve their economic circumstances, and to acquire education. By 1898 three state laws had been passed prohibiting racial discrimination in public accommodations, although occasional discrimination remained. By 1900 the black population had reached about five thousand, and it doubled in the following forty years.

The Great Depression: By the late 1920s many blacks were unemployed, and educated African Americans were forced to leave the state in search of work. Housing remained scarce and often substandard. By 1936 an estimated 62 percent of the Twin Cities' (Minneapolis and St. Paul) black population was on welfare relief or dependent on charity. The coming of **World War II** (1939–45), however, brought prosperity as well as thousands of black immigrants to Minnesota.

Civil Rights Movement: The **Civil Rights movement** began full-scale in Minnesota in 1960, when members of the Youth Council of the Minneapolis chapter of the **National Association for the Advancement of Colored People (NAACP)** began picketing lunch counters that refused to serve African Americans. Rising racial tensions resulted in racial disturbances in the summers of 1966 and 1967.

Current African-American Population: According to U.S. Census Bureau estimates, the total black population in Minnesota was 140,644 (3 percent of the state population) as of July 1, 1998.

Key Figures: Civil rights leader and journalist **Roy Wilkins** (1901–1981); **Alan Cedric Page** (1945–), former football player and state Supreme Court justice; Pulitzer Prize–winning playwright **August Wilson** (1945–); singer and composer **Prince** (Prince Rogers Nelson) (1958–).

(SEE ALSO NIAGARA MOVEMENT.)

Mississippi

Slave Population: Upon statehood in 1817, more than four in ten Mississippi residents were black. Thereafter, as the state entered the boom years of the cotton economy, Mississippi's black population soared; by 1840 slaves outnumbered whites statewide, and by 1860 the ratio of slaves to whites in some counties was greater than nine to one. The state's slave code was considered the harshest of all states; as one **expatriate** put it, "Mississippi was everybody's choice as the state that was the South at its worst."

Free Black Population: During the pre Civil War years a tiny fraction (0.2 percent in 1860) of black Mississippians were free. In 1840 **free blacks** totaled 1,366 (compared to 195,211 slaves); by 1860 that number had fallen to 773 after all free blacks not certified by county courts to be of "good character" were expelled from the state.

Civil War: During the **Civil War** (1861–65) black Mississippians fled the plantations to Union (Northern) lines at the first opportunity.

Reconstruction: During **Reconstruction,** Mississippi's freedmen briefly entered the body politic as full citizens, helping to send two blacks to the U.S. Senate and one to the House. Under the blatantly white-supremacist state constitution of 1890, however, African-American Mississippians were disfranchised (denied the right to vote) and faced harsh discrimination, segregation, and exclusion.

The Great Depression: Between 1910 and 1960 over one million blacks left the state in protest of the oppressive political conditions and lack of economic opportunity. In 1940 0.4 percent of all eligible black Mississippians were registered to vote, a figure that rose only to 6.7 percent by 1964.

Civil Rights Movement: Mississippi was the arena for some of the bloodiest racial conflicts of the 1950s and 1960s, becoming the symbol of white resistance to changing federal policy. Conflict climaxed during the **Freedom Summer** of 1964, when black and white college students led civil rights and voter registration efforts in the face of large-scale white harassment and violence.

Current African-American Population: According to U.S. Census Bureau estimates, the total black population in Mississippi was 1,003,175 (36 percent of the state population) as of July 1, 1998.

Key Figures: Hiram Rhoades Revels (1822–1901), the first African American to sit in the U.S. Senate; Isaiah Montgomery (1841–1924), founder of the independent black town Mound Bayou; blues musicians Charley Patton (c. 1887–1934) and **Robert Leroy Johnson** (c. 1911–1938);

Chicago native **Emmett Louis Till** (1941–1955), who was lynched for whistling at a white woman; civil rights activists **Fanny Lou Hamer** (1917–1977) and **James Meredith** (1933–).

(SEE ALSO EMANCIPATION; BLUES, THE.)

Missouri

First African-American Settlers: African Americans have lived in Missouri since 1717, when slave-owning Jesuit (Catholic) missionaries settled in the state.

Slave Population: Missouri was admitted to the Union as a slave state in 1819. Most slave owners kept only one or two slaves, who grew grains, tobacco, hemp, and flax or worked as craftworkers. In 1860, 114,931 slaves lived in Missouri.

Free Black Population: In 1860 the **free black** population was 3,572 (3 percent of Missouri's African-American population).

Civil War: Missouri was a border state during the **Civil War**, meaning it was between the Union states to the north and the Confederate states to the south. Although many Missourians supported **slavery** and sympathized with the South, the state remained tied to the Union. Approximately 8,344 African Americans from Missouri served in the Union army. Slavery was ended in Missouri by state proclamation on January 11, 1865.

Reconstruction: During the early part of **Reconstruction,** Missouri's 1865 constitution banned slavery but required a segregated (racially separate) educational system. It also prohibited racial intermarriage and mandated separate libraries, public parks, and playgrounds. During the 1920s Missouri became a center for the **Ku Klux Klan,** and in 1924 a particularly brutal **lynching** (hanging) occurred in Charleston.

The Great Depression: In the 1930s Missouri was the focus of a national campaign by the **National Association for the Advancement of Colored People (NAACP)** to equalize education. In 1948 St. Louis University opened its doors to African Americans, and in 1950 the University of Missouri admitted its first African-American student. Statewide school desegregation did not begin to occur in Missouri until the 1954 *Brown v. Board of Education of Topeka, Kansas* decision by the U.S. Supreme Court.

Civil Rights Movement: In 1960 **sit-ins** forced stores and restaurants in St. Louis, Kansas City, and Jefferson City to serve blacks, and in 1963 further sit-ins forced city authorities to pass equal rights laws. Federal civil rights legislation led to increased economic and educational opportunity for black Missourians, but continued discrimination led to frustration and anger. In 1968, after the assassination of the Rev. Dr. **Martin Luther King Jr.** (1929–1968), Kansas City erupted, and authorities were compelled to call out the entire 900-man police force as well as 1,700 National Guardsmen and 168 state troopers to stop the violence. Jefferson City and other areas had smaller racial outbreaks.

Current African-American Population: According to U.S. Census Bureau estimates, the total black population in Missouri was 612,788 (11 percent of the state population) as of July 1, 1998.

Key Figures: Jean Baptiste Du Sable (c.1750–1818), founder of Chicago; Dred Scott (c. 1795–1858), a St. Louis slave who launched a suit for his freedom that resulted in the famous U.S. Supreme Court decision *Dred Scott v. Sandford*; **Scott Joplin** (1868–1917), a pianist and composer who popularized **ragtime** with his best-selling "Maple Leaf Rag"; bandleader and composer **Count Basie** (1904–1984); musicians **Mary Lou Williams** (1910–1981) and **Charlie "Yardbird" Parker** (1920–1955); Dr. J. Edward Perry (1870–1962), physician and activist who organized the first black private hospital in Kansas City; **George Washington Carver** (c.1864–1943) scientist and educator; **Josephine Baker** (1906–1975), entertainer; writer **Langston Hughes** (1902–1967); **Coleman Hawkins** (1904–1969), **jazz** artist; **Roy Wilkins** (1901–1981), chair of Kansas City branch of the NAACP; sociologist Oliver Cromwell Cox (1901–1974); **Chester Himes** (1909–1984), writer; William Clay (1931–), the state's first black U.S. congressman in 1969.

(SEE ALSO LINCOLN UNIVERSITY; ST. LOUIS, MISSOURI.)

Mitchell, Arthur Adams Jr.

DANCER, CHOREOGRAPHER
March 27, 1934–

Born in New York City, dancer Arthur Mitchell began **tap dance** lessons at the age of ten and attended the High School of Performing Arts as a modern-dance major. He made his first professional appearances before graduation, when he was the first male to receive his school's prestigious Dance Award.

Mitchell won a scholarship to the School of American Ballet in 1952. In 1955, after only three years of concentrated **ballet** study, he toured with the John Butler Company. He returned to New York to join the New York City Ballet (NYCB).

Within his first week with NYCB, Mitchell landed a featured role in the famed choreographer George Balanchine's *Western Symphony*. In 1957 Balanchine created a prominent dance in *Agon* for Mitchell and ballerina Diana Adams, which earned the dancer international recognition.

Mitchell stayed with the NYCB for fifteen years, dancing a range of leading roles. In 1962 his role as Puck in Balanchine's *A Midsummer Night's Dream* won praise for his dramatic skill and charisma.

Mitchell also performed in several Broadway productions, did choreography for **Eartha Kitt** at the 1957 Newport (Rhode Island) Jazz Festival, and appeared at the Festival of Two Worlds in Spoleto, Italy. In 1967 he helped organize the National Ballet Company of Brazil.

Mitchell often encouraged others to learn classical ballet. He taught at several schools, and in 1968 he and ballet master Karel Shook reacted to the

An African-American FIRST

When Arthur Mitchell joined the New York City Ballet (NYCB) in November 1955, he became the first African-American principal dancer permanently associated with that company, as well as the first African-American male principal dancer in a major ballet company. Mitchell made news for the groundbreaking work he did with choreographer George Balanchine, but he asked that the NYCB issue no publicity about breaking a color barrier.

Arthur Mitchell standing in front of a poster for the Dance Theatre of Harlem, the organization he co-founded (AP/Wide World Photos. Reproduced by permission)

assassination of the Reverend Dr. **Martin Luther King Jr.** by forming the school that became the **Dance Theatre of Harlem**. Mitchell says he wanted to prove "that there is no difference, except color, between a black ballet dancer and a white ballet dancer."

Mitchell's numerous awards include the Image Award of Fame, presented by the **National Association for the Advancement of Colored People (NAACP)**, several honorary doctorates, a MacArthur Fellowship (1994), and a place in the Dance Hall of Fame (1999).

Modern Jazz Quartet

MUSIC GROUP

Composed of harpist Milt Jackson, pianist-composer John Lewis, bassist Percy Heath, and drummer Connie Kay, the Modern Jazz Quartet (MJQ) displays the style known as "cool jazz," marked by a strong, flexible rhythm and complex harmony. Jackson and Lewis were originally members of famous jazz musician **Dizzy Gillespie's** (1917–1993) big band.

The quartet's music combines **jazz** with elements of European chamber music (music intended for a small auditorium, with one player performing each part). It remains firmly rooted in African-American culture, however, blending soul music and the **blues**.

Early songs include "Vendome" (1952) and "Concorde" (1955). In 1966 the quartet released *Blues at Carnegie Hall*. The Modern Jazz Quartet disbanded in 1974, only to reunite for tours and recordings in 1981.

Monk, Thelonious Sphere

JAZZ PIANIST, COMPOSER
October 10, 1917–February 17, 1982

Thelonious Monk was admired as a **jazz** composer, but early in his career many dismissed him as a pianist because his highly original melodies and harmonies often sounded like wrong notes. However, his compositions attracted the attention of the most adventurous jazz musicians and placed Monk at the center of the new bebop movement during **World War II** (1939–45).

Born in Rocky Mount, North Carolina, Monk grew up in the San Juan Hill district of Manhattan, in New York City. He began playing piano professionally in the mid-1930s. By 1940 he was a member of the house rhythm section at Minton's Playhouse, a nightclub in New York City's **Harlem** district well known among musicians for its nightly jam sessions. Live recordings from this period show that Monk's style was firmly rooted in the "stride" piano style of ragtime music and that he was already leaning toward creating unusual new harmonies for standard songs.

By 1944 Monk had already written several of his best-known compositions, such as "Epistrophy," "Round Midnight," and "Hackensack," which

Jazz pianist Thelonious Monk (Courtesy of the Library of Congress)

was recorded as "Rifftide" in Monk's first professional recording, with the **Coleman Hawkins** (1904–1969) Quartet.

Although he was well known among fellow bebop musicians, Monk did not become generally known until 1947, when he made a series of recordings for the Blue Note record label showing a wide range of his compositions, like "Criss Cross," "Ruby, My Dear," and "Straight, No Chaser."

In 1951 Monk was accused of drug possession and was barred from performing in New York City until 1957. But he recorded the famous "Bags Groove" session with jazz trumpeter **Miles Davis** (1926–1991) in 1954 and the album *Brilliant Corners* in 1956.

Throughout the summer of 1957 Monk played at the Five Spot, a New York nightclub, with saxophonist **John Coltrane** (1926–1967). These performances finally earned him attention as one of the most important figures in modern jazz.

From the late 1950s through the 1960s Monk worked mainly with his quartet, featuring tenor saxophonist Charlie Rouse (1924–1988). The group toured the United States and Europe and recorded for Columbia Records. Monk increasingly turned to piano solos, recording his own compositions as well as old popular songs.

After a world tour in 1971 Monk retired from public life, but his reputation continued to grow as a younger generation of musicians discovered his compositions and took on the challenge of adding their own interpretations to his distinctive melodies and harmonies.

The 1988 film *Thelonious Monk: Straight, No Chaser* (executive producer, Clint Eastwood; director, Charlotte Zwerin) documents Monk's music and life in the late 1960s.

Montana

First African-American Settlers: The first blacks to enter Montana were explorers and fur trappers. Montana's first permanent black settlers were gold miners who arrived following gold discoveries in the early 1860s. The 1870 census reported seventy-one blacks in Helena, with smaller concentrations of African Americans in six other counties.

Free Black Population: Montana had few African-American homesteaders (settler-farmers) because of the expense of high-plains agriculture. Nevertheless, some blacks staked land claims. Nineteenth-century black Montanans included retired soldiers and cowboys, but black servants made up the largest occupational group.

Reconstruction: Helena was home to the first black community in Montana, beginning as a gold-mining camp and later giving rise to black fraternal groups, literary societies, and churches. Although the African-American population rose steadily from 346 in 1880 to 1,834 in 1910, it decreased over the next three decades as many blacks left because of declining employment opportunities and growing racial restrictions.

The Great Depression: The shrinking populations of Montana cities took their toll on community institutions such as churches. The Great Falls chapter of the **National Association for the Advancement of Colored People (NAACP),** established in 1922, shut down by 1930.

Civil Rights Movement: Montana's small black population crusaded for civil rights legislation in the late 1940s and early 1950s. A successful campaign was initiated by Arcella Hayes to repeal discriminatory statutes and enact the Fair Employment Practices Law in 1949. Four years later, Hayes began a successful campaign to repeal the state's forty-four-year-old ban on interracial marriages.

Current African-American Population: According to U.S. Census Bureau estimates, the total black population in Montana was 3,219 (0.4 percent of the state population) as of July 1, 1998.

Key Figures: Frontiersman James Beckwourth (1798–1866).

Martin Luther and Coretta Scott King lead the march from Selma to Montgomery, Alabama (Corbis Corporation. Reproduced by permission)

Montgomery, Alabama, Bus Boycott

The Montgomery, Alabama, bus boycott began on December 5, 1955, as an effort by black residents to protest the trial of **Rosa Parks.** She had been arrested for violating the city's law that required blacks to sit in the back of city buses when she refused to give up her seat to a white person. The boycott was intended to last for only a day, but local black support of the strike proved so great that black community leaders decided to continue the boycott until city and bus company authorities met their demands. The boycotters wanted the authorities to desegregate the buses, hire black bus drivers for predominantly black routes, and insist that bus drivers show greater courtesy to their passengers. The leaders formed the Montgomery Improvement Association (MIA) to run the extended boycott. At a mass meeting in the evening of the first day of the boycott, several thousand blacks supported these decisions.

The Reverend Dr. **Martin Luther King Jr.** was chosen as the MIA's president. Rufus Lewis organized car pools to transport blacks to their jobs without having to use buses. The Reverend **Ralph Abernathy** headed the committee negotiating with the city and the bus company.

Throughout the thirteen months of negotiations, the boycott was sustained by mass meetings and its car pool operation. The weekly mass meetings, rotated among the city's black churches, continually reinforced the high level of emotional commitment to the movement among the black population. Initially, the car pool consisted of private cars whose owners volunteered to participate. But as contributions flowed in from sympathetic northerners, the MIA eventually purchased a fleet of station wagons, assigned ownership of them to the various black churches, hired drivers, and established regular routes.

On November 13 the U.S. Supreme Court agreed with a previous ruling by a lower federal court that bus segregation was unconstitutional. The city petitioned the Supreme Court for rehearing, and a final order was delayed until December 20. On December 21, 1956, the buses were integrated and the boycott ended.

The Montgomery Bus Boycott marked the beginning of the **Civil Rights movement**'s direct action phase, and it made the Martin Luther King Jr. a national figure. Although the integration of the buses was actually produced by the federal court ruling rather than by the boycott, it was the boycott that demonstrated that ordinary African Americans possessed the power to change society.

Moody, Ann

CIVIL RIGHTS ACTIVIST, WRITER
September 15, 1940–

Anne Moody was a civil rights activist and writer who wrote what is widely believed to be one of the best works on the **Civil Rights movement,** her **autobiography** *Coming of Age in Mississippi.*

Born near Centreville, Mississippi, Moody was raised on a sharecropping farm (an arrangement in which a farmer rents land to farm, paying the rent with a share of the crop). She attended segregated schools and graduated from Tougaloo College (Edwards, Mississippi), which she attended on a basketball scholarship.

Moody became involved in the Civil Rights movement in college and worked for the **Congress of Racial Equality (CORE)** from 1961 to 1963. In 1964 she became the coordinator of civil rights activities at Cornell University (Ithaca, New York). Moody then moved to New York City, believing she would have more of an impact as a writer.

Coming of Age in Mississippi (1968), Moody's best-known work, describes the hardships of growing up in a racist society. It won the Best Book of the Year Award in 1969. Moody continues to write, although her work does not receive the attention it once did.

Moore, Archibald Lee "Archie"

BOXER
December 13, c. 1913, 1916–December 9, 1998

Boxer Archie Moore was born in Mississippi in either 1913 or 1916. "Old Mongoose," as he liked to call himself, had more fights than any lightheavyweight champion in boxing history and was still knocking out people

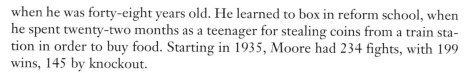

when he was forty-eight years old. He learned to box in reform school, when he spent twenty-two months as a teenager for stealing coins from a train station in order to buy food. Starting in 1935, Moore had 234 fights, with 199 wins, 145 by knockout.

The phenomenal success of **Joe Louis** in the heavyweight division did not sit well with white boxing promoters, who were always convinced that a white champion could outdraw a black one. They continually denied the hard-punching Moore a title shot throughout the 1940s and early 1950s. He was thirty-nine years old when he finally took the title, beating Joey Maxim, the tough veteran champ, in 1952. Moore held on to that title for a decade. Eager for the top rung on the ladder, he fought twice for the heavyweight title, but was knocked out by Rocky Marciano and **Floyd Patterson.** His eleventh-round knockout of Yvonne Durelle in 1958, after being floored five times, is considered one of the great comebacks in ring history.

Moore spent much of his retirement promoting the sport of boxing and advising young men to avoid drugs. He died in 1998 after heart surgery.

Morehouse College

Founded: Morehouse College was established in 1867 as the Augusta Baptist Seminary through funding provided by the National Theological Institute.

History Highlights:

- 1867: Augusta Baptist Seminary is founded in Augusta, Georgia, and soon becomes associated with the American Baptist Home Mission Society (ABHMS). The first class is composed of thirty-seven men and women.

- 1879: The seminary moves to Atlanta, Georgia, and is renamed the Atlanta Baptist Seminary. It also becomes an all-male institution.

- 1897: The school develops a college program and becomes the Atlanta Baptist College.

- 1906: John Hope is the first African-American president of the college; he serves until 1931.

- 1913: The school is again renamed and becomes Morehouse College, in honor of Henry Lyman Morehouse, a longtime ABHMS benefactor.

- 1929: Because it is facing financial difficulties, Morehouse pools its resources together with **Spelman College** (Atlanta's women's college) and **Atlanta University.**

- 1957: The cooperation between Atlanta colleges that began in 1929 is expanded when Spelman, Atlanta University, and Morehouse are joined by several other Atlanta colleges to form the **Atlanta University Center.**

- 1978: The Morehouse School of Medicine is established.

Location: Atlanta, Georgia

Known For: Morehouse is the only private historically black college for men in the United States.

Number of Students (1999–2000): 3,000

Grade Average of Incoming Freshman: 3.0

Admission Requirements: SAT or ACT scores; admissions interview; four years of English, three years of math, two years of science, two years of social studies; recommended two years of foreign language and two years of history; personal essay; letters of recommendation from a teacher and a counselor.

Mailing Address:
Morehouse College
Office of Admission
830 Westview Dr., SW
Atlanta, GA 30314

Telephone: (800) 851-1254

URL: http://www.morehouse.edu

Campus: Morehouse's 61-acre campus is located in downtown Atlanta. Buildings include the Martin Luther King chapel, which contains a memorial to Martin Luther King and a wall of honor depicting former presidents and black historians. Because Morehouse is part of the Atlanta University Center, students are eligible to use many of the facilities located throughout Atlanta, including the Robert Woodruff Library, which contains over 500,000 volumes.

Special Programs: African studies; Caribbean studies; courses in Swahili; combined art and education programs with Spelman College; combined architecture program with University of Michigan; Morehouse Research Institute; International Power Institute; Center for Science and Math Education.

Extracurricular Activities: Student government, student newspaper, the *Maroon Tiger*; literary magazine; five fraternities; over forty organizations, including honor societies, Radicals for Christ Posse, Black Scholars Association, a glee club, and the United Men of Morehouse; athletics (men's basketball, football, tennis, track-and-field).

Morehouse Alumni: Civil rights leader **Martin Luther King Jr.** (1929–1968); Olympic athlete **Edwin Moses** (1955–); filmmaker **Spike Lee** (1957–).

Morgan, Garrett Augustus

INVENTOR
March 4, 1875–July 7, 1963

The inventor Garrett Morgan was born in Kentucky. In his teens he traveled to Cincinnati, Ohio, where he found work as a handyman. Six years later, he moved to Cleveland, Ohio, and briefly worked fixing sewing machines for a clothing manufacturer. Morgan then began several successful enterprises, including a sewing machine repair service and a tailor shop. He also tried his hand at a number of inventions, the most important being a "breathing device" that he patented in 1914. Morgan's device enabled firefighters to breathe in smoke-filled buildings and protected those who labored near noxious fumes and dust. The apparatus consisted of a hood that fit over the head with two tubes leading from the face mask around the left and right sides of the body to a bag of fresh air.

In 1912 Morgan, along with several Cleveland business executives, formed the National Safety Device Company to manufacture and advertise the Morgan Safety Hood. In 1916 Morgan's hoods were worn when he and others entered a smoke-filled tunnel, 250 feet below Lake Erie, to rescue workers trapped after an explosion in the Cleveland waterworks system. The following year, Morgan received a contract from the U.S. Navy to produce his gas mask for combat use.

In 1922 Morgan patented another important invention, the three-way automatic traffic signal. The "go-stop" signals used before Morgan's invention had no intermediate or neutral signal position; there was no "yellow light" as it was later known. Without a traffic officer present, the "go" and "stop" signals could change too abruptly, leading to accidents. Morgan's signal caused the "go" and "stop" arms to pause briefly in a half-mast position to caution drivers to slow down. Morgan sold the rights to his signal to the General Electric Company for $40,000 in 1923. General Electric then converted the signal into the now commonly used three-way light.

Aside from his inventions, Morgan published an African-American newspaper in the early 1920s. He was a longtime member of the Cleveland **NAACP** and in 1931 ran unsuccessfully for city council. In 1943, Morgan contracted glaucoma, from which he gradually lost most of his sight. He died in Cleveland in 1963.

Mormons

The Church of Jesus Christ of Latter-day Saints, more commonly known as the Mormon Church, was established in 1830. Since its founding, very few African Americans have adopted this religion.

Mormonism was founded in Fayette, New York, by American religious leader Joseph Smith (1805–1844). During the 1830s there were an estimated twelve to twenty-four black Mormons. A few key factors explain why black participation has been low. First, there was little interaction between blacks and whites during this time. Second, and more important, the religious writings (scriptures) of the Mormons, put forth by Smith, claimed that blacks were lesser human beings than whites. These two factors prevented blacks from becoming priests in the Mormon Church. In addition, the Mormon Church took a position against the abolition of slavery, which discouraged blacks from joining.

African Americans who were associated with Mormonism left a lasting impression. Among them were Elijah Abel, who developed a close friendship with Smith. Abel was ordained a priest of the Mormon Church before the 1847 ban on African-American priests was enacted. The fact that a black was ordained as a priest—along with Abel's close relationship with Smith—gave the impression that the religion was more open to black membership than its policies suggested.

Shortly after Smith's death in 1844, Brigham Young (1801–1877) became head of the Mormon Church. One of his first decisions was to ban blacks from the priesthood. Young's decision was a result of the behavior of William McCary, who was of African-Indian ancestry and was associated briefly with the church in Nebraska. McCary practiced polygamy (marriage to more than one wife).

In the 1850s the Mormons moved their headquarters to Salt Lake City, Utah. Because there were a number of white practicing Mormons who owned black slaves, Young decided to legalize **slavery.** His decision made Utah the only U.S. territory west of the Mississippi River where slavery was legal before the American **Civil War** (1861–65).

During the next fifty to seventy-five years the number of black Mormons continued to be low. Even though slaves throughout the United States were freed by 1865, the Mormon Church upheld its ban on black priests and continued to enforce policies of segregation.

In the 1950s the population of blacks in Utah doubled, and Utah's chapter of the **National Association for the Advancement of Colored People (NAACP)** began to address Utah's race policies. By 1963 the NAACP persuaded the Mormon Church to issue a statement in favor of civil rights. In the late 1960s non-Mormon blacks began pressuring the church to change its policies on race, and by 1971 the church developed a special organization for its black members called "the Genesis group." In addition, blacks were allowed to sing in the famous Mormon Tabernacle Choir and were recruited to play on athletic teams at Brigham Young University in Provo, Utah. In 1978 the Mormon Church formally lifted its ban on black priests. The lifting of the ban resulted in greater participation among blacks in Central America and South America and in parts of Africa. However, a limited number of blacks within the United States have joined the Mormon Church.

Morrison, Toni

WRITER
February 18, 1931–

An African-American FIRST

In 1993, when Toni Morrison was awarded the Nobel Prize for literature, she became the first African American in history—and the first black woman of any nationality—to be awarded this most prestigious of international literary awards.

Toni Morrison, now considered one of the finest modern American novelists, was born in Lorain, Ohio, to a family she describes as a group of storytellers. After graduating from **Howard University** (Washington, D.C.) in 1953, Morrison moved to Cornell University for graduate work in English and received a master's degree in 1955. She taught at Texas Southern University from 1955 to 1957 and then at Howard University (until 1964), where she met and married Harold Morrison, a Jamaican architect, and gave birth to two sons. Those were years that Morrison has described as a period of almost complete powerlessness, when she wrote quietly and participated in a writers' workshop, creating the story that would become her first novel, *The Bluest Eye.*

Toni Morrison, the first African-American winner of the Nobel Prize for literature, poses with a copy of her novel *Beloved* (AP/Wide World Photos. Reproduced by permission)

In 1964 Morrison divorced her husband and moved to Syracuse, New York, where she began work for the publisher Random House. She later moved to a senior editor's position at the Random House headquarters in New York City—continuing to teach, along the way, at various universities. Since 1988 she has been a professor of the humanities at Princeton University.

The Bluest Eye was published in 1970 to critical acclaim but did not enjoy much public attention. Slowly, over the next two decades, Morrison began to build her repuation with the novels *Sula* (1973), *Song of Solomon* (1977), *Tar Baby* (1981), and *Beloved* (1987), a novel that shows how storytelling and history conflict when one's imagination tries to make sense of slavery. *Beloved* won the Pulitzer Prize for fiction, and by this time Morrison was being discussed internationally as one of the greatest American writers of all time.

In 1992 Morrison published her sixth novel, *Jazz*, as well as a collection of previous lectures on American literature, *Playing in the Dark*. The following year, Morrison received the highest honor a writer can receive, the international Nobel Prize for literature, confirming her status as an American treasure. Morrison's critical praise finally met with commercial success in 1998 after her novel *Paradise* was promoted by television personality **Oprah Winfrey**. After Winfrey's endorsement, *Paradise* became a best-seller. In 1998 Winfrey also produced and starred in a film adaptation of Morrison's novel *Beloved*.

Morton, Ferdinand Joseph "Jelly Roll"

JAZZ PIANIST, COMPOSER
October 20, 1890–July 10, 1941

Although the facts of his early life and his claim to have singlehandedly invented **jazz** are disputed, Jelly Roll Morton was a crucial figure in connecting the musical styles of the late nineteenth and early twentieth centuries—**blues**, vaudeville, and **ragtime**—with the small jazz ensembles of the 1920s. He was also the first great jazz composer and the most important pianist with roots in New Orleans-style jazz. His skill as an arranger and composer made him an important model for later jazz composers.

Morton was born Ferdinand Joseph LaMothe in Gulfport, Mississippi. His father, a carpenter who played classical music on the trombone, left the family when Ferdinand was a child. The boy was raised in New Orleans, Louisiana, and took the last name of his stepfather, Ed Morton, a porter who also played the trombone. Ferdinand played guitar and trombone before taking up the piano as a teenager. He began performing in the Storyville district of New Orleans and later traveled along the Gulf Coast as far as Florida, learning from pianists along the way. He studied music with a Louisiana professor, but it was his 1902 meeting in New Orleans with ragtime pianist Tony Jackson that set the course for his career.

Morton left New Orleans in 1906 and traveled throughout the South, playing piano in vaudeville shows. He eventually went to Chicago, Illinois, where he settled for three years, leading his own band. He published his first composition, "Jelly Roll Blues," in 1915. The title refers to the nickname he gave himself, "Jelly Roll," which had a sexual meaning during the early 1900s.

Between 1917 and 1923 Morton traveled and worked up and down the West Coast, from Tijuana, Mexico, to Alaska, and to Colorado and Wyoming. He also worked in Los Angeles, California, as a boxing promoter.

In 1923 he returned to Chicago and made the recordings that earned him his reputation as a musician, including "London Blues," "Grandpa's Spell," and "The Pearls" (1923–1924). He also worked with a white group called the New Orleans Rhythm Kings.

From 1926 to 1930 Morton and his band the Red Hot Peppers—which included trombonist Kid Ory (c. 1889–1973), clarinetist Johnny Dodds

(1892–1940), and drummer Baby Dodds (1898–1959)—recorded songs like "Kansas City Stomp," "Mournful Serenade," and "Pontchartrain Blues." During this time Morton also continued to travel and perform, playing with artists like trumpeter and bandleader **W. C. Handy** (1873–1958).

Other well-known Morton compositions are "New Orleans Blues," "Mamanita," and "Black Bottom Stomp." He played an artful blend of ornamental saloon music and stomping blues. His arranging allowed for improvisation (creating musical passages as a piece is played) to liven up carefully composed sections, always within the style of New Orleans instrumental ragtime.

In 1928 Morton moved to New York City and continued to record with the Red Hot Peppers. In 1934 he worked as the house pianist at the Red Apple Club in New York's Harlem district. By the early 1930s, in spite of his busy schedule, his health and his career began to decline. Audiences were losing interest in New Orleans jazz, and the Great Depression (1929–39) had caused a collapse of the record industry. Morton also lost all of his money after investing in a cosmetics company that failed.

He moved to Washington, D.C., in 1935, and in 1938 he recorded music and stories about his life for American folklorist John Lomax (1867–1948) at the Library of Congress. These recordings raised many questions, however, because Morton claimed he had invented jazz in New Orleans in 1902 and that many famous jazz tunes had been stolen from him. Still, the interviews provide a valuable glimpse into the creation of New Orleans jazz and into Morton's insights into the workings of his music. *Mister Jelly Roll* (1950), released by John Lomax's son, folklorist Alan Lomax, is a condensed version of the Library of Congress interviews.

Morton continued to work until shortly before his death from heart disease in 1941. His life was the subject of a Broadway musical by George C. Wolfe, called *Jelly's Last Jam* (1992).

Moseley-Braun, Carol

POLITICIAN
August 16, 1947–

Carol Moseley-Braun was the first African-American woman to win a seat in the U.S. Senate. She is known for her firm commitment to civil rights, education, and gender equality.

Born in Chicago, Illinois, Moseley-Braun earned a bachelor's degree from the University of Illinois at Chicago and a law degree from the University of Chicago (1972). In 1978 she began her political career by winning a seat in the Illinois House of Representatives. While in the state legislature, she focused her efforts on improving education and banning discrimination in housing and private clubs. Moseley-Braun became the first woman and the first black to be elected assistant majority leader in the Illinois legislature.

After working for Cook County, which includes Chicago, she made a run for the U.S. Senate in 1992, winning a close election. During her first term in the Senate, she drafted civil rights legislation aimed at achieving educational equality for women and preventing violence against them. Speculation about the misuse of campaign funds and her support for a dictatorship in Nigeria contributed to her defeat in a bid to be elected again in 1998. In 1999 Moseley-Braun continued her political career when she was nominated to become ambassador to New Zealand and Somoa, island nations located in the southwestern Pacific Ocean.

An African-American FIRST

In 1992 Carol Moseley-Braun became the first female African American to serve in the U.S. Senate. She defeated Alan Dixon and wealthy Chicago attorney Al Hofeld for the Democratic Party's nomination. She defeated Republican Rich Williamson in a close election for the seat. Moseley-Braun sponsored two important bills while in the Senate: the Gender Equity in Education Act and the 1993 Violence Against Women Act.

Moses, Edwin Corley

TRACK-AND-FIELD ATHLETE
August 31, 1955–

Born and raised in Dayton, Ohio, track star Edwin Moses began running hurdles at Dayton Fairview High School. An excellent student, Moses accepted an academic scholarship to **Morehouse College** in Atlanta,

Georgia. In his junior year at Morehouse, he began to compete in the 400-meter hurdles and qualified for the United States Olympic Team. Moses was the first hurdler to perfect a thirteen-step approach between each hurdle (most runners required fourteen or fifteen steps). At the 1976 Montreal Summer Olympics, he won the 400-meter hurdles in the world-record time of 47.64 seconds. Following the Olympics, Moses returned to Morehouse to finish his degree in aerospace engineering. He graduated in 1978.

Beginning in 1977, Moses won 122 consecutive races, establishing a record for the most consecutive victories in track-and-field competition. In 1983 he set a new world record in the 400-meter hurdles (47.02 second). The following year, he won his second Olympic gold medal at the Los Angeles Games and was named Sportsman of the Year by both the U.S. Olympic Committee and *Sports Illustrated*. In 1985 Moses was elected to the U.S. Olympic Hall of Fame. He retired from competition in 1988. Moses was one of several track and football stars who joined the United States Olympic bobsled program in the early 1990s. A brakeman for the sled for the United States, he won a bronze medal at a 1990 World Cup event. Moses attempted to compete in the 1992 Summer Games in Barcelona, Spain, but was injured. He maintained his ties to the United States Olympic movement, however, through his involvement with the U.S. Olympic Committee's Athletes' Advisory Council.

Moses retired from sports and returned to Atlanta, where he is a successful financial planner.

Motley, Archibald John Jr.

PAINTER
1891–January 19, 1991

The painter Archibald John Motley Jr. was born in New Orleans, Louisiana, and later lived in Chicago, Illinois. Motley received his initial art training in high school and began four years of study at the School of the Art Institute of Chicago, graduating in 1918. During his work at the Institute, Motley created highly accomplished figure studies. He used subdued coloring, careful attention to modeling, and slightly broken brushwork. In the late 1910s and 1920s, as racial barriers thwarted his ambition to be a professional portraitist, Motley hired models and asked family members to pose for him. His sensitive portraits show his strong feeling for composition and color.

The young painter was honored in a commercially successful one-man exhibition of his work at New York City's New Gallery in 1928, and he spent the following year in Paris, France, on a Guggenheim Fellowship. For the New Gallery show, Motley painted several imaginative scenes of African ethnic myths. Following the exhibition, he visited family members in rural Arkansas, where he painted portraits as well as landscapes of the region. During his stay in Paris, Motley portrayed the streets and cabarets of the French capital. In *Blues*, perhaps his best-known painting, he captured the vibrant and energetic mood of nightlife among Paris's African community.

After finding little outlet for his ambitions as a portraitist, Motley at an early point in his career turned his talents to the subject of everyday life in Chicago's Black Belt. Deeply influenced by **jazz,** his paintings evoke the streets, bars, dance halls, and outdoor gathering spots of Chicago's Bronzeville during its heyday of the 1920s and 1930s.

A figure in Chicago's **New Negro** movement, Motley used a modern painting style to portray his ethnic roots. Between 1938 and 1941 he joined numerous other Illinois artists as an employee of federally sponsored arts projects. For institutions in Chicago and other parts of the state, he painted easel pictures and murals.

Motley visited Mexico several times in the 1950s, where he joined his nephew **Willard Francis Motley** (1909–1965), the writer, and other American artists living outside the United States. His Mexican work ranges from brightly colored, small-scale landscapes to large, mural-size works.

At the end of his career, Motley experimented in several new directions. In his long lifetime he produced a relatively small number of works, of which the most important, *The First One Hundred Years*, is his only painting with an overt political message. Today Motley is recognized as one of the founders of twentieth-century African-American art. Motley died on January 19, 1991. (*See also*: **Painting and Sculpture**)

Motley, Constance Baker

LAWYER, JUDGE
September 14, 1921–

Constance Baker Motley was the first black woman to be appointed a federal judge. Her distinguished career has opened the door of opportunity for African Americans and women in legal and political professions.

Born in New Haven, Connecticut, Motley graduated from high school with honors. She could not afford college, but a wealthy businessman discovered her brilliance and offered to pay for her education. She earned a bachelor's degree from New York University (1943) and a law degree from Columbia Law School (1944) in New York. During and after law school, Motley worked for future U.S. Supreme Court Justice **Thurgood Marshall** (1908–1993) at the **National Association for the Advancement of Colored People (NAACP)**. Although she began as a clerk (legal assistant) for Marshall, she eventually began trying cases on her own. Motley went on to try some of the most important desegregation cases in American history, including cases that allowed blacks to attend the University of Mississippi and the University of Georgia. She also helped write the legal briefs (a summarized legal argument) for the landmark decision in ***Brown v. the Board of Education of Topeka, Kansas*** (1954), which allowed blacks to attend the same public schools as whites.

Motley left the NAACP in 1964 and earned a seat in the New York State Senate. In 1965 she was elected president of the Manhattan (New York) borough, and a year later she was appointed to a federal judgeship

An African-American FIRST

Constance Baker Motley was the first female African American to be elected to the New York State Senate and the first woman to be elected president of the Manhattan borough (one of the five political divisions, or boroughs, of New York City). Perhaps her greatest accomplishment came on January 25, 1966, when President Lyndon B. Johnson appointed her judge for the U.S. District Court of Appeals for the Southern District of New York. She was both the first black and the first woman to be confirmed a federal judge for that district.

by President Lyndon B. Johnson (1908–1973; president 1963–69). In 1982 she became the chief judge of her court, serving until 1986, when she became senior judge. She published an **autobiography** titled *Equal Justice under Law* in 1998. Motley continues to serve on a U.S. district court in New York.

Motley, Willard Francis

NOVELIST
July 14, 1909–March 4, 1965

Born and raised in a middle-class Chicago, Illinois, neighborhood, Willard Motley decided to become a writer after traveling around the United States for many years working at odd jobs and observing the life of the working class during the bleak economic years of the **Great Depression** of the 1930s. He worked as a ranch hand, cook, migrant laborer, shipping clerk, photographer, interviewer for the Chicago Housing Authority, and writer for the Office of Civil Defense.

In the 1940s Motley lived in Chicago's slums, an experience that provided the material for his first novel, *Knock on Any Door* (1947), which involved white characters involved in criminal activity and drug use in an impoverished urban environment. This novel became commercially successful and was made into a Hollywood film in 1949.

In 1951 Motley published *We Fished All Night*, a novel that examines the experiences of three **World War II** (1939–45) veterans as they struggle to cope with postwar life. Motley's last novel, *Let Noon Be Fair* (1966) examines the gradual corruption of a Mexican fishing village that becomes popular with North American tourists. Motley lived in Mexico for the last twelve years of his life and died of gangrene (decay of body tissue caused by loss of blood supply) in Mexico City in 1965.

Motown, which began as a small record company in 1959, became the largest black-owned company in the United States. Motown nurtured many prominent figures of American popular music, including **Smokey Robinson** (1940–), **Marvin Gaye** (1939–1984), **The Temptations, The Four Tops, Diana Ross** (1944–), **Stevie Wonder** (1950–), The Jackson 5, and The Commodores.

Motown was founded in the basement of Berry Gordy Jr.'s (1929–) Detroit, Michigan, home. Gordy, a former boxer and record store owner, had written several of **Jackie Wilson's** (1934–1984) hit songs. By 1962 Gordy was comparing Motown with the Detroit auto industry that gave the label its name, a shortened form of "Motor Town."

Gordy and his producers created dozens of classic soul music records in Motown's basement studio. Gordy prepared his acts for performances on tours known as the Motown Revue by hiring a consultant to teach them everything from makeup to manners. In 1965 Motown hired tap dancer **Cholly Atkins** (1913–) to arrange dance steps for its performers. He created such well-known features as the "Temptations Walk" and the **Supremes'** modest half turns.

Smokey Robinson was the first of Motown's songwriter-producers, writing and producing six of Motown's first top ten hits. He wrote and produced hits for The Miracles, The Temptations, Marvin Gaye, and many other artists.

The most famous version of the "Motown Sound" was largely the creation of two brothers, Eddie and Brian Holland, and a third songwriter, Lamont Dozier. This team was known as "H-D-H." Starting in 1963 the Hollands and Dozier created a recognizable style that included drums and tambourines, vibraphone and piano, baritone saxophone, pulsating bass guitar, and melodies that set off the lyrics. Examples are The Supremes' songs "Where Did Our Love Go?" and "Back in My Arms Again."

The early 1970s saw important career changes for musicians who had been with Motown almost from the start, like Marvin Gaye and Stevie Wonder, who began writing and producing their own albums. Motown's last discovery of the 1960s was the Jackson 5, a family group featuring young **Michael Jackson** (1958–), who became a pop superstar in the 1980s and 1990s. The group's first four singles went to number one on the music charts.

Gordy involved Motown in the **Civil Rights movement** as early as 1963, releasing *The Great March to Freedom*, containing **Martin Luther King Jr.'s** (1929–1968) "I Have a Dream" speech. In the early 1970s Motown started a new spoken-word label, Black Forum, which produced records of many of King's speeches as well as albums by African-American poet **Langston Hughes** (1902–1967), activist **Stokely Carmichael** (1941–1998), poet and playwright **Amiri Baraka** (1934–), and actor-comedian **Bill Cosby** (1937–).

In the early 1970s Gordy moved Motown to Los Angeles, California, where he became involved in television specials and films. In 1973 Motown was the biggest black-owned company in the United States, and Gordy

Blues legend Muddy Waters (AP/Wide World Photos. Reproduced by permission)

helped finance and produce the movies *Lady Sings the Blues* (1972), *Mahogany* (1975), and *The Wiz* (1978), all of which starred Diana Ross. Despite the departure of many of Motown's key musical and financial figures, the company remained strong. Diana Ross, Stevie Wonder, The Commodores, and Rick James continued to put Motown's records on the charts.

By the 1970s Motown had become a financial giant as well as a dominant musical influence. After many more years of producing musical television and movie hits, Gordy decided to sell the company. In 1988 MCA bought Motown, then the fifth-largest black-owned business in the United States. In 1993 MCA sold the company to Polygram. Polygram revitalized Motown, developing acts, including the group Boyz II Men.

Since 1985 Motown's original headquarters in Detroit has been a museum dedicated to the history of the company. (*See also*: **Jackson Family**)

Waters, Muddy

BLUES SINGER, GUITARIST
April 4, 1915–April 30, 1983

Born McKinley Morganfield, Muddy Waters grew up in Clarksdale, Mississippi, and began playing guitar at seventeen. He recorded both as a soloist and with a string band in 1941–42 for a Library of Congress field-recording project. Moving to Chicago, Illinois, in 1943, he began playing the electric guitar. By 1947 he was playing under the name Muddy Waters, and had added a rough, aggressive edge to the urban **blues** that had been established there. Waters's band eventually featured harmonica player Little Walter, and their recording "Louisiana Blues" (1950), became a nationwide hit. The band had many top ten hits in the 1950s, including "I'm Your Hoochie Coochie Man" (1953) and "I'm Ready" (1954).

Muddy Waters continued to tour throughout the United States and Europe in the 1960s and received much praise as a primary influence on many rock musicians of the "British Invasion," such as The Rolling Stones, who named themselves after one of Waters's songs. Waters remained active as a performer for the rest of his life, winning Grammy Awards for several later recordings. He was inducted into the Rock and Roll Hall of Fame in 1987.

Muhammad, Elijah

RELIGIOUS LEADER
October 10, 1897–February 25, 1975

Born Robert Poole in Georgia, Elijah Muhammad was one of thirteen children. In 1919 he married Clara Evans and they joined the black migration to Detroit, Michigan, where he worked in the auto plants. In 1931 he met Master **Wallace D. Fard** (c. 1934–), founder of the **Nation of Islam** (NOI; a religious movement), who eventually chose Muhammad as his chief aide. Fard named him "Minister of Islam," dropped his "slave name," Poole, and restored his true Muslim name, Muhammad. As the movement grew, a Temple of Islam was established in a Detroit storefront. It is estimated that Fard had close to eight thousand members.

After Fard mysteriously disappeared in 1934, the NOI was divided by internal struggles and Elijah Muhammad led a major faction to Chicago, where he established Temple of Islam No. 2 as the main headquarters for the NOI. He also instituted the worship of Master Fard as Allah and himself as the Messenger of Allah and head of the Nation of Islam. Muhammad built on the teachings of Fard and combined aspects of **Islam** and Christianity with a strong racial slant. The Honorable Elijah Muhammad's message of racial separation focused on the recognition of true black identity and stressed economic independence. The beliefs of the Black Muslims have been described as hard work, frugality, the avoidance of debt, self-improvement, and a conservative lifestyle. The disciples also followed strict dietary rules outlined in Muhammad's book *How to Eat to Live.*

Muhammad's ministers of Islam found the prisons and streets of the ghetto a fertile recruiting ground. His message struck a responsive chord in the thousands of black men and women whose hope and self-respect had been all but defeated by racial abuse. Muhammad had an uncanny sense of the vulnerabilities that black people felt. He diagnosed the problem as a confusion of identity and self-hatred caused by white racism. The cure he prescribed was the formation of a separate black nation.

After spending four years in a federal prison for encouraging draft refusal during **World War II**, Elijah Muhammad was assisted by **Minister Malcolm X** (1925–1965) in building the movement and encouraging its rapid spread in the 1950s and 1960s. During its peak years, the NOI had more than half a million devoted followers and accumulated an economic empire worth an estimated $80 million. Besides his residence in Chicago, Muhammad also lived in a mansion outside Phoenix, Arizona, since the climate helped to reduce his respiratory problems. He had eight children with his wife but also fathered a number of illegitimate children with his secretaries, a circumstance that was one of the reasons for Malcolm X's final break with the Nation of Islam in 1964.

With only a third-grade education, Elijah Muhammad was the leader of the most enduring black militant movement in the United States. He died in Chicago and was succeeded by one of his six sons. After his death, Muhammad's estate and the property of the NOI were involved in several lawsuits over the question of support for his illegitimate children.

Muralists

African-American murals are among the most widely reproduced and easily recognized forms of black art. A mural is a large-scale work of art, painted or carved on a wall, ceiling, or floor or on panels painted in a studio and then installed in these spaces. Because murals are usually placed in public places, they can communicate a message to people from all walks of life. Many murals use visual images to tell the stories of heroes or events in African-American history and are preserved as cultural treasures.

African-American muralists were greatly influenced by Mexican muralists, such as Diego Rivera (1886–1957), who began painting in the 1920s and 1930s to teach the poor people of Mexico about their history and heritage. Most African-American mural painting began in the 1930s, but a few black artists painted murals during the 1800s and early 1900s.

Early African-American Muralists

The best example of African-American murals from the nineteenth century is the work of **Robert S. Duncanson** (1821–1872). Between 1848 and 1850 he painted a series of eight landscape frescoes for the entrance hallway of a former Cincinnati, Ohio, mansion, now the Taft Museum.

In 1913 William Edouard Scott (1884–1964) painted two murals for public schools in Indianapolis, Indiana. In 1933 he completed two murals for the Harlem Young Men's Christian Association (YMCA) in New York City.

Renaissance

The New Negro Renaissance and the **Harlem Renaissance** of the late 1920s and 1930s was a turning point for African-American visual arts. **Aaron Douglas** (1899–1979) was the first to successfully combine African imagery with European modernist styles, creating a new African-American art. He also produced the most African-American murals. Early in his career he

Famous African-American Muralists and Selected Works

Charles Alston:
canvas panels for Harlem Hospital, New York City (1936–37)

Romare Bearden:
six-panel collage *The Block*, Harlem, New York City (1971);
mosaic *Baltimore Uproar*, Baltimore, Maryland (1983);
mosaic *Pittsburgh Recollections*, Pittsburgh, Pennsylvania (1984)

John T. Biggers:
The Contribution of Negro Women to American Life and Education, YWCA, Blue Triangle branch, Houston, Texas (1953);
mural *Family Unity*, Student Center, Texas Southern University, Houston, Texas (1983);
panels *House of the Turtle* and *Tree House*, Harvey Library, Hampton University, Hampton, Virginia (1992)

Houston Conwill (with Estella Conwill Majozo and Joseph De Pace):
floor mural *Rivers*, Langston Hughes Auditorium, Schomburg Center for Research in Black History, New York Public Library, New York City (1990);
The New Ring Shout, African burial ground, New York City (1995)

Jeff Donaldson and other members of the Organization of Black American Culture:
Wall of Respect, Chicago, Illinois (1967)

painted murals for nightclubs in the Harlem district of New York City. In his later works Douglas told the story of his people's journey from ancient Africa to modern American cities, celebrating their hopes and achievements. His style is known by its larger-than-life figures on flat, geometrically broken backgrounds.

Hale Woodruff (1900–1980), who in 1939 painted three panels commemorating the centennial of the **Amistad mutiny,** and Charles Alston (1907–1977), who was interested in ancient healing and modern medicine, are among other important muralists of this era. Woodruff's Amistad murals are considered some of the finest African-American murals.

The 1930s and the New Deal

Increased interest in the arts during the late 1930s and President Franklin Roosevelt's (1882–1945) New Deal government work programs allowed more murals to be created during this time. Many black muralists started their careers with these projects. The Public Works of Art Project and the Federal Arts Project, among others, hired artists to decorate public buildings across the United States. The Harlem Artists Guild's efforts significantly increased the number of black artists hired by New Deal agencies. Most black women artists, however, were placed in teaching positions, which may explain why so few black women muralists became well known.

The 1940s to the 1970s

After New Deal programs ended, there was less work for black muralists, and most of their commissions came from within the black community. Aaron Douglas painted murals for private residences in Delaware, and Charles Alston and Hale Woodruff painted murals for a California life insurance company. Historically black colleges and universities were an important source of work for muralists during this period. Charles White (1918–1979) painted a fresco at **Hampton Institute** (now Hampton University), Hampton, Virginia, showing the faces and figures of more than twenty great African-American men and women. White inspired a number of students to become muralists.

The Black Arts Movement

During the **Black Arts movement** of the late 1960s and 1970s, young artists in cities across the United States began painting murals in poor neighborhoods to communicate with a large number of people. They often organized group projects to create this "people's art." Muralists covered buildings with colorful images of black pride, African heritage, and African-American heroes and heroines. The best known is Chicago's *Wall of Respect*, created in 1967 by Jeff Donaldson (1932–) and other artists. Donaldson was an art professor and leader of the African Commune of Bad Relevant Artists, or **AfriCobra.**

The Late Twentieth Century

Romare Bearden (1912–1988) and **Jacob Armstead Lawrence** (1917–2000) were two prominent black artists of the late twentieth century.

CREATING MURALS: MATERIALS AND METHODS

African-American muralists work with both traditional and new materials and methods. Murals painted on plaster are called frescoes. Artists work from a small-scale drawing called a cartoon, enlarging the design and transferring its outline to the prepared surface. For a "buon" (true) fresco, a smooth layer of plaster must be applied to the surface a small section at a time so that it is still wet when painted. The artist must work quickly and cannot go back and make changes. More commonly used today is "fresco secco," which is made by applying water-based paint to dry plaster. Many muralists today also paint the fresco on large canvas panels in their studio and then install the panels in the spaces for which they were created.

Famous African-American Muralists and Selected Works

Aaron Douglas:
frescoes for **Fisk University**'s Cravath Library, Nashville, Tennessee (1930);
nightclub murals for Sherman Hotel, Chicago, Illinois (1930);
panel commemorating **Harriet Tubman** for Bennett College, Greensboro, North Carolina (1931);
fresco for Harlem's 135th Street YMCA, New York City (1933);
canvas panels for New York Public Library, 135th Street branch, New York City (1934);
murals for the Texas Centennial Exposition (1936)

Jacob Lawrence:
ten-panel mural *Games*, Kingdome Stadium, Seattle, Washington (1979);
two series of enamels on steel panels, *Exploration* (1980) and *Origins* (1984), Blackburn University Center, **Howard University**, Washington, D.C.;
panel mural *Theater*, University of Washington, Seattle (1985)

Archibald Motley:
United States Mail, Wood River, Illinois, post office (1937)

Charles White:
The Contribution of the Negro to American Democracy, Hampton University, Hampton, Virginia (1943)

Hale Woodruff:
panels commemorating centennial of Amistad slave mutiny and trial, Talladega College, Talladega, Alabama (1939);
panel series *Art of the Negro*, Arnett Library, Atlanta University, Atlanta, Georgia (1950)

Both began painting murals late in their careers. Bearden was nearly sixty when he created *The Block* (1971), showing city life on one block of a busy Harlem street. A tape recording of street sounds is part of the mural.

Lawrence spent the early part of his career painting long series of small images that tell stories from African-American history. When he was in his sixties, he began combining multiple images into murals. Among his most famous are a series of twelve enamels on steel panels, called *Exploration* (1980). Lawrence was still painting until a few weeks before his death in June 2000, at age 82, and was scheduled to exhibit new work later that year.

Houston Conwill (1947–) and John T. Biggers (1924–)—one of the students who watched Charles White paint his fresco at Hampton University during the 1940s—are two well-known muralists of the 1990s. Conwill's 1990 floor mural *Rivers*, installed at the New York Public Library was inspired by black poet **Langston Hughes**'s (1902–1967) poem "The Negro Speaks of Rivers." Known for his "cosmograms," or floor diagrams of black history, Conwill has worked on these projects since 1984 with his sister, poet Estella Conwill Majozo, and architect Joseph De Pace. They completed *The New Ring Shout* in 1995. It commemorates blacks buried at an eighteenth-century African burial ground in New York City.

Biggers returned to Hampton University in 1992 to paint two panels for the university's new Harvey Library and painted murals in Houston, Texas, in the mid-1990s.

Murphy, Carl

PUBLISHER
January 17, 1889–February 26, 1967

Carl Murphy was born in Baltimore, Maryland, in 1889. His father was the publisher of the *Baltimore Afro-American*. After attending high school in Baltimore, Murphy graduated from **Howard University** (Washington, D.C.) in 1911. He continued on to Harvard University (Boston, Massachusetts), receiving a master's degree in German in 1913. Murphy studied in Germany for several months after his graduation and then returned to the United States to become a professor of German at Howard University.

Because of the poor health of his father, Murphy started to work at the *Baltimore Afro-American*, becoming editor in 1918. After his father's death in 1922, Murphy was suddenly thrust into the leadership of one of the most influential African-American newspapers in the country. By the end of Murphy's tenure in 1961, the newspaper chain had grown to include newspapers in Newark, New Jersey; Philadelphia, Pennsylvania; Washington, D.C.; and Richmond, Virginia. At its peak, the paper had a circulation of over 200,000.

Murphy was an active supporter of African-American civil rights. As a member of the board of directors of the **National Association for the Advancement of Colored People (NAACP),** he vigorously supported the NAACP's legal challenges to discrimination. He was also active in professional associations and committees on education. His commitment to education and civil rights issues earned him the NAACP's highest award, the Spingarn Medal, in 1955. Murphy died in Baltimore in 1967.

Murray, Albert L.

CRITIC, NOVELIST
May 12, 1916–

Albert Murray: Selected Publications

Born and raised in Alabama, Albert Murray received degrees in education and English. He joined the U.S. Air Force in 1943, serving during **World War II** (1939–45), and retired from the military with the rank of major in 1962. During his career as an educator, Murray taught at **Tuskegee Institute** in Alabama, New York City's Columbia University, Colgate University (Hamilton, New York), the University of Massachusetts at Boston, the University of Missouri, and Barnard College (New York City).

Criticized by some for conservative views, Murray's writings focus on the positive aspects of African-American culture rather than on the negative effects of **slavery**. He has an interest in the blues tradition and emphasizes the rich complexity of a culture that defined itself regardless of oppression. Murray argues that race should not be the prime aspect that determines identity.

Murray achieved new popularity in the mid-1990s. He was a principal adviser to **Wynton Marsalis** (1961–) in the administration for the Lincoln Center (New York) **Jazz** Program. He received increased publicity following the publication of a book of criticism, *The Blue Devils of Nada* (1994), and his third novel, *The Seven League Boots* (1995).

Music. *See* **Blues, The; Concert Music; Folk Music and Singers; Gospel Music; Jazz; Motown; Opera; Ragtime; Rap; Reggae; Rhythm and Blues**

NAACP. *See* National Association for the Advancement of Colored People

NAACP Legal Defense and Educational Fund

The NAACP Legal Defense and Educational Fund, Inc. (LDF) has been the central organization for gaining African-American civil rights through the legal system. It was created in 1940 by the **National Association for the Advancement of Colored People (NAACP),** but from the beginning it had its own board of directors and a separate means of raising funds. Popularly known as the Inc. Fund, it was set up to launch a legal attack on segregation in public education.

The first director-counsel of the LDF was former NAACP attorney **Thurgood Marshall** (1908–1993), who in 1965 would become the first African-American U.S. Supreme Court justice. The LDF started with a staff of five lawyers. Based in New York City, with regional offices in Washington, D.C., and Los Angeles, California, the LDF in 2000 had some twenty-five staff attorneys assisted by cooperating attorneys throughout the United States. It offers four scholarship programs to aid African-American law students.

Early Civil Rights and Education Cases

During the 1940s and 1950s the LDF brought a variety of landmark civil rights and education cases before the U.S. Supreme Court. In *Sweatt v. Painter* (1950), the Court ruled that segregated school facilities led to discrimination. LDF lawyers also sued to eliminate differences in pay between white and black teachers. By 1951 the LDF was working on some twenty elementary and high school cases and a dozen higher-education cases as a direct challenge to segregation. Its efforts were rewarded in 1954 with the Supreme Court's decision in ***Brown v. Board of Education of Topeka, Kansas,*** argued by Marshall, which ordered the desegregation of public schools "with all deliberate speed."

Much of the LDF's work was done not in the Supreme Court but in small southern towns, on a shoestring budget and often under dangerous conditions. Lawyers received death threats as they defended blacks who had been arrested, and they sometimes had to run from lynch mobs. Even though they frequently lost their cases, their presence helped gain a fair trial for many blacks. In 1950 the Supreme Court ruling in *Shepard and Irvin v. Florida* helped establish the law that says defendants must be tried in a court free of prejudice against them.

During the late 1950s southern lawmakers claimed the LDF created cases in it which it had no rightful interest or standing. But in 1963 the Supreme Court ruled that the LDF's filing of legal cases was protected by the U.S. Constitution. By 1965 LDF lawyers had taken education cases in every southern state. In the 1968 case *Green v. County School Board of New Kent County,* the Supreme Court ordered immediate and total desegregation of schools.

Split from the NAACP

By 1954 personal differences between staff members and a disagreement over the LDF's mission led to a total split with the NAACP, which believed the LDF should argue civil rights cases, while the LDF believed its mission was to achieve equality in education. The LDF and the NAACP formally parted in 1956.

After its victory in school desegregation, the LDF began to fight segregation in other areas. In 1956 it began a central involvement in the **Civil Rights movement** when it won *Gayle v. Browder*, the case of the **Montgomery bus boycott** led by the Reverend Dr. **Martin Luther King Jr.** (1929–1968).

Change of Leadership

In 1961 Marshall was appointed to the U.S. Circuit Court and left the LDF. His white assistant, Jack Greenberg (1924–), who had come to the LDF in 1949, succeeded him as new director-counsel. He would hold the position for the next twenty-three years.

During the 1960s the LDF continued as an active force in the Civil Rights movement, defending sit-in protesters and freedom riders and providing bail funds for the many activists who were arrested during the struggle.

During the Black Power movement of the late 1960s and early 1970s, there was conflict within the LDF over its white leadership and its refusal to defend black radicals except in the few cases where civil rights were involved.

The LDF in the Late Twentieth Century

Since the 1970s the LDF has concentrated on other areas of civil rights, such as affirmative action, "reverse discrimination," and racially biased employment testing and student exams. Capital punishment (the death penalty) has also been a particular focus, especially in cases where a black man was given the death penalty for raping a white woman. The death penalty in cases of rape was finally declared unconstitutional in *Coker v. Georgia* (1977).

In 1984 Julius LeVonne Chambers (1936–) took over as director-counsel of the LDF, and it continued to focus on the areas of poverty law, education, fair housing, capital punishment, fair employment, environmental justice, and voting rights. A California housing-discrimination suit filed in 1992 brought the victims $300,000, one of the largest awards ever granted to victims of racial bias in housing.

Chambers resigned in 1992 and was replaced by Elaine Ruth Jones, former head of the LDF's Washington, D.C., office, who had helped create the Civil Rights Restoration Act (1988), the 1988 Fair Housing Act, and the Civil Rights Act of 1991. Jones—who won an International Human Rights Law Group Award for lifetime achievement in 1996—turned the LDF's focus toward environmental and health-care discrimination cases. It worked to get equal treatment for blacks victimized by toxic wastes and to get free lead-poisoning testing for poor children.

RACE AND THE DEATH PENALTY

In preparing for the Supreme Court case *Maxwell v. Bishop* (1970), which involved an Arkansas African-American man convicted of raping a white woman, the LDF organized a study of race in death-penalty sentencing. It showed that 89 percent of men given the death penalty for rape between 1930 and 1962 were black. It also showed patterns of racial discrimination in Arkansas death sentences for rape between 1945 and 1965. The Court refused to rule on the basis of the statistics that the death penalty was racially discriminatory.

In *Coker v. Georgia* (1977) the death penalty in rape cases was declared unconstitutional, but the LDF continued to fight the death penalty for African Americans in other cases. It commissioned a larger study on race and the death penalty in the early 1980s (called the Baldus Study), but in a 1987 case the Court still refused to rule on the basis of the statistics alone.

In 2000, however, the U.S. Justice Department conducted a study that showed minorities make up three-fourths of the defendants in federal cases where the crime is punishable by death and that about half of those sentenced to the death penalty from 1988 to 2000 were black. These data were expected to raise questions in the twenty-first century about the racial fairness of the death penalty.

The LDF continues to be involved in poverty law and sued to block New Jersey from stopping welfare payments to women who have more children while on welfare. It settled a suit against the Los Angeles County Metropolitan Transportation Authority in 1996, charging that city bus systems discriminated against poor minorities.

The LDF also continues to fight discrimination in education and voting rights. In the mid-1990s it was a prominent supporter of public schools and an opponent of private-school voucher plans.

Nash, Diane Bevel

CIVIL RIGHTS ACTIVIST
May 15, 1938–

Diane Nash's prominent role in the student **sit-in** movement made her one of the few well-known female activists of the **Civil Rights movement.** Nash was born in Chicago, Illinois. She attended **Fisk University** in Nashville, Tennessee, where she was confronted by rigid racial segregation for the first time in her life, and later that year, she joined with other students from local colleges to organize protests against racism and segregation. Nash found the concept of moral resistance highly compatible with her strong religious beliefs and came to embrace nonviolence as a way of life.

In April 1960 Nash was one of the founding members of the **Student Nonviolent Coordinating Committee (SNCC)** in Raleigh, North Carolina. In February 1961 she and a group of ten other students were arrested in Rock Hill, South Carolina, for civil rights activities and refused the opportunity for bail. Their actions dramatized racial injustice, popularized the plight of African Americans in the South, and set a precedent of "jail, no bail" that was followed by many other activists during the Civil Rights movement.

In 1961 Nash left school to devote herself full-time to the movement. She played an important role as coordinator of the SNCC **freedom rides.** Later that year, she was appointed head of direct action in the SNCC and moved to Jackson, Mississippi, where she continued her commitment to social activism. In August 1962 Nash moved to Georgia and became involved in the **Southern Christian Leadership Conference (SCLC).**

Nash and her husband proved to be a highly effective organizing team and played an integral role in organizing many SCLC campaigns, including the 1964–65 Selma, Alabama, voting rights campaign. In 1965 they were awarded the Rosa Parks Award from the SCLC for their commitment to achieving social justice through nonviolent direct action.

Nash has maintained a commitment to black empowerment and over the years has broadened the scope of her activism to include engaging in antiwar protests and addressing issues of economic injustice. She also teaches and lectures on women's rights and the Civil Rights movement.

Nat Turner's Rebellion

Virginia slave Nat Turner (1800–1831) led the most significant slave revolt in U.S. history. Some say Nat Turner's Rebellion represented the first major battle of the long struggle to end **slavery.**

Turner was born in Southampton County, Virginia. His mother was said to have been born and raised in Africa. She told her young son that his intelligence and the distinctive lumps on his head were signs that he had been chosen for a great purpose. Turner was born five days before the execution of Virginia slave Gabriel Prosser (c. 1776–1800), who had planned the first major slave revolt in U.S. history. Prosser's plan failed when a great storm scattered his men, and he was tried and hanged. Turner probably heard stories about Prosser as a child.

Nat Turner learned to read as a boy and built a strong religious faith from the African beliefs of his family and the Christian values of his first master, Benjamin Turner. As he grew, he became convinced that his special purpose was to end the enslavement of black people.

Shortly before his death, Turner told his story to a young lawyer named Thomas Ruffin Gray. Called Turner's "Confessions," it is one of the finest firsthand texts in American history.

According to this account, Turner had a vision in 1825 in which he saw "white spirits and black spirits engaged in battle." The sun was "darkened," and "thunder rolled in the Heavens, and blood flowed in streams." Turner had another vision three years later that told him to prepare to kill his enemies with their own weapons.

THE NAT TURNER CONTROVERSY

William Styron's novel *The Confessions of Nat Turner* (1967) is a fictionalized version of Nat Turner's revolt. The book takes the form of Turner's story as told to a white lawyer prior to his execution. Styron's book was awarded a Pulitzer Prize in 1968 and was popular among critics. However, it soon became the subject of a major controversy. Many African-American authors questioned Styron's motives and abilities, calling into question whether a white author could write about a black man. Their arguments culminated in the collection *William Styron's Nat Turner: Ten Black Writers Respond* (1968). Critics such as John Henrik Clarke and Vincent Harding accused Styron of committing a deliberately racist act and showing "moral cowardice" for having attempted the narrative depiction of Turner, claiming he distorted history and denied Turner's true character and motives.

Styron countered his detractors by noting his lifelong interest in Nat Turner, whose actual rebellion took place only a few miles from the author's childhood home, and his careful research. He also emphasized that the work was a novel and that he relied on imagination over strict fact where the historical record was unclear or incomplete. Meanwhile, several African-American writers, notably **James Baldwin,** defended Styron and his work. The long-term effect of Styron's novel and the attacks it prompted were to increase popular interest in the historical Nat Turner and his actions. However, the strong disagreement between various white and black views on how Turner should be portrayed served as one of the first indicators of the difference in racial attitudes that characterized the last decades of the twentieth century.

In February 1831 a solar eclipse signaled to Turner that it was time to begin. On August 13 he woke to see a dim sun changing hazy colors. Taking this as a sign he gathered a few men on August 21 and told them of his plan to attack white families. His intention was to move from house to house through the countryside, killing all whites in each household, regardless of age or sex. Turner hoped this show of force would convince other slaves to join the rebellion. His goal was to take the county arsenal at Jerusalem, Virginia, and then get slaves throughout the South to join the fight for freedom. Once the slaves had gained a foothold, Turner intended to stop the slaughter of women and children and of men who showed no resistance.

Shortly after midnight on Monday, August 22, 1831, Turner's band attacked his master Joseph Travis's household, killing everyone. By nightfall some seventy-five slaves had joined the rebellion, and by Tuesday morning at least fifty-seven whites had been killed in a twenty-mile path.

When Turner's men stopped to rest within three miles of Jerusalem, local militia (citizens who banded together to fight) attacked, catching them off guard. Virginia cavalrymen soon arrived to crush the rebellion. They killed more than one hundred blacks in two days and mounted severed heads atop poles as a warning to other slaves who might be tempted to revolt.

Turner managed to hide from authorities for six weeks. After a huge manhunt, he was captured in a swamp on October 30. He was publicly

In "The Confessions of Nat Turner" the slave rebel describes the 1831 uprising in Southampton, Virginia (Courtesy of the Library of Congress)

THE
CONFESSIONS
OF
NAT TURNER,
THE LEADER
OF
THE LATE INSURRECTION
IN SOUTHAMPTON, VA.
AS FULLY AND VOLUNTARILY MADE TO
THOMAS R. GRAY,
In the prison where he was confined, and acknowledged by him to be such, when read before the Court of Southampton: with the certificate, under seal of the Court convened at Jerusalem, Nov. 5, 1831, for his trial.

ALSO,

AN AUTHENTIC ACCOUNT

OF THE

WHOLE INSURRECTION,

WITH

Lists of the Whites who were Murdered,

AND OF THE

Negroes brought before the Court of Southampton, and there sentenced, &c.

RICHMOND:
PUBLISHED BY THOMAS R. GRAY.

hanged twelve days later. Among African Americans, Turner became a martyr (one who dies for his or her beliefs) and a folk hero never to be forgotten.

Nat Turner's rebellion forced Virginia's legislature to consider the possibility of gradual **emancipation,** or freeing, of slaves. It also attracted some whites to the colonization movement, whose members proposed freeing slaves but sending them to Africa to live. They thought resettlement would remove dangerous slaves from the United States and reduce the free black population. Black and white abolitionists (those working to end slavery) in the North saw that slaves were willing and able to fight for their freedom if provided with weapons and outside support. (*See also* **Gabriel Prosser Conspiracy.**)

National Association for the Advancement of Colored People (NAACP)

Since its organization in 1909, the National Association for the Advancement of Colored People (NAACP) has been the most important civil rights organization in the United States.

Founding of the NAACP

In 1908 white socialist and labor activist William English Walling (1877–1936) wrote a newspaper article calling on citizens to fight for racial equality. White journalist and social worker Mary White Ovington (1865–1951) read the article and responded to Walling's plea. The two met with labor reformer and social worker Dr. Henry Moskowitz (1879–1936) to discuss "the Negro Question." They became the principal founders of the NAACP.

Two other white men were members of the core group—Charles Edward Russell, also a socialist, and Oswald Garrison Villard, a publisher who was a grandson of the abolitionist William Lloyd Garrison.

The group issued a statement on February 12, 1909, combining ideas about equal rights from the **Niagara movement**—formed in 1905 by African-American writer **W. E. B. Du Bois** (1868–1963) and others—with a platform to protect the civil and political rights of African Americans as guaranteed under the Fourteenth and Fifteenth Amendments to the U.S. Constitution. Of the sixty people in the original organization, only seven were black: William L. Bulkley; Du Bois; the Reverend Francis J. Grimké (1850–1937), **Mary Church Terrell** (1863–1954), Dr. J. Milton Waldron (1863–c. 1925), Bishop Alexander Walters (1858–1917), and **Ida Bell Wells-Barnett (1862–1931)**.

The organization's permanent name was adopted in 1910. The group chose the term "colored people" to emphasize the broad concerns of its founders and to allow the organization to reach beyond the United States. The NAACP's first president was Moorfield Storey (1845–1929), one of the nation's top constitutional lawyers. Joel E. Spingarn (1874–1939), a professor, became the New York branch's first president in 1911.

In November 1910 Du Bois launched *The Crisis* as the NAACP's journal. It soon became one of the most important tools in the civil rights struggle, educating both blacks and whites about racial oppression.

By the end of 1919, through the efforts of field secretary **James Weldon Johnson** (1871–1938), the NAACP had 310 branches, including thirty-one in the South.

Activities of the NAACP

Stopping violence against blacks was the first task of the NAACP. **Walter White** (1893–1955) began by investigating lynchings. Congress never outlawed **lynching**, but the NAACP eventually helped end this crime through publicizing its horrors.

CHRONOLOGY

NAACP

1933
NAACP forms the Scottsboro Defense Committee in alliance with the International Labor Defense to save the lives of the Scottsboro Boys, eight young black men convicted of raping two white women.

1933
Second Amenia Conference is held. Whites are barred from attending. A committee formed after the conference declares that black and white workers have the same interests. As a result, the Congress of Industrial Organizations (CIO) is formed. Unlike the American Federation of Labor (AFL), it opens its ranks to black workers and is closely allied with the NAACP.

1946
U.S. President Harry Truman appoints the President's Committee on Civil Rights and makes Walter White a key adviser.

1948
Following NAACP pressure, Truman issues an order barring segregation in the U.S. armed forces. In 1954, the Department of Defense reports that there are "no longer any all-Negro units in the services."

1956
Louisiana leads the South in barring the NAACP from operating there after the NAACP refuses to give the Louisiana attorney general its membership lists. Not until 1964, after four appeals, does the NAACP win the right, through the Supreme Court, to operate again in these states.

The NAACP used legal action to address many issues throughout its history. It had two criteria for accepting a case: (1) it involved discrimination and injustice based on race or color, and (2) it would establish a legal precedent for protecting the rights of African Americans as a group. The organization took cases that involved the death penalty, housing discrimination, election practices that prevented blacks from voting, unfair working conditions and wages, and segregation of schools.

NAACP branches also used boycotts and picketing, publicity campaigns, and official protests successfully in areas such as job discrimination, discrimination in federal programs, segregation of the U.S. **military,** and black stereotypes in movies and television.

The NAACP created its own legal department in 1935 and hired Charles H. Houston (1895–1950) as its first special counsel. He and his trainee, **Thurgood Marshall** (1908–1993), began the legal attack on separate schools for black and white students. Their work resulted in the landmark U.S. Supreme Court case *Brown v. Board of Education of Topeka, Kansas* (1954), setting the framework for the desegregation of schools throughout the United States. Marshall became the first director-counsel of the NAACP Legal Defense and Educational Fund on its founding in 1940. In 1961 he became the first African-American Supreme Court justice.

Civil Rights in the 1950s and 1960s

During the 1950s the NAACP's trailblazing victories in the courts, especially the *Brown* decision, made it a target of white groups in the South, like the terrorist **Ku Klux Klan** and the White Citizens' Council in Mississippi. There were bombings and shootings of NAACP regional officials.

The passing of the Civil Rights Act of 1957 paved the way for further legislation, and the NAACP continued to work for civil rights through the courts. At the same time, the Reverend Dr. **Martin Luther King Jr.** (1929–1968) and student groups carried out nonviolent protests, such as **sit-ins,** in the South.

Events of 1963 reshaped the civil rights struggle. On June 11, President John F. Kennedy (1917–1963) delivered a televised speech about civil rights. The following night, NAACP Mississippi field secretary **Medgar Evers** (1925–1963) was assassinated in Jackson. The day he was buried, Kennedy sent a strong civil rights bill to Congress. On August 28 the civil rights March on Washington was held at the Lincoln Memorial in Washington, D.C.

On November 22, 1963, President Kennedy was assassinated in Dallas, Texas. His successor, President Lyndon B. Johnson (1908–1973), vowed to get Kennedy's civil rights bill passed. The passing of the Civil Rights Act of 1964 and the Voting Rights Act of 1965 were immense victories for the NAACP and for every group that had worked for civil rights.

The final struggle to get the 1968 Fair Housing Act passed was overshadowed by King's assassination in Memphis, Tennessee, on April 4. The following day, at a meeting of civil rights leaders at the White House, the NAACP agreed to urge Congress to pass the fair housing bill as a tribute to King.

The NAACP in the Late Twentieth Century

After the late 1960s the NAACP encouraged **affirmative action** and minority hiring programs, campaigned against the death penalty, helped defeat unfavorable nominees to the Supreme Court, and continued to work for more favorable portrayal of blacks in the media.

Civil rights activities slowed during the presidential administration of Ronald Reagan (1981–88). Controversial leadership by the Reverend **Benjamin Chavis Jr.** (1948–) from 1993 to 1994 caused the NAACP to reconsider its role during the late 1990s.

In 1995 Representative **Kweisi Mfume** (1948–) left Congress to take over the NAACP presidency. Under his leadership the organization cleared its debt and renewed its activism in human rights, environmental racism, and justice for African Americans. In February 1998 civil rights veteran **Julian Bond** (1940–) became chairman of the board. His focus on voting earned the NAACP credit for the increased number of blacks voting in the 1998 congressional elections.

National Baptist Convention

The National Baptist Convention, U.S.A., founded on September 24, 1895, makes up the largest body of African-American Christian organizations in the world, with over 7.5 million members. Its roots date from 1834, when African Americans in Ohio organized the Providence Baptist Association to strengthen the work of local Baptist churches. This organization set a trend for local churches, resulting in the forming of other associations, state and regional conventions, and national bodies.

In 1895 a group of clergymen successfully encouraged numerous African-American Baptist organizations to merge into the National Baptist Convention. The newly formed convention had multiple purposes. It increased the work of the National Baptist Educational Convention through aggressive involvement in the **education** of blacks. It encouraged local churches to increase their support of secondary schools and colleges throughout the southern region of the United States. Internationally, the National Baptist Convention advanced foreign missionary projects in Africa, Central America, and the West Indies, expanding mission schools, churches, and medical institutions.

The convention's leaders organized its work through specialized boards, including the Foreign Mission Board, the Home Mission Board, the Educational Board, the Baptist Young People's Union, and the Publishing Board. Problems developed within several of the boards, and a split in leadership occurred in 1915. But the National Baptist Convention emerged from these troubles as the majority convention among African-American Baptists.

In 1956 a serious debate erupted when the convention's president, Rev. Joseph H. Jackson (1900–1990), reached the end of his allowed term in office. A majority of the convention's leaders and delegates wanted this term extended so he could continue as leader. A group favoring the election of

CHRONOLOGY

NAACP

1957
Civil Rights Act of 1957 is passed.

1960
Four North Carolina college students, two former officers of the NAACP's college chapter, sit at a segregated lunch counter in Greensboro, North Carolina, and refuse to leave until they are served. The sit-in movement soon spreads throughout the South.

June 12, 1963
NAACP Mississippi field secretary Medgar Evers is assassinated.

August 28, 1963
March on Washington for Jobs and Freedom is held. Led by the NAACP, it is the largest civil rights demonstration in U.S. history.

1964
Civil Rights Act of 1964 is passed.

1965
Voting Rights Act of 1965 is passed.

1968
Fair Housing Act is passed.

1969
NAACP begins *Head v. Timken Roller Bearing Co. of Columbus, Ohio,* a landmark affirmative action antidiscrimination lawsuit.

Rev. Gardner C. Taylor (1918–) of Brooklyn, New York, challenged Jackson's leadership. Jackson emerged the winner, but his victory did not calm the troubled waters. On September 11, 1961, a national call was issued for the organization of a separate group, the Progressive National Baptist Convention. The new convention protested some of Jackson's policies and rallied to give stronger support to the **Civil Rights movement** under the leadership of Rev. **Martin Luther King Jr.** (1929–1968).

Although the National Baptist Convention remained the largest convention of African-American Baptists, its leadership role was challenged. When Rev. T. J. Jemison became president of the convention after King's assassination in 1968, he worked to restore that role.

National Urban League

The National Urban League is an organization designed to improve the economic and employment conditions within the African-American community. From its founding in New York City in 1911, the league has worked to improve government programs and increase job opportunities for blacks.

The National Urban League was originally a combination of different groups with a common goal—the general improvement of the African-American community. During the early 1900s there were two major black organizations: the **National Association for the Advancement of Colored People (NAACP),** and the **National Urban League.** The two groups decided to share the fight against racial inequality in the United States. The NAACP took on the responsibility of working on the legal rights of blacks, and the National Urban League set out to improve the economic condition of blacks.

The National Urban League attacked the problem of limited economic opportunity for blacks from several angles. The group addressed private-sector employment and racism in labor unions. It also sponsored job training programs. In the 1930s and 1940s the group expanded its efforts to include public policy (the programs put forth by federal, state, and local governments). The National Urban League fought for legislation for welfare programs for blacks, worked to end discrimination in the defense industry, and lobbied for desegregation of the U.S. **military.** By the 1960s, with the help of civil rights laws, the organization was helping tens of thousands of blacks find jobs in the private sector. By the 1970s and 1980s the league was offering several training and job placement programs for blacks.

Some of the ways the National Urban League has tried to meet its goal of improving economic conditions for blacks include publishing reports; providing social service training for blacks; and encouraging black colleges to teach about important social, political, and economic issues facing blacks. In the 1960s the league began taking a more active approach to solving economic issues, and by the 1970s it began securing contracts with the government to provide social services (programs designed to help people in need). The organization also began publishing reports—such as *The Urban League Review*—on the economic condition of blacks. The league lost some of its influence during the 1980s, when funding for social programs was cut.

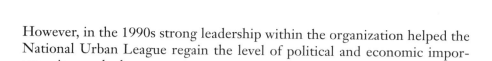
However, in the 1990s strong leadership within the organization helped the National Urban League regain the level of political and economic importance it once had.

Nation of Islam (NOI)

The Nation of Islam (NOI) was founded in 1930 by **Wallace D. Fard** (died 1934), who called himself Farrad Mohammed. A salesman who sold raincoats and silks, Farrad Mohammed also preached to poor African Americans in Detroit, Michigan. He told them the "true" religion of African Americans was not Christianity, but **Islam,** the "religion of the Black Men" of **Africa** and Asia. Master Fard, as he came to be called, taught his followers about white "blue-eyed devils," who had gained power through brutality, murder, and trickery.

He told his followers that they were not Americans and therefore owed no allegiance to the American flag. Fard established several organizations: the University of Islam, an elementary and high school; the Muslim Girls Training Corps Class, where female members learned home economics and were taught how to be proper Muslim women; and the Fruit of Islam, consisting of men who provided security for Muslim leaders.

One of Fard's most trusted officers was a man named **Elijah Muhammad** (1897–1975). After Fard was mysteriously murdered in 1934, Muhammad moved his family and close followers to Chicago, Illinois, in 1936, where they established Temple of Islam Number 2. This temple eventually became the national headquarters of the movement. Muhammad continued with his own teachings, proclaiming that God is black and that he, the Honorable Elijah Muhammad, had been appointed as God's messenger.

Under Muhammad's leadership, the NOI encouraged economic and racial independence. "Do for Self" became the rallying cry. The NOI stressed hard work, careful money management and the avoidance of debt, self-improvement, and a conservative lifestyle. During the forty-one-year period of his leadership, Muhammad and his followers established more than one hundred temples nationwide and many grocery stores, restaurants, bakeries, and other small businesses.

The beliefs of the NOI had a profound effect on **Malcolm X** (1925–1965). Born Malcolm Little, he was converted to Islam while in prison in 1947. He went on to become one of the most effective leaders for the Nation. Elijah Muhammad, recognizing Malcolm's organizational talents and enormous appeal, named him national representative of the NOI, second in rank to Muhammad himself. Malcolm X challenged the Reverend **Martin Luther King Jr.'s** (1929–1968) philosophy of integration and nonviolence. By contrast, Malcolm urged his followers to defend themselves by any means necessary.

In 1964, however, Malcolm X had an argument about political philosophy and morality with Elijah Muhammad. As a result, Malcolm left the NOI to form his own organization. Malcolm X was assassinated in 1965 while delivering a lecture in the African-American neighborhood of **Harlem** in New York City.

After Elijah Muhammad's death in 1975, his son Wallace Deen Muhammad was named supreme minister of the NOI. Within months Wallace shocked his followers by declaring that whites were no longer viewed as devils and could join the movement. He made other changes in the beliefs of the NOI and, as a result, many of his followers left the movement.

In 1978 **Louis Farrakhan** (1933–) began a new temple in Chicago. Farrakhan's Nation of Islam retains the beliefs of Elijah Muhammad. In 1995 Farrakhan organized the **Million Man March** in Washington, D.C. Farrakhan's leadership and his speech at the event brought him new respect as a black leader. During this period the Nation of Islam gained some notable new members, including boxer **Mike Tyson** (1966–). However, Farrakhan could not seem to avoid controversy. In 1998, for example, he upset many by appointing Muhammad Abdul Aziz, the man convicted of killing Malcolm X, to lead Harlem's Mosque Number 7—the very mosque that was headed by Malcolm X during his rise to fame.

In 2000, despite the Nation of Islam's nationwide visibility, its membership remained small. However, it has become the longest-lasting black militant and separatist movement in African-American history. It is also important for having introduced Islam as a fourth major religion in the United States, next to Protestantism, Catholicism, and Judaism. (*See also* **Black Nationalism.**)

Native Americans. *See* American Indians

Naylor, Gloria

January 25, 1950–
WRITER

Gloria Naylor was born in New York City. As a youth she traveled through parts of the United States as a missionary for the **Jehovah's Witnesses** (1968–1975). She later returned to the eastern United States to receive degrees from Brooklyn College (New York) in 1981 and Yale University (New Haven, Connecticut) in 1983. Her first published work, *The Women of Brewster Place* (1982), won the American Book Award for best first novel in 1983. The novel relates the lives of seven black women who live on one ghetto street and the oppression and spiritual strength shared by African-American women.

Naylor wrote a television screenplay adaptation of her first novel, which starred television personality **Oprah Winfrey** and was aired in 1984. Her later novels include *Linden Hills* (1985), *Mama Day* (1988), and the best-selling *Bailey's Cafe* (1992). Naylor wrote a play based on *Bailey's Cafe*, which was produced and performed by the Hartford Stage Company in 1994. She also wrote the screenplay for the PBS presentation *In Our Own Words* (1985). Naylor edited the volume *Children of the Night: The Best Short Stories by Black Writers, 1967 to the Present* (1995) A follow-up to her first novel, *The Men of Brewster Place*, was published in 1998.

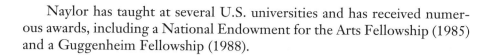
Naylor has taught at several U.S. universities and has received numerous awards, including a National Endowment for the Arts Fellowship (1985) and a Guggenheim Fellowship (1988).

Neal, Larry

WRITER
September 5, 1937–January 6, 1981

Larry Neal, one of the most prominent figures of the **Black Arts movement** of the 1960s and 1970s, was born in Atlanta, Georgia, and earned degrees from Lincoln University in Pennsylvania (1961) and the University of Pennsylvania (1963). His early articles, including "The Negro in the Theatre" (1964) and "Cultural Front" (1965), were among the earliest to express the need for blacks to develop their art and culture separately from a racist white society.

Neal's books and essays, many written or edited in collaboration with the poet **Amiri Baraka,** argued that the purpose of black art was to develop a new method of expression. The only way to do this, he argued, was to rid black art of all white and European influences. His and Baraka's 1968 essay "The Black Arts Movement," gave a name and a direction to a developing national trend. His books include *Black Boogaloo: Notes on Black Liberation* (1969) and *Hoodoo Hollerin' Bebop Ghosts* (1971). Though known primarily for his social and artistic criticisms, Neal also wrote several plays, screenplays, and television scripts.

Neal was an instructor at the City College of New York from 1968 to 1969 and subsequently taught at Wesleyan University (Middletown, Connecticut) and Yale University (New Haven, Connecticut). By the mid-1970s, he was reconsidering his view of black culture. In his essay "The Black Contribution to American Letters" (1976), he argued that while all African-American writers must be in some way political, it was important to separate their public personalities from their private experiences, which often include much more than simply a rejection of nonblack influences. Neal died of a heart attack in Hamilton, New York, in 1981.

Nebraska

First African-American Settlers: The Kansas-Nebraska Act of 1854 opened the territory to settlement. Slaves were first bought and sold in the 1850s in Nebraska City, although Nebraska escaped the violence that plagued the early settlement of Kansas, as very few slaveholders migrated to the area.

Slave Population: The census of 1860 listed only eighty-two blacks in the territory, fifteen of whom were slaves. That year, however, the territorial legislature abolished **slavery.** Nebraska joined the Union as the thirty-seventh state on March 1, 1867.

Free Black Population: Most **free blacks** moved to Omaha, where chances of finding work were greater. Many African Americans were railroad workers, packers, or general laborers.

Reconstruction: Some blacks took up homesteads in the post–**Civil War** (1861–65) years, but most settled in towns. For the most part, African Americans were accepted, or at least tolerated, although some violent incidents occurred (for example, 150 black migrants were driven out of the state capital of Lincoln in 1879). According to the 1910 census, blacks composed 0.6 percent of the state population (7,689) and 3 percent of Omaha's population (4,426).

The Great Depression: Patterns of segregation intensified from 1920 to 1940 despite the influx of African Americans during the Great Migration in the first decades of the twentieth century. Large-scale black migration resumed during **World War II** (1939–45), primarily to Omaha. In the 1940s civil action groups such as the Lincoln and Omaha Urban Leagues led efforts to end segregation and public-housing discrimination.

Civil Rights Movement: Regardless of efforts by regional civil action groups, the state of Nebraska did not institute open-housing or fair-employment laws until such laws were federally mandated. Violence hit Omaha during the 1960s' **Civil Rights movement**, with significant riots occurring in 1966 and 1968.

Current African-American Population: According to U.S. Census Bureau estimates, the total black population in Nebraska was 67,173 (4 percent of the state population) as of July 1, 1998.

Key Figures: Malcolm X (1925–1965), born Malcolm Little, black nationalist leader who was assassinated during a speech; baseball Hall of Fame pitcher **Robert Gibson** (1935–).

(SEE ALSO **EXODUSTERS; RED SUMMER.**)

Nevada

First African-American Settlers: African-American men accompanied fur traders and explorers to early Nevada. Black explorer James P. Beckwourth went through the area; a mountain pass was later named after him.

Free Black Population: Most nineteenth-century African Americans lived in the chief silver-producing area in Nevada, although they were almost entirely barred from mining. Most did menial labor, although some operated businesses, from barbershops to cafes and hotels.

Reconstruction: Nevada achieved statehood on October 1, 1864. In the mid-1870s protests from the African-American community helped to eliminate most governmental discrimination against black Nevadans. The African-American population declined in the 1880s, however, when silver mines ceased producing heavily; the population did not recover until the 1940s.

The Great Depression: Rising private discrimination in the late 1930s earned Nevada the nickname "the Mississippi of the West." Branches of the **National Association for the Advancement of Colored People (NAACP)** were organized in Las Vegas and Reno. During **World War II** (1939–45) substantial numbers of African-American workers were hired for defense-related jobs.

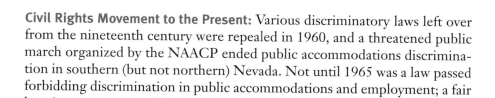
Civil Rights Movement to the Present: Various discriminatory laws left over from the nineteenth century were repealed in 1960, and a threatened public march organized by the NAACP ended public accommodations discrimination in southern (but not northern) Nevada. Not until 1965 was a law passed forbidding discrimination in public accommodations and employment; a fair housing act was passed in 1971.

Current African-American Population: According to U.S. Census Bureau estimates, the total black population in Nevada was 133,396 (nearly 8 percent of the state population) as of July 1, 1998.

Key Figures: Poet James Whitfield (1822–1871).

New Hampshire

First African-American Settlers: African Americans have been in New Hampshire since the first known African slave arrived in Portsmouth from Guinea in 1645.

Slave Population: According to census records, the number of slaves was 70 in 1707 and peaked at 656 in 1775. Slaves were imported to New Hampshire by prosperous residents, who typically owned one to three. Men worked in the shipyards, aboard ships at sea, in shops, and in the fields, while women performed domestic service. In 1788 New Hampshire became a state; by 1800 there were only eight slaves in the state, and none soon after.

Free Black Population: Laws restricting activities of Negroes and mulattoes (persons of mixed white and black ancestry) applied equally to enslaved and **free blacks.** Some blacks earned freedom by serving in the colonial wars, while others purchased their freedom.

Civil War: After decades of effort by abolitionists to end **slavery,** the state supreme court in 1861 affirmed that a person's color should not deny that person the full rights of citizenship, including the right to vote. Slavery was abolished, and slaves brought into the state were considered free.

Reconstruction: The first black church in the state was founded in Portsmouth in 1896. By the 1920s the influx of tourists to the state brought black chauffeurs, maids, and cooks, some of whom remained permanent residents. Black laborers migrated to Nashua from the southern states in the 1920s to work in wood-treating plants.

The Great Depression: Following the outbreak of **World War II** (1939–45), black soldiers and sailors were stationed at various military installations in southern New Hampshire, and civilian jobs at the Portsmouth Naval Shipyard became plentiful and accessible to African Americans. A new wave of black migrant workers and professionals arrived in the 1950s with the growth of the electronics industry and the opening of Pease Air Force Base.

Civil Rights Movement to the Present: A branch of the **National Association for the Advancement of Colored People (NAACP)** was chartered in the late 1950s to address the problems of housing and employment discrimination. It persuaded the state legislature to pass laws against discrimination in 1961.

Current African-American Population: According to U.S. Census Bureau estimates, the total black population in New Hampshire was 8,504 (0.7 percent of the state population) as of July 1, 1998.

Key Figures: Revolutionary war veteran Wentworth Cheswill (1746–1817); **Alexander Crummell** (1819–1898), abolitionist and missionary; author **Harriet E. Adams Wilson** (c. 1830–1870), who wrote what may have been the first novel by an African American published in the United States.

(SEE ALSO **UNDERGROUND RAILROAD.**)

New Jersey

First African-American Settlers: Although it is not clear when persons of African descent first arrived on New Jersey soil, Dutch colonists received an incentive of additional land for every slave imported between 1664 and 1666. The first documented arrival of black slaves to New Jersey occurred in 1680.

Slave Population: Throughout the eighteenth century, New Jersey slaves—who numbered about twenty-six hundred in 1726, forty-seven hundred in 1745, and twelve thousand in 1790—constituted roughly 8 percent of the overall population. Most worked on small farms that averaged about three slaves and produced grain and raised livestock. The state's slave population peaked at thirteen thousand in 1800; by 1860 that number had dwindled to eighteen.

Free Black Population: By 1800, in Quaker-dominated South Jersey, **free blacks** outnumbered slaves by almost five to one. Under the gradual provisions of the 1804 **abolition** law, all children born of slaves after July 4 of that year were to be emancipated (freed) after serving apprenticeships to their mother's master.

Civil War: By the time of the **Civil War** (1861–65), black New Jerseyans numbered nearly twenty-six thousand and had structured a vibrant institutional life that included churches, schools, literary societies, fraternal lodges, and charities.

Reconstruction: After the Civil War, increased discrimination and insensitivity from the white community stirred African Americans to build alternative institutions; by 1915 the black network included newspapers, homes for the elderly and orphans, political and social clubs, and businesses. The Great Migration triggered by **World War I** (1914–18) led to an influx of blacks from the southern states; between 1910 and 1930 the black population grew from 90,000 to 209,000.

The Great Depression: While the **Great Depression** slowed migration during the 1930s, **World War II** (1939–45) renewed immigration to the state. A new state constitution adopted in 1947 outlawed racial segregation in public schools and the state militia, making New Jersey the first state to make such provisions constitutional.

Civil Rights Movement to the Present: A doubling in the size of the black population, from 318,565 in 1950 to 770,292 in 1970, coincided with the

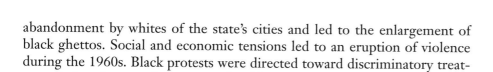

abandonment by whites of the state's cities and led to the enlargement of black ghettos. Social and economic tensions led to an eruption of violence during the 1960s. Black protests were directed toward discriminatory treatment in housing, employment, and public accommodations.

Current African-American Population: According to U.S. Census Bureau estimates, the total black population in New Jersey was 1,188,236 (nearly 15 percent of the state population) as of July 1, 1998.

Key Figures: Actor and singer **Paul Robeson** (1898–1976); **William James "Count" Basie** (1904–1984), bandleader and jazz pianist.

(SEE ALSO **UNDERGROUND RAILROAD**.)

New Mexico

First African-American Settlers: In 1539 explorer Stephen Dorantes was one of the first persons of African descent to enter the territory of New Mexico. When New Mexico was colonized at the end of the sixteenth century, Africans arrived with Spanish General Juan de Oñate.

Slave Population: Black men and women were imported to pre–Civil War New Mexico as forced laborers in mining and agriculture. In 1821, when New Mexico passed from Spain to Mexico, slavery continued on a small scale. In 1850, the year New Mexico became a U.S. territory, twenty-two blacks lived there, most of whom were domestic servants who worked for military or government officials.

Free Black Population: In the mid-nineteenth century, black fur traders and trappers arrived in New Mexico, the most famous of which was explorer James Beckwourth, who married a New Mexican and opened a hotel in Santa Fe. During the **Mexican War** (1846–48) more blacks arrived in the area with military forces.

Civil War: During the **Civil War** (1861–65) Confederate troops from the South invaded New Mexico, hoping to conquer the territory, but they were driven off and the territory remained in the hands of the Union army (the North).

Reconstruction: Between 1866 and 1900 from 3,000 to 3,800 black infantrymen and cavalrymen in the U.S. Army served at one time or another at eleven of the sixteen forts in New Mexico. Called "buffalo soldiers," a term of honor originated by Indians who thought the hair of black soldiers resembled the fur of buffalo, the black troops protected the growing white population and enforced the laws. The civilian black population remained under 200 until the 1870s, when many Civil War veterans and blacks from the South migrated west to work in the cattle industry. By 1912, when New Mexico achieved statehood, discrimination against blacks had become more blatant following the influx of southern whites to the state.

The Great Depression: Except for a temporary influx of African Americans after **World War I** (1914–18) to work on the railroad, blacks accounted for less than 1 percent of New Mexico's population through 1940. Most worked in coal mines or on farms. **World War II** (1939–45) led a great number of blacks to move to the state, some for military service and others for government jobs or jobs in the defense industry.

Civil Rights Movement to the Present: Despite the influence of New Mexico's branch of the **National Association for the Advancement of Colored People (NAACP)**, the state did not pass civil rights legislation until 1964.

Current African-American Population: According to U.S. Census Bureau estimates, the total black population in New Mexico was 45,124 (3 percent of the state population) as of July 1, 1998.

Key Figures: Nobel Prize–winning statesman **Ralph Bunche** (1904–1971); jazz musician **John Lewis** (1940–).

(SEE ALSO **SPANISH-AMERICAN WAR**.)

New Negro

The term "New Negro" has been used differently throughout U.S. history. During the 1700s and early 1800s, whites used the term to refer to Africans who had been newly enslaved. By the end of the 1800s, it was used to describe blacks who had been newly freed by the **Emancipation** Proclamation (1863). Into the twentieth century, both white and African-American leaders, journalists, writers, and artists, discussed the "New Negro" in articles and books. By then the term referred to a new generation of blacks who were educated and who displayed racial pride and political and cultural awareness.

A New Negro for a New Century, published in 1900, was one of earliest books to discuss the New Negro. It consists of historical and social essays written by educator **Booker T. Washington** (c. 1856–1915), activist Fannie B. Williams (1855–1944), and other prominent African Americans. Washington's chapter stresses the importance of education in empowering blacks, and Williams's essay focuses on the role of African-American women in the future development of the United States.

During the 1920s the idea of the New Negro became an important symbol of racial progress. It was during this time that a number of African-American political groups were established, and each claimed that it best represented the ideal of the New Negro. Such organizations included the **National Association for the Advancement of Colored People (NAACP)**, the **National Urban League**, and the **Universal Negro Improvement Association (UNIA)**.

But the term "New Negro" did not refer only to politics. In 1925 **Alain L. Locke** (1885–1954), a philosophy professor at **Howard University**, in Washington, D.C., and a leading promoter of black writers and artists, published a book of essays called *The New Negro, An Interpretation*. It contained essays and articles by important African-American political leaders, including **W. E. B. Du Bois** (1868–1963), yet Locke's essays, "Enter the New Negro" and "Negro Youth Speaks," focused exclusively on a group of young writers and artists. According to Locke, it was through the drawings, poetry, and writings of African Americans that the "voice of the New Negro is

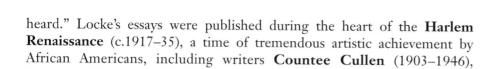

heard." Locke's essays were published during the heart of the **Harlem Renaissance** (c.1917–35), a time of tremendous artistic achievement by African Americans, including writers **Countee Cullen** (1903–1946), **Langston Hughes** (1902–1967), and **Zora Neale Hurston** (c. 1891–1960).

After the 1920s, as society shifted and racial attitudes changed, the expression "New Negro" stopped being used. Scholars, however, still debate about which of the various political and artistic philosophies best represented the ideal of the New Negro.

New Orleans, Louisiana

Early History

New Orleans was founded in 1718 by Jean Baptiste, Sieur de Bienville, governor of the French Colony of Louisiana, and was made the capital of the colony in 1722. By 1721 the town contained 145 white men, 65 white women, 38 children, 29 white servants, 172 black slaves, and 21 Indian slaves. The first imported slaves, five hundred Africans bought on credit from the St. Domingue colony (now Haiti), came in 1719. In the following twelve years, twenty-three slave ships arrived in Louisiana.

While only a few slaves were imported in the following forty years, the black inhabitants, mainly Senegalese (brought directly from Africa, unlike most blacks in British North America) helped build a distinct Afro-French culture in New Orleans. The enslaved black community soon included most of the town's skilled laborers, and the "donated" labor of blacks built much of the city. Black Creoles—the term usually refers to native Louisianian francophones—borrowed heavily in their cuisine and art from African models, and passed them along to whites. Africans contributed words to the creole dialect. The first code noir (black code), passed in 1724, prohibited mixed-race marriage, provided for Roman Catholic religious training, outlawed Sunday labor, and allowed slaves to own property and marry. Many slave owners ignored the code.

New Orleans grew slowly into a major port. In 1763, along with the rest of the Louisiana Territory, it was ceded to Spain in the Treaty of Paris. In 1791, slave revolts in St. Domingue, plus smaller ones in rural Louisiana, brought large numbers of whites, free mulattos, and enslaved blacks to New Orleans. Further immigrants from St. Domingue entered in 1809, when they were expelled from Spanish Cuba. In 1795, Spain granted the United States free navigation of the Mississippi River and use of the large depot at New Orleans. Americans began to settle in the city. In 1800 France regained Louisiana in a secret treaty; three years later, however, New Orleans and the Louisiana Territory were sold by Napoleon to the United States.

Throughout the years of Spanish rule, New Orleans remained largely French in culture. However, while slavery continued, the nature of the town's African-American population began to change, as a new, free colored community, mostly composed of mulattos, came into being. In 1769, the town contained 1,225 slaves, but only 100 free persons of color. The latter number would grow to 1,200 by the end of the Spanish era, against a slave population of 3,000, as a result of natural increase plus a huge Caribbean influx. The Spanish encouraged the growth of a free colored community as a buffer between blacks and whites. Spanish law made manumission easy and slaves worked to purchase their own freedom. Some earned their freedom by serving in militia units. Though most free blacks had enslaved relatives, authorities made use of them as city guards, in slave patrols, and as informers.

Cultural Development

Under American rule, New Orleans became the most important city in the South, and a major port and banking center for the Mississippi River region. The city's French character, and its large black and immigrant population, highlighted its distinctiveness. Gen. Andrew Jackson recruited black troops from the city for the Battle of New Orleans in 1815, and in the mid-1840s black contingents fought in the Mexican War. Antebellum African-American culture in New Orleans took diverse forms. Congo Square in the center of the city, which took its name from the slaves who established a market there for their own produce, was the scene of funerals and public dances, with dances such as the *carabiné*, and music provided by African instruments. The voodoo religion, a syncretic combination of African snake worship, Haitian rituals, and Christian elements, attracted followers of all races and religions. Dr. John was dubbed the "king" of his voodoo, while his rival, Madame Marie Laveau, was acclaimed the "queen." Even the dominant Catholic religion was affected by African traditions. The famous Mardi Gras, the carnival preceding Lent, is adapted in part from African festivals. Blacks offered for sale at the slave auctions under the giant rotunda of the St. Louis Hotel often were presented in Mardi Gras-style costumes.

Although the Louisiana Civil Code of 1808 forbade mulattos from marrying either whites or black slaves, New Orleans became famous for its quadroon balls where white men trysted with mixed-race women. Mulatto women were kept under the arrangement known as plaçage. Under this system, white men took mulatto mistresses as "second wives," buying houses for the women and any children that resulted from their union. Mulatto children often legally inherited their parents' money and property, including slaves, and frequently traveled to France to vacation or be educated. Prominent mulatto citizens included Bastile Croquière, who instructed elite whites in fencing; Norbert Rillieux, inventor of the vacuum pump for sugar refining; Aristide Mary, philanthropist and real estate tycoon; Victor Sejour, a playwright; the doctors Louis Charles Roundanez, James Derham, and Alexandre Chaumette; the composer/conductor Edmond Dédé who later led the Alcazar Orchestra in France; and the sculptor Eugene Warbourg. In 1845, a circle of writers, led by Armand Lanusse, published a volume of verse entitled *Les Cenelles*.

The free black community prospered and continued to grow. Job opportunities for skilled black laborers were reasonably plentiful, since few white immigrants were trained artisans. Legal manumission remained simple. Free Anglo-American blacks continued to migrate to the city, although they remained largely separate from the creole community. They formed Baptist and Methodist churches, and joined several Masonic groups.

Despite New Orleans's reputation for tolerance, segregation and discrimination hindered the lives of free people of color. Blacks were officially excluded when the New Orleans public school system was established in 1841, although some white fathers enrolled their mulatto children. Roman Catholic schools were established for blacks, such as the Couvent Institute. The Institute, funded by a legacy from an ex-slave, was established in 1847. As the city's Anglo-American population became dominant and whites aligned themselves with the other southern states, prejudice against free people of color increased. By the 1850s black organizations such as churches and fraternal societies were forced to lead increasingly clandestine existences. The French code noir was officially abrogated in the mid-1850s. Laws against free black migration were enforced, and manumission became difficult.

The Civil War and Its Effect on the City

The coming of the **Civil War** in 1861 dramatically changed the situation of African Americans in the city. When the war began, some 1,400 free people of color (eventually 3,000), acting variously out of southern patriotism, slaveholder interest, and/or fear of white wrath, entered the Confederate Army as an unarmed unit, the New Orleans Home Guards. The Union takeover of New Orleans in 1862 galvanized the city's black population and that of the surrounding area. Slavery became almost extinct in the area, as slaves left their masters and poured into the city. Union Army Gen. Benjamin Butler, commanding the city, originally opposed efforts by blacks to enlist in the Union Army. By September 1862 this policy was reversed, and eventually three black New Orleans units, including the Corps D'Afrique, were established.

Despite the military ability of African Americans, and the creoles' evident dignity and social standing, civil rights efforts lagged. The Union occupation forces retained the harsh Black Codes of the 1850s. Since President Abraham Lincoln had exempted Louisiana from the Emancipation Proclamation (see **Emancipation**), free people of color began to lobby to formally end slavery throughout the United States, and in March, 1864, two creole delegates, E. Arnold Bertonneau and Jean-Baptiste Roudanez, went to Washington to press Congress and President Lincoln to extend suffrage rights to Louisiana's blacks. Their efforts were unsuccessful. Black creole opinion had as its major forum *L'Union*, a French (later bilingual) biweekly journal that became the major black newspaper. It folded in mid-1864, but Paul Trvigne, its editor, quickly began the bilingual *Tribune*, which in fall 1864 became the first African-American daily newspaper. The creole elite and black Americans joined together at that time to form the National Equal Rights League of Louisiana. In 1864, league members lobbied in Congress against the bill readmitting Louisiana to the Union, since the government denied blacks suffrage. The end of the war brought fresh conflict to New Orleans.

Early Civil Rights Action

In July 1866, a Radical Republican convention, organized to consider changing the 1864 state constitution to grant black suffrage, was held at the Mechanics' Institute, Louisiana's capitol building. A group of freed blacks, led by a marching band, attempted to cross Canal Street, the city's wide main artery, to protest outside the convention. They were jeered by a white mob, organized by conservatives trying to break up the convention. A white protester shot at the blacks, who fired back. Police opened fire into the crowd of black marchers. Antiblack violence spread across the city. Neither the Union Army nor the Freedmen's Bureau intervened. By the time order was restored, 37 people were dead, 34 of them black; 136 people were wounded, 119 of them black; and police had made 293 arrests. Outrage over the violence in Congress led in part to the Civil Rights Act of 1866.

The following year, 1867, after African American William Nichols was thrown off a streetcar, New Orleans black leaders organized a successful sit-in campaign, and a mob of 500 blacks stoned segregated "star cars." Gen. Philip Sheridan, commanding the region, refused to support segregated facilities, and desegregation was achieved. The same year, Congress passed the Reconstruction Act (see **Reconstruction**), which dissolved the Louisiana government. The interim government enfranchised blacks. The next year, 1868, Sheridan organized a "Black and Tan" Radical Republican constitutional convention, of which two-thirds of the delegates were African-American. The new constitution provided for racial equality and integrated public schools, which opened in 1869. That same year, the Republican legislature passed a public accommodations law, which creoles and others enforced through large damage suits against violators.

In 1868, however, the race for the Republican nomination for governor, then tantamount to election, destroyed the fragile creole-American black alliance. That year, the black creole Francis Dumas, a Union army veteran and former slaveholder, ran for the gubernatorial nomination with the support of the Tribune, which refused to back a white candidate, Henry Warmoth. Warmoth, with the support of P.B.S. Pinchback, a powerful army veteran and political broker who had recently come to New Orleans, won a very close race. Warmoth named the black Oscar Dunn his lieutenant governor, but broke with the creoles, ending the public subsidies that kept the Tribune afloat. His ally, Pinchback, named lieutenant governor in 1871, briefly became the first African-American state governor after Warmoth's impeachment in 1872. Pinchback was later elected to the U.S. Senate.

New black and creole institutions were set up in the post-bellum era. Blacks formed their own churches and Scots rite Masonic lodges and benevolent societies, although creoles generally stayed in interracial Catholic churches and French rite Masonic lodges. Three colleges opened in New Orleans: Straight University (1869), founded under the aegis of the American Missionary Association; Leland University (1869), a private college; and New Orleans University (1873), a state-funded institution. Originally integrated, eight of the ten graduates of its first Law School class in 1878 were white. Another college, Southern University, opened in 1879 (after it moved in 1914, its buildings housed Xavier University). The colleges remained intellectual centers through the Jim Crow era and helped take the place of city high schools, which excluded blacks from 1879 to 1917 and segregated them afterwards.

A Cultural Flowering

Reconstruction also brought a cultural flowering in African-American New Orleans. Theaters opened, and public lectures—especially those of the African-American female suffragist and poet, Frances E. W. Harper— were popular among creoles. Dance halls such as the Brown, the Natural, the Economy, and the Union were popular among blacks. There were even large dances held at the state capitol. Many people enjoyed horse races and regattas, often organized through the city's many social clubs. Baseball had a wide following in the city. There were interracial games in the 1870s.

Perhaps most importantly, music was played throughout the city: A New Orleans University group gave concerts of spirituals; minstrel shows and vaudeville were popular, as were many brass bands, the most famous of them Sylvester Decker's Excelsior Brass Band; and Professor Louis Martin's Negro Symphony Orchestra and black concert performers, such as Victor Eugene Macarthy, played classical music. When a French opera company was stranded in the city in 1875, the black creole community sponsored a season of performances.

Struggles Intensify

In 1874, white rioters rose up against Louisiana's biracial government in the so-called Battle of Liberty Place. In 1876 white Democrats won a disputed election and immediately started "redeeming" the state. City schools and public accommodations were resegregated almost immediately, although public transportation remained integrated. Most blacks were now restricted to older, squalid and segregated residential areas. During the 1880s, the creole elite, led by real estate tycoon and philanthropist Aristide Mary and lawyer/journalist Rodolphe Desdunes, began new efforts against discriminatory legislation. In 1887, Desdunes formed *L'Union Louisianaise*, which with creole financial support, grew into a newspaper, the New Orleans *Crusader*, for a time the nation's only African-American daily. In 1890, after the passage of a law segregating railroad transportation, the creoles formed a Comite des Citoyens to challenge the law in court and raised money to defer legal expenses. A member of the Comite, Homer Plessy, agreed to serve as defendant. In 1896, however, the U.S. Supreme Court ruled in the ***Plessy v. Ferguson*** decision that "separate but equal" facilities were constitutional. The turn of the century brought the final decline of the creole community. The strict color bar eliminated the vestiges of their privileges, and promoted assimilation with blacks.

Despite official segregation and continuing racial tension, which broke into a major riot in 1900, New Orleans remained a culturally interracial city. One locus of interracial contact in these years, though clandestine and exploitative, was Storyville, the legal red-light district. Despite the romantic aura of Storyville, it played only a small part in African-American life in the city. The prostitutes, the majority of whom were African Americans, ranged in their pigmentation. The most expensive houses, which attracted an exclusively white clientele, usually featured light-skinned women. The owners of the larger brothels, except for "Miss Lulu" White, were all white.

Jazz Flowers and Labor Conflicts

The lively entertainment scene in New Orleans—of which Storyville was only one aspect—nurtured the growth of distinctive African-American musical forms, especially **jazz**. Early jazz, as played in the first years of the twentieth century by pioneers such as Buddy Bolden, **Jelly Roll Morton**, and King Oliver, developed from a melange of ragtime, marching bands, and the music of popular entertainment halls. New Orleans' unusual multiracial culture promoted its development. Early jazz was primarily collectively improvised polyphonic versions of rags and of blues melodies. After 1915, with the emergence of the white Original Dixieland Jazz Band (who made the first jazz recordings in 1917), and after 1920, with King Oliver and **Louis Armstrong**, jazz soon became successively a national and international craze. However, the lure of larger entertainment markets elsewhere, such as Chicago and New York City, led to an exodus of jazz musicians to the North. By 1925, New Orleans was largely depleted of its first-rank jazz musicians, and the dominance of "New Orleans Jazz" was essentially over.

The depression of 1893 brought conflict and rioting by whites over apportionment of labor on the docks, and destroyed the uneasy decade-long alliance between black and white unionized labor. The two sides recognized their interest in alliance, though, and by 1901 made fresh agreements, which held through a general strike in 1907, and lasted until the decline of the unions in 1923. During the following years, a few blacks were promoted to supervisory positions, but eventually the absence of union work rules and wage scales led to a steep decline in wages and working conditions. Beginning in 1929, the **Great Depression** further eroded black labor influence in the port.

Meanwhile, the city continued as a musical center. Traditional jazz remained a mainstay of New Orleans culture. In places such as Preservation Hall, early New Orleans jazz was lovingly preserved, primarily for the benefit of tourists. In 1969, the popular New Orleans Jazz and Heritage Festival was inaugurated. New Orleans also helped spawn other popular African-American musical forms. The great gospel singer **Mahalia Jackson** came from New Orleans, though the bulk of her career was spent in Chicago. In the 1930s and '40s local musicians, influenced by Latin and Caribbean rhythms, developed an infectious, fast-paced, piano-centered blues style generally known as New Orleans **rhythm-and-blues**. The pioneers include **Professor Longhair**, Lloyd Price, and Dave Bartholomew, though the best-known exponent in the style was **Fats Domino**, one of the leading rock-and-roll performers of the 1950s. The Neville Brothers had a successful rhythm and blues career stretching from the 1950s through the 1990s. New Orleans is the hometown of a number of contemporary black musicians; avant-garde drummer Ed Blackwell hailed from New Orleans, and in the 1980s, natives Branford and Wynton Marsalis came to national prominence as jazz artists. In tribute to its musical heritage, in the 1990s the city was selected as the home of the Black Music Hall of Fame and Museum.

The movement for black equality never completely died in New Orleans. During the 1920s the black Federation of Civic Leagues, an organization of social clubs led by creole activist A. P. Tureaud, sponsored a New Orleans branch of the **NAACP**. The NAACP successfully challenged

a 1924 residential segregation ordinance in the U.S. Supreme Court, won salary equalization for African-American teachers in the early 1940s, and paid residents' poll taxes to further an unsuccessful electoral challenge to voter registration laws. In 1946, Tureaud sponsored a lawsuit, *Hall v. Nagel*, which eased white interference with black voter registration. In 1953, after another lawsuit, *Tureaud v. Board of Supervisors*, Tureaud opened the doors of Louisiana State University to blacks.

New Orleans in the Late Twentieth Century

During the 1950s, a moderate mayor, Chep Morrison, eased police harassment of blacks. However, only a few small gains were made in desegregation. Blacks remained largely excluded from downtown areas. The NAACP, led by Ernest "Dutch" Morial, faced constant white opposition, although white harassment increased the NAACP's prestige in the black community. In 1958, following a suit in court, Judge Skelly Wright voided streetcar/bus segregation, and in 1960, despite Morrison's strong opposition, the first schools were desegregated. The same year, activists from the **Congress of Racial Equality (CORE)** sponsored **sit-ins** and direct action on Canal St. White storeowners challenged the legality of the sit-ins, but the U.S. Supreme Court ruled in *Garner v. Louisiana* (1960) that they were constitutionally protected. The sit-ins eventually brought about the desegregation of city lunch counters in 1962. The NAACP joined CORE and other black groups in a short-lived Citizen's Committee, which sponsored a march on City Hall in September 1963. Nevertheless, the process of desegregation was slow. In 1965, African-American players staged a walkout at an American Football League All-Star game in New Orleans to protest racial discrimination in the city.

The U.S. Voting Rights Act of 1965 altered the city's political landscape. In 1967, Dutch Morial won a seat in the Louisiana legislature, and two years later, almost won a seat as councilman-at-large. The same year, with his support and that of two important black political clubs, Community Organization for Urban Politics (COUP) and Southern Organization for Unified Leadership (SOUL), the moderate liberal Moon Landrieu was elected mayor. Landrieu ended discrimination in public accommodations and awarded city patronage to black allies in COUP and SOUL, particularly jobs connected with the Superdome, the city's giant new sports arena. During the early 1970s, a combination of white flight and new economic opportunity, transformed New Orleans into an African-American majority city.

In 1978, Dutch Morial ran for mayor and won by a narrow margin, mostly on the strength of the black vote. Ironically, due to past personal and political disagreements, Morial was opposed or only halfheartedly supported by COUP and SOUL, whose leaders he proceeded to prosecute for corruption once in office. Morial served two terms, retaining popularity among his black constituency despite opposition from both whites and black leaders over his independent policy-making, including color-blind merit hiring. In 1985, Sidney Barthelemy of COUP, running as a moderate against another black candidate, became New Orleans' second African-American mayor. Ironically, he received barely 25 percent of the black vote, but won 85 percent of the white vote. With help from an overwhelmingly strong black vote, Marc Morial, Dutch Morial's son, was elected New Orleans's new Mayor in 1994. Despite opposition by white business interests and accusations of past drug use, he was easily reelected in 1998.

While racial divisions continue to plague New Orleans, there has been progress in certain areas. In 1989, city officials voted to store the Liberty Monument, an obelisk commemorating the Battle of Liberty Place, on the grounds that it commemorated prejudice and served as a rallying point for the **Ku Klux Klan**. White supremacists led by gubernatorial candidate David Duke challenged the removal. In 1993, after a court ordered the monument restored, the city's Human Rights Commission voted unanimously that it be removed. The same year, under pressure from the city council, the Rex organization, one of the four prestigious secret societies that plan the city's annual Mardi Gras festival, invited its first three blacks to become members.

New York

First African-American Settlers: A black population first developed in 1626 in the city of New Amsterdam, part of the Dutch colony of New Netherland, later called New York City after the English conquest of 1664.

Slave Population: The Dutch imported and enslaved Africans to work on farms, estates, and public works. By 1790 the enslaved African population stood at 21,324, giving New York the largest black population and the most well developed institution of **slavery** in the North.

Free Black Population: A gradual emancipation law was passed in 1799 that freed all children born to slave women after July 4 of that year. Central New York contained many routes and stations on the **Underground Railroad** through which fugitives passed on their way to Canada.

Civil War: Following the Emancipation Proclamation of January 1, 1863, the war to preserve the Union also became the war of **emancipation,** one in which blacks would finally be allowed to become soldiers. The worst urban riot in U.S. history occurred in New York City in the summer of 1863 when immigrant workers hostile toward blacks from years of job competition, and unable to escape having to fight in the Civil War, directed their anger toward blacks.

Reconstruction: While the years between the **Civil War** (1861–65) and **World War I** (1914–18) were ones of economic expansion and industrial growth for the state, New York's black population did not benefit equally, in part because of segregated unions that kept blacks out of most skilled industrial jobs. The Great Migration in the early part of the 1900s increased the black population in urban areas such as New York City and Buffalo, which experienced an increase in its African-American population from 1,698 in 1900 to 13,563 in 1930. In 1918 the Civil Rights Act of New York State was passed, prohibiting discrimination in certain areas, such as public accommodations.

The Great Depression: The **World War II** years (1939–45) increased the flow of black migrants from the South to northern cities looking for work in a labor market recovering from the **Great Depression.** The economic picture for African Americans in the state brightened significantly during the war years, but race relations still required much improvement, as was evidenced by a major riot in **Harlem** in 1943.

Civil Rights Movement to the Present: After World War II, New York was part of the nationwide movement to pass laws banning discrimination in employment and housing. Black New Yorkers became increasingly involved in the state and federal governments; by 1966 the state assembly contained eight blacks, 5.3 percent of the total number of people serving.

Current African-American Population: According to U.S. Census Bureau estimates, the total black population in New York was 3,219,676 (18 percent of the state population) as of July 1, 1998.

Key Figures: Poet **Jupiter Hammon** (1711–c. 1806); **Sojourner Truth** (c. 1797–1883), one of the leading antislavery speakers; clergyman and civil rights activist **Adam Clayton Powell Jr.** (1908–1972); **David Norman Dinkins** (1927–), the first black mayor of New York City.

(SEE ALSO **NEW YORK CITY DRAFT RIOT OF 1863; HARLEM RENAISSANCE.**)

New York City

New York's Beginnings

The founding by the Dutch of the colony of New Netherland in 1624 and its principal city, New Amsterdam, was soon followed by the importation of African slaves in 1626 (see **Slave Trade**). Africans were an integral part of the economic development of the colony as the Dutch West India Company enslaved Africans for use on public works. Unlike other colonies in the New World, those in bondage to the company had certain basic rights such as baptism, marriage, and some legal standing afforded by the courts in a colony that operated without a formal slave code. Indeed, some Africans occupied a status termed "half-freedom," which released them from bondage for an annual payment to the company and the use of their labor at unspecified times. The precise extent of African slavery is unclear during this period, but it was increasing in the late 1650s.

A more restrictive form of bondage was introduced with the English conquest of New Netherland in 1664. Under the English, the colony became New York and the main city was renamed New York City. By 1741, blacks numbered 20 percent of the city's 11,000 population. English fears of a slave uprising became quite pronounced after the April 6, 1712 insurrection of approximately two dozen slaves. The hysteria following the insurrection resulted in the temporary closing of Elias Neau's Catechism School for Negroes, the first school for blacks in British North America, opened in 1704. In March of 1741 a rash of ten fires occurred (eight in six days) which many residents construed to be the beginning of a slave rebellion. Whether a form of protest against slavery or a revolt to overthrow slavery, some thirteen blacks were burned at the stake, sixteen hung along with four whites, and seventy-one deported. Since the area's early settlement by the Dutch in the seventeenth century, blacks resided not only on Manhattan Island, or the city itself, but also lived in Brooklyn. A 1698 census of the province revealed no free blacks in Kings County (then a collection of independent villages that included Brooklyn), but indicated that there were 296 slaves, which constituted 15 percent of the county's population of 2,017. By 1738, Kings County was the leading slave holding county in New York, and by 1790 blacks accounted for more than one-third of the population. The agricultural economy of King's County accounts for the small number of free blacks—only 46—and the large number of slaves, 1,482. In comparison, 33 percent, or 1,036, of New York City's black population was free. By 1820, only seven years before mandatory emancipation in the state, half of Kings County's black population remained enslaved. In 1820, more than 60 percent of white families in Kings County owned slaves, compared to 18 percent in New York City.

New York Abolishes Slavery and Black Institutions Emerge

Slavery in New York City was not overthrown by overt rebellion, but by those in the state who recognized the contradiction between a slave society and the democratic rhetoric of the Revolutionary War; this recognition culminated in the passage of the gradual abolition law of 1799. In the final years of the institution in New York City most slave holding units were of small size. In 1790, 75 percent of slave holders in the city owned only one or two slaves. The gradual emergence of a free black population led to the formation of a separate black institutional life in the 1790s and early nineteenth century. Black members dissatisfied with the discriminatory treatment they received within white churches left to form their own churches. African Americans attended segregated schools since they were excluded from most white schools. The best known school in early New York City was the African Free School, founded by the largely white New York Manumission Society in 1787. Blacks also started their own schools and formed mutual aid societies like the New York African Society for Mutual Relief in 1810, which was designed to aid the poor, widows, orphans, and disabled. The creation in 1827 of the nation's first black newspaper, *Freedom's Journal*, by John Russwurm and Samuel Cornish, provided a means of communication and discussion relevant to free blacks and the antislavery movement. In 1800 black Methodists in New York City, led by Peter Williams, consecrated the Zion Church, which in time became the founding congregation of the African Methodist Episcopal Zion Church. His son, Peter Williams, Jr., founded the first black Episcopal church in New York City, St. Phillips African Church in 1819.

Some free blacks prospered in this period of transition from slavery to freedom which occurred simultaneously with the movement of New York City's economy toward "metropolitan industrialization." These opportunities, however, decreased over the next decades as prejudice and discrimination from employers, the consuming public, native workers, and a poor competitive immigrant working class combined to drive blacks out of recently acquired skilled jobs and exclude them from newly developing industrial jobs. The economic position of blacks was fragile in the early nineteenth century. Attacks on individual black property owners by poor whites had begun during the first two decades of the nineteenth century and

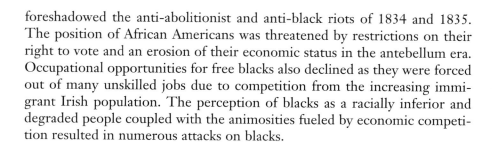

foreshadowed the anti-abolitionist and anti-black riots of 1834 and 1835. The position of African Americans was threatened by restrictions on their right to vote and an erosion of their economic status in the antebellum era. Occupational opportunities for free blacks also declined as they were forced out of many unskilled jobs due to competition from the increasing immigrant Irish population. The perception of blacks as a racially inferior and degraded people coupled with the animosities fueled by economic competition resulted in numerous attacks on blacks.

President Lincoln's Emancipation Proclamation of 1862 (see **Emancipation**) had turned the **Civil War** from one to preserve the Union to one to end slavery. Immigrant workers unable to pay the $300 "commutation fee" to avoid the draft and fearful of the job competition from emancipated blacks took out their racial prejudices and economic fears upon the city's small black population. Blacks fleeing the draft riots in 1863 were driven from downtown Brooklyn and New York City. Some found refuge in the Weeksville-Carrsville area of Kings County, named after local blacks. This area is located in present-day Bedford-Stuyvesant. The Weeksville-Carrsville area dates from the 1830s and was an acknowledged neighborhood by the 1840s. A sense of community existed in the neighborhood; Weeksville blacks petitioned, albeit unsuccessfully, in 1869 to have a black appointed to the Brooklyn Board of Education so that they could have a say in the governance of the five "colored" schools. (In 1882 Phillip A. White became the first black on the Brooklyn Board of Education.) The distinctive black character of Weeksville and other parts of the Ninth Ward (which included part of present-day Bedford-Stuyvesant) was lost by 1870 as whites purchased property and moved into the area touted as excellent for "genteel suburban residences." However, more was lost than the character of the neighborhood, for as immigrants came to Brooklyn and New York City they and their offspring forced blacks out of skilled and semi-skilled jobs.

Postwar Strife and the Rise of Harlem

Despite the contributions of black New Yorkers to the Union victory, including the formation of the Twentieth United States Colored Infantry, efforts to grant voting rights to minorities failed. Equal suffrage for black New Yorkers would not come until the passage of the Fifteenth Amendment to the U.S. Constitution in 1870. Between 1870 and the turn of the century African Americans continued to contribute to the establishment of new institutions and organizations in their community. *The New York Age*, founded in 1887 under the editorship of T. Thomas Fortune, became one of the leading black newspapers in the nation. In the early years of the twentieth century Charles Anderson, a close ally of **Booker T. Washington**, was a leading black Republican politician. During the same years Tammany Hall organized the United Colored Democracy, its black auxiliary. During these years the black population in the city grew significantly. Nevertheless, blacks remained less than 2 percent of the total population as southern and eastern European immigrants swelled the city's population.

In 1900, New York City had 60,000 black residents. By 1920, it had the largest black population of any city in the country, though less than 3 percent of the population was black. The city's ethnic diversification was accompanied by considerable social upheaval as groups contended for jobs and living space. The worst disturbance during these years was the August 1900 anti-black riot when policemen joined the white mobs in attacking blacks all along Eighth Avenue between Twenty-seventh and Forty-second streets. Seeking the security of new neighborhoods, better housing, and equal social status, blacks took the opportunity to move into the middle-class community of Harlem, created by vacant apartments in an overbuilt housing market, and the entrepreneurial skills of a black realtor, Philip A. Payton, and his Afro-American Realty Company organized in 1904. Many of the major African-American social, fraternal, and religious institutions relocated from their downtown quarters to Harlem by the early 1920s.

The "Great Migration" of blacks from the South and the Caribbean was intensified by the demand for labor in the North during the World War I years; many of these new immigrants settled in Harlem. New York City also became the center of increased Caribbean immigration. Approximately 25 percent of Harlem's black population were foreign-born by the mid-1920s, with the vast majority of the foreign-born composed of Caribbean immigrants. Although the foreign-born percentage decreased 16.7 percent by 1930 due to restrictive immigration laws, West Indian immigrants continued to play an important role in the economic, intellectual, and political life of New York City. By 1930, an estimated one-third of New York City's black professionals were from the Caribbean. In 1919 Caribbean immigrants founded New York City's leading black newspaper, the *Amsterdam News*.

The Harlem Renaissance and African Repatriation

By this time, Harlem had become the center of New York's black life, containing not only the working class, but also the small but influential black middle class. In 1919, the Equitable Life Assurance Society placed on the market the beautiful brownstones on W. 139th Street designed by Stanford White which had been off limits to black buyers. Within eight months, members of the black bourgeoisie had purchased them and they became known as "Striver's Row." Other streets, such as Edgecomb Avenue and St. Nicholas Place, became middle- and upper-income black enclaves. The diverse black nationalities and artistic communities of Harlem contributed to its heterogeneous class composition and cosmopolitan reputation in the 1920s. Throughout the first half of the twentieth century Harlem was the cultural and ideological capital of black America. In the 1920s, it became the center of both a literary renaissance (see **Harlem Renaissance**) and the black nationalistic movement of **Marcus Garvey**—a Caribbean immigrant—and his Universal Negro Improvement Association (UNIA). From his Harlem headquarters, Garvey instilled a new racial pride while advocating the decolonization of Africa from European rule. The UNIA established several businesses, including the ill-fated Black Star Line of ships, which was intended to facilitate commerce between Africa and African-Americans. Its promoters hoped the UNIA would play a role in the repatriation of blacks from the racially repressive climate of the United States to freedom in an independent Africa. Garveyism was the nationalistic manifestation of the New Negro movement's search for racial pride and assertiveness in the struggle for freedom.

The literary ferment of the Harlem Renaissance produced numerous authors and poets who celebrated their African and African-American heritage. Black writers extolled the culture and character of Africa. The cosmopolitan nature of the Renaissance is seen in the number of West Indian artists who played an instrumental role in the literature, such as Claude McKay and Eric Walrond. Artists and their literary promoters, such as the black sociologist and editor of the National Urban League magazine *Opportunity*, (1923-1944), Charles S. Johnson, sought to create a new and more positive image for African Americans through the arts which might be absorbed by the larger society. The **National Association for the Advancement of Colored People** (NAACP), the leading civil rights organization in the United States, had its offices in Harlem, as did its journal, the *Crisis*. Harlem had a vibrant nightlife which was soon discovered by white theatergoers, critics, publishers, and intellectuals. The dominant form of black popular music was **jazz.** New York City soon became a music center for jazz. White New Yorkers found black music and entertainers readily available in Harlem nightclubs. Connie's Inn and the **Cotton Club** were two of the most famous clubs in Harlem in the twenties. Owned by white underworld figures, they featured black bands, singers, and chorus-line dancers.

Political Advances and the Great Depression

The appreciation of black music did not carry over into the human sphere, however, and many of the white-owned clubs excluded black patrons. The period of the twenties and thirties was one in which the city's black population demanded greater participation or control of the institutions in their communities. In Harlem, blacks demanded positions at Harlem Hospital from which they had been excluded, as well as control of Harlem's district leaderships, clubhouses, and representation. In 1929, Charles Fillmore, a Republican, became the city's first black district leader. In 1935, Herbert Bruce, a West Indian immigrant, became the Democratic Party's first black district leader. In the first five years of the Great Depression, West Indian politicians made significant gains in the Democratic party. By 1952, four of the five Democratic district leaders in Harlem were West Indians. Four of the five founding members of the Harlem branch of the Communist Party were West Indians.

In part these trends were the result of African-American domination of the black posts within the Republican party and the greater accessibility of the Democratic party, which had far less black involvement until the New Deal. West Indians cooperated with African-American Democrats in attempts to gain black control over the Harlem Nineteenth and Twenty-first Assembly Districts. Despite some degree of tension between African Americans and West Indians, race far more than nationality determined the condition of blacks in the city and nation. By the 1930s, the first wave of West Indian immigrants that entered the country at the beginning of the twentieth century lived in neighborhoods segregated by race but not divided by black ethnic or class differences. By the latter half of the 1920s the Garvey movement had collapsed with his imprisonment and deportation. The stock market crash of 1929 and accompanying depression eroded interest in the Renaissance. Still, Harlem remained dynamic, as the struggle for equality intensified as the black unemployment rate in the city grew to nearly double that of whites and threw nearly half of Harlem's families onto relief. The injustice of employment discrimination in Harlem retail and chain stores in the midst of the depression added insult to injury. Blacks initiated successful boycotts in Harlem in the 1930s, forcing department stores, utilities, and transportation companies to reverse their policies and hire blacks. Boycotts and protest marches were important weapons in breaking down the prejudice-induced barriers that existed during the Great Depression. Riots and black violence directed at white businesses helped sensitize political and civic leaders to the need for change.

With the onset of the preparedness drive for World War II, New York City became the headquarters for A. Philip Randolph's movement for the March on Washington in 1941 to protest discrimination in the armed forces and among federal contractors. This led to the creation of a Federal Fair Employment Practices Committee in 1941 to insure blacks their fair share of jobs in defense industries. World War II ended the depression and illustrated the contradiction of a country fighting against racist Nazi ideology with two armies, one white and one black. The shooting of a black soldier by a white policeman in the Hotel Braddock in Harlem touched off another riot on August 1, 1943. The human cost of the riot was significant, with 6 people killed, all black, and 185 people injured, mostly black. Arrests of blacks numbered more than 550, with most in custody for burglary and reception of stolen goods. Estimates were that some 1,450 stores were damaged. In comparison to the Detroit riot of June 21 of the same year, the loss of life and physical injury were considerably less, but the events of August 1st and 2nd came as a surprise in America's most cosmopolitan city in which the mayor, Fiorello La Guardia, was popular in the black community. Frustration with the continuation of racism was the underlying cause of the riot. Pictures of the earlier Detroit riot showing black victims of white mobs and police were carried by New York newspapers along with numerous articles on white violence and discrimination against black servicemen. On the local level the riot was in part sparked by black discontent with employment discrimination, with police brutality, and La Guardia's apparent retreat from liberal policies. Following the riot, La Guardia moved to implement policies that the black community had advocated. Within one week of the riot, the Office of Price Administration announced the opening of an office to investigate food price-gouging in Harlem. Within two weeks, La Guardia inaugurated a series of radio broadcasts to promote racial harmony. The New York City Board of Education created a course on Intercultural Relations for teachers which emphasized African-American contributions. The mayor also announced that any discrimination in tenant selection for Stuyvesant Town was illegal. The riot stimulated greater efforts at improving race relations.

The Post-World War II Era

World War II had a positive effect upon the black condition, stimulating African-American migration to the North and the acquisition of industrial jobs. In 1944, the election of **Adam Clayton Powell, Jr.** to the United States Congress, and the election of Powell's successor to the New York City Council, Communist party member Benjamin J. Davis, contributed to the growth of militant black political leadership in Harlem. In the post-World War II era, the black population grew, heavily augmented by migration from the South and the Caribbean. The passage of state and federal discrimination legislation in housing and employment aided the expansion of the black middle class and black outmigration to other boroughs and suburbs. Between 1940 and 1950, Bedford-Stuyvesant emerged as an overwhelmingly black ghetto and by 1960 black residents had expanded into parts of Crown Heights and Brownsville. The Greater Bedford-Stuyvesant area developed into the largest black community in New York City. Nearly 40 percent of the city's blacks made their home in Brooklyn by 1970. The South Jamaica-St. Albans-Cambria Heights area of Queens also blossomed as a large area of black settlement after World War II. The black populations in other boroughs were significantly augmented by the increase in black immigration from the Caribbean following the reform of immigration laws in 1965. The 1980 census indicated that 300,000 New Yorkers were born in the non-Hispanic Caribbean, 80 percent of whom had arrived since 1965.

The center of the Caribbean black community shifted in the 1970s from the Harlem and Bedford-Stuyvesant neighborhoods to Crown Heights, East Flatbush, and the Flatbush sections of central Brooklyn. In 1980, 54.8 percent of the city's West Indian population lived in Brooklyn, with only 7.4 percent living in Manhattan. Large West Indian settlements have developed in southeastern Queens and the northeast Bronx. By the mid-1980s, many of the more prosperous West Indians had moved to the Springfield Gardens, Cambria Heights, and Laurelton sections of Queens. The rise of West Indians to national prominence was evidenced in the careers of former congresswoman, presidential candidate, and daughter of Barbadian immigrants, **Shirley Chisholm**, and **Colin Powell**, the first black chairman of the Joint Chiefs of Staff and son of Jamaican immigrants. Postwar New York City continued to serve as a beacon for black immigrants from the South and Caribbean immigrants alike, but many did not find northern cities to be the urban promised land. Employment discrimination, housing segregation, periodic instances of police brutality, and inadequate education served to disillusion some with life in New York. In the 1950s, the **Nation of Islam** had sent its most talented organizer, minister, and spokesman, **Malcolm X**, to New York City. Malcolm X not only built the Harlem Mosque into a major force in the city, but he also significantly increased the national following of the Nation of Islam through his vehement condemnations of America's history of virulent racism. His assassination in upper Manhattan in 1965 was a major setback to the advocates of black nationalism and black empowerment.

New York Art and Culture Flourishes in the late Twentieth Century

Despite their disillusionment, blacks continued their quest for empowerment in the city. The expanding black population helped elect black politicians to many new offices. In 1989, the greatest triumph of black political power in New York City was the election of David Dinkins, a product of Harlem's vital political scene, to the mayor's office. The administration of Dinkins, however, was plagued with the problems troubling all major cities. Some of these problems included the continuation of crime at unacceptable levels, an overburdened educational system, a growing underclass, a deteriorating physical infrastructure, poor minority-community relations with the police, and stagnating black impoverishment. Despite its many problems, New York City continues to be the center of African-American cultural life in the United States. In almost every area of the arts, New York City remains one of the centers for innovations, and black New Yorkers, both native and transplanted, continue to make enduring contributions. The city has a long history of black classical and theatrical music, dating back to the early decades of the century, when Will Marion Cook, Harry T. Burleigh, J. Rosamund Johnson, **Scott Joplin**, and **Eubie Blake** composed for the theater and concert hall. In the second half of the century, musicians such as William Grant Still, **Paul Robeson**, **Leontyne Price**, Martina Arroyo, and **André Watts** have had significant associations with New York. New York City has both been a home of numerous jazz movements and the place of residence for musicians such as Bud Powell, **Charlie Parker**, **Sonny Rollins**, **Max Roach**, **Miles Davis**, **Ornette Coleman**, and Cecil Taylor. Popular rhythm and blues groups such as Frankie Lymon and the Teenagers and Little Anthony, starting as street corner harmonists, were formed in New York City. Folk musicians associated with New York City include **Leadbelly**, Josh White, Sonny Terry, Brownie McGhee, and calypso and popular singer **Harry Belafonte**. There have also been a number of important dancers in New York City, including **Florence Mills**, **Pearl Primus**, and Asadata Dafora, along with more recent performers such as Arthur Mitchell and the Dance Theater of Harlem, **Alvin Ailey**, and his successor **Judith Jamison**, and modern dancer **Bill T. Jones**. New York City has also been home to tap dancers such as **Bill "Bojangles" Robinson** and **Charles "Honi" Coles** (see also **Tap Dance**).

Beginning in the late 1970s, the most significant contribution of black New Yorkers to popular music was the creation and development of rap music (see **Rap**), which originated in the housing projects of the Bronx, Manhattan, and Queens. Among the first important rap artists were Afrika Bambaata, Grand Master Flash and the Furious Five, the Sugar Hill Gang, and Run-DMC. Other important New York City rappers include LL Cool J, Kool Moe Dee, Krs-One, and Public Enemy. There have also been a number of important black writers and artists associated with New York City since the Harlem Renaissance. **James Baldwin**, a native of Harlem, used the city for the setting of several of his novels, including *Go Tell It on the Mountain* (1953). **Ralph Ellison** lived in New York for most of his adult life, and much of his novel *Invisible Man* (1952) is set in the city. Other writers associated with New York City for significant portions of their careers include **Zora Neale Hurston**, **Nella Larsen**, **John O. Killens**, **Lorraine Hansberry**, **Samuel R. Delany**, **Paule Marshall**, **Audre Lorde**, **Albert Murray**, **Gloria Naylor**, **Melvin Tolson**, and **Ann Petry**. African-American painters and sculptors from New York City include Romare Bearden, Jacob Lawrence, Richmond Barthé, Augusta Savage, and Jean-Michel Basquiat.

Racial Strife Continues

Despite the flowering of its African-American culture, New York in the late twentieth century remained a troubled racial hotbed. The divide in races was perhaps highlighted by the electoral defeat of Mayor Dinkins by former

U.S. District Attorney Rudolph Giuliani in 1993. An important factor in the election was the criticism directed at Dinkins by those who believed he excessively restrained the police when rioting broke out in Crown Heights in August 1991 between blacks and Jews after the accidental death of a black youth hit by a Hasidic driver and the subsequent murder of a Jewish rabbinical student. The event polarized the city, and brought militant community-based black protest, largely led by Brooklyn minister Al Sharpton.

Despite the city's long history of progessive social policy and massive anti-poverty spending, New York's citizens of African ancestry endured rising difficulties in the last years of the twentieth century. Among the underlying causes was the erosion of the city's base of manufacturing jobs; New York's economic problems were masked by the glittering midtown prosperity generated during the 1990s stock market boom, but the explosion in Wall Street profits held few benefits for ordinary African Americans. Dinkin's mayoral defeat inaugurated a long reign of aggressive police tactics that bred mistrust of the police in parts of the African-American community even as crime dropped sharply. Two incidents in particular received national publicity. In 1997, Haitian immigrant Abner Louima was tortured and sexually brutalized by a group of New York police officers, some of whom were later convicted of criminal offenses in connection with the incident. In 1999 an unarmed African immigrant, Amadou Diallo, was shot to death by police; the officers claimed that they had mistaken Diallo's wallet for a weapon, and they were acquitted in February of 2000.

(SEE ALSO COTTON CLUB; DAVID DINKINS; HARLEM RENAISSANCE; NEW YORK; SPIKE LEE)

New York City Draft Riot of 1863

The New York City Draft Riot, lasting five days beginning July 13, 1863, was the most violent of several protests in Northern U.S. cities during the American **Civil War** (1861–65). When the federal government announced the military conscription (or draft) act, which required all young, healthy men to register to become soldiers in the war, angry white mobs paralyzed the city.

The men protested being forced to leave their jobs and families. Adding to their anger was the long-standing economic competition between working-class whites and African Americans, as well as a strong local Democratic Party and racist newspapers that turned residents against the federal government's policies.

Mobs numbered in the thousands and were scattered throughout the city, overwhelming New York's small police force. They attacked offices and threatened the lives of whites who favored Union (federal) policies. But most of their anger was turned against blacks in the city, who were harassed, brutally beaten in the streets, and driven from their homes. The mobs burned a black orphanage and looted the Colored Seamen's Home and other black institutions. Blacks fled from their homes and took refuge outside the city. Some had themselves locked in jail for protection. The rioters murdered at least eleven blacks and injured hundreds of others.

Union army soldiers were brought in to restore order. By the time the riots were over, at least 105 people had been killed and hundreds of others had been wounded. Most of the dead and wounded were rioters. Property damage totaled millions of dollars; in some cases the mobs had destroyed entire city blocks.

New York City merchants raised money to help the black victims and to rebuild the orphanage. But no amount of money could relieve the fear caused by the lawlessness of an angry mob. After the five days of terror, many blacks left the city. By 1865 New York City had lost 20 percent of its black population.

Newspapers. *See* Liberator, The

Newton, Huey

POLITICAL ACTIVIST
February 17, 1942–August 22, 1989

Huey Newton was a revolutionary during the **Civil Rights movement** who helped found the **Black Panther Party for Self-Defense.** He is known for leading the violent wing of political activists in the fight for racial equality.

Born in Monroe, Louisiana, Newton moved with his family to California at an early age. He attended Merritt College, where he participated in civil rights activism. At the time (the 1960s), college students across the country were staging protests against racism. Some blacks began to question the ability of the Civil Rights movement to peacefully solve problems like racism, poverty, and police brutality. In the fight for black equality, Newton adopted a strategy based on "guerilla warfare," which involves use of unconventional tactics to take the enemy by surprise, such as hit-and-run attacks and ambushes.

Newton and his friend **Bobby Seale** decided to create the Black Panther Party, whose primary goal, they said, was to protect blacks from police brutality. The Panthers began making "justice patrols," carrying shotguns (which was legal at the time) and monitoring the way police treated blacks. Many police officers were opposed to this practice, and there were several violent clashes between the two forces. Newton was involved in one such clash in 1967 and was charged with murdering a police officer. Although the actual events of the incident are unclear, Newton was sentenced to two to fifteen years in prison. The event brought attention to the problem of police brutality, and protesters began a "free Huey" campaign. Newton was released from prison after an appeals court took a closer look at the incident. Upon his release, Newton tried to revive the Panther Party, which was falling apart.

In 1977 Newton was charged with another murder and decided to flee to Cuba because he feared an unfair trial. He returned to the United States in 1977 and faced the charges, which were then dropped. Newton earned a Ph.D. degree from the University of California and tried to revive his political activism. However, drug use and recurring problems with the law plagued him; he was killed in a drug-related incident in 1989.

Niagara Movement

The Niagara Movement, which was organized in 1905, was the first significant organized black protest movement in the twentieth century, and represented the attempt of a small but articulate group of radicals to challenge the then-dominant accommodationist ideas (see Accommodationism) of **Booker T. Washington**.

The Niagara Movement developed after failed attempts at reconciling the two factions in African-American political life: the accommodationists, led by Booker T. Washington, and the more militant faction, led by **W. E. B. Du Bois** and William Monroe Trotter. A closed-door meeting of representatives of the two groups at Carnegie Hall in New York City in 1904 led to an organization, the Committee of Twelve for the Advancement of the Interests of the Negro Race, but the committee fell apart due to the belief of Du Bois and Trotter that Washington was controlling the organization.

In February 1905, Du Bois and Trotter devised a plan for a "strategy board" which would fight for civil rights and serve as a counterpoint to Washington's ideas. Since they knew Washington was most popular among whites, they resolved to form an all-black organization. Along with two allies, F. L. McGhee and C. E. Bentley, they set a meeting for that summer in western New York, to which they invited fifty-nine businessmen and professionals who were known to be anti-Washingtonites.

In mid-July 1905, Du Bois went to Buffalo. He had difficulty arranging hotel reservations, and crossed to the Canadian side of Niagara Falls. Fearing reprisals by Washington, who had sent spies to Buffalo, the radicals kept their conference secret. On July 11-14, 1905, twenty-nine men met and formed a group they called the Niagara Movement, both for the conference location and for the "mighty current" of protest they wished to unleash. Du Bois was named general secretary, and the group split into various committees, of which the most important was Trotter's Press and Public Opinion Committee. The founders agreed to divide the work among state chapters, which would "cooperate with congressmen and legislators to secure just legislation for the colored people," and pursue educational and informational programs. Movement members would meet annually.

The Niagara Movement's "Declaration of Principles," drafted by Du Bois and Trotter and adopted at the close of the conference, was a powerful and clear statement of the rights of African Americans: "We believe that this class of American citizens should protest emphatically and continually against the curtailment of their political rights." The declaration went on to urge African Americans to protest the curtailment of civil rights, the denial of equal economic opportunity, and denial of education; and the authors decried unhealthy living conditions, discrimination in the military, discrimination in the justice system, **Jim Crow** railroad cars, and other injustices. "Of the above grievances we do not hesitate to complain, and to complain loudly and insistently," they stated. "Persistent manly agitation is the way to liberty, and toward this goal the Niagara Movement has started. . . ."

At the end of its first year, the organization had only 170 members and was poorly funded. Nevertheless, the Niagarites pursued their activities, distributing pamphlets, lobbying against Jim Crow, and sending a circular protest letter to President Theodore Roosevelt after the Brownsville Incident in 1906. That summer the movement had its second annual conference, at Harpers Ferry, West Virginia. This was an open meeting, and the conference speeches, and the tribute to John Brown (see **John Brown's Raid**), aroused much publicity.

The Niagara Movement, despite its impressive start, did not enjoy a long life. There was, from the start, determined opposition by **Booker T. Washington**—he prevented sympathetic white newspapers, and even many black ones, from printing the declaration—which dissuaded many blacks from joining or contributing funds. The loose organization, with only token communication between state chapters, and the radical nature, for the time, of such forthright protest, also contributed to the movement's decline. Not long after the Harper's Ferry Conference, factional struggles broke out between Du Bois and Trotter, as well as disagreements over the role of women in the movement. By the end of the summer of 1907, Trotter had been replaced as head of the Press Committee, and his supporters grew disenchanted with the movement. Du Bois tried to keep it going, guiding the movement through annual conferences in 1908 and 1909, after which it largely ceased to exist.

However, even in its decline, the movement left a lasting legacy. In 1908, Du Bois had invited Mary White Ovington, a settlement worker and socialist, to be the movement's first white member; by 1910 he had turned to the search for white allies by joining the newly organized **National Association for the Advancement of Colored People**. Despite its predominantly white leadership and centralized structure, the NAACP was really the successor to the Niagara Movement, whose remaining members Du Bois urged to join the NAACP. (However, William Monroe Trotter and his faction of the Niagara Movement never affiliated with the new organization.) The NAACP inherited many of the goals and tactics of the Niagara Movement, including the cultivation of a black elite which would defend the rights of African Americans through protest and lobbying against oppression and the publicizing of injustice.

Nicholas Brothers

TAP DANCERS

Fayard (1914–) and Harold (c. 1921–2000) Nicholas were born in Philadelphia, Pennsylvania, to parents who were entertainers. Fayard gravitated toward show business at a young age, later stating that the live performances he saw as a child were his first great influences. Fayard and Harold would go on to become one of the most popular **tap dance** acts of the twentieth century.

The children began their professional career as the Nicholas Kids and for a short time danced with their sister Dorothy in shows on the East Coast. During an appearance at the Pearl Theater in Philadelphia, the brothers were recruited to dance in New York. Their name was changed to the Nicholas Brothers, and they joined the ranks of the famous "brothers" tap acts of the twentieth century.

On April 10, 1932, they moved to the **Cotton Club** in New York's **Harlem** neighborhood, where they performed with such top bands of the period as **Cab Calloway's** (1907–1994). Throughout the 1930s the Cotton Club was their "home." The Nicholas Brothers were known as "the Show Stoppers" because they literally stopped the show each night as the closing act.

Perhaps because Fayard and Harold were children, they were the only African-American performers permitted to mingle with the exclusively white patrons of the Cotton Club. The elegant rhythms of the young stars quickly propelled them to fame. Fayard and Harold frequently left their regular act at the Cotton Club to tour with international shows and to perform in films.

From the time they were small, both Fayard and Harold danced with agility, grace, and sophistication. They choreographed many of their own dance routines and improvised (made up dance steps while performing) on stage with assurance and flair. The full use of their limber bodies and the use of their hands distinguished their dancing. The Nicholas Brothers perfected the innovative technique of doing full splits (as opposed to half splits), and they popularized acrobatic moves such as alternately jumping over each other's head in splits while descending a staircase. Their "classic" tap style blended ballet, eccentric dancing, flash, and acrobatics.

During nearly five decades in show business, Fayard and Harold toured the world from Africa to Europe. In the 1960s they appeared as guests on numerous TV shows and in 1965 performed as part of veteran entertainer Bob Hope's Christmas special for the troops fighting in the **Vietnam War** (1959–75). In the 1970s Fayard won a Tony Award for his choreography (creation and arrangement of dance steps) in the Broadway hit *Black and Blue*. The Lifetime Achievement Award of 1991 crowned the brothers' career as one of the best tap dance acts of the twentieth century. A Public Broadcasting Service (PBS) documentary (*We Sing, We Dance: The Nicholas Brothers*) tells the story of their career.

Norman, Jessye

OPERA SINGER
September 15, 1945–

Born in Augusta, Georgia, Jessye Norman was an **opera** soprano singer of promise from an early age. She graduated from **Howard University** in 1967 with a bachelor's degree in music and studied at the Peabody Conservatory before enrolling at the University of Michigan. A travel grant allowed Norman to enter the International Music Competition in Munich, Germany, in 1968, where she won first place.

She made her operatic debut as Elisabeth in German composer Richard Wagner's (1813–1883) *Tannhäuser* in 1969. In 1972 she sang *Aida* in an English production of French composer Hector Berlioz's (1803–1869) *Les Troyens*. Norman made her recital debuts in London, England, and New York City in 1973.

Diva Jessye Norman performs in Paris, France (AP/Wide World Photos. Reproduced by permission)

Norman's U.S. stage debut came on November 22, 1982, when she appeared as both Jocasta in *Oedipus Rex* (Stravinsky, 1927) and Dido in *Dido and Aeneas* (Purcell, 1689) with the Opera Company of Philadelphia. The following year she made her debut with the Metropolitan Opera.

As a recitalist, guest orchestral soloist, presenter of master classes, and recording artist, Norman is acknowledged as a musician of the highest rank. She was heard in nearly every major U.S. city by 1990 and appeared frequently on television, starting in 1979, when she gave a concert version of the first act of Wagner's *Die Walküre* (1856) with the Boston Symphony Orchestra.

Norman has excelled in French and German opera, while remaining faithful to her roots in the African-American spiritual. With a voice ranging

from a dark mezzo-soprano to a dramatic soprano, she has not hesitated to reintroduce works outside of the mainstream repertory or to perform songs of the musical theater. She has appeared on numerous recordings, including both classical and spiritual pieces.

North Carolina

First African-American Settlers: The black presence in North Carolina dates from 1526, when a large Spanish expedition from the West Indies tried to plant a colony near Cape Fear.

Slave Population: The English settlement of North Carolina in the 1650s and the Fundamental Constitutions of 1669 fixed the status of Africans as slaves. By 1790, a year after North Carolina was admitted to the Union, there were 100,572 slaves in the state; by 1860 that number had reached 331,059, one-third of the total population. Most slaves worked producing cotton, tobacco, and rice.

Free Black Population: North Carolina produced a number of exceptional blacks during the pre–**Civil War**) period, including **David Walker**, a free black from Wilmington who in 1829 published a tract demanding the immediate **abolition** of slavery.

Civil War: During the **Civil War** (1861–65) thousands of slaves defected to northern troops in eastern North Carolina. As many as five thousand black North Carolinians bore arms for the Union army.

Reconstruction: During **Reconstruction** the **Ku Klux Klan** launched a reign of terror across the state to destroy the biracial coalition of blacks and whites in the Republican Party. Despite political setbacks, efforts at black community building advanced, leading to black clubs, societies, and churches. Most African Americans served as agricultural or domestic workers; blacks composed three-fourths of the labor force in the tobacco industry.

The Great Depression: The black middle class became increasingly active in politics during the 1930s as it deserted the Republican Party for the party of Franklin D. Roosevelt and the promise of his New Deal program to end the **Great Depression**. The Great Migration of southerners to the northern states that had begun during **World War I** (1914–18) accelerated in the 1940s, and North Carolina lost 14.8 percent of its black population.

Civil Rights Movement: The **sit-in** movement that began in 1960 spread across the southern states. North Carolina contributed a number of key national figures to the **Civil Rights movement**, including **Floyd B. McKissick, Ella Baker**, and **Jesse Jackson**.

Current African-American Population: According to U.S. Census Bureau estimates, the total black population in North Carolina was 1,665,273 (22 percent of the state population) as of July 1, 1998.

Key Figures: Ella Baker (1903–1986), founder of the **Student Nonviolent Coordinating Committee**; minister and civil rights activist Jesse Jackson (1941–).

(SEE ALSO **SOUTHERN CHRISTIAN LEADERSHIP CONFERENCE**.)

North Dakota

First African-American Settlers: The Missouri River brought the first handfuls of black Americans from New Orleans, Louisiana, and St. Louis, Missouri, to the Dakotas in the early 1800s.

Free Black Population: African Americans in early North Dakota lived in a region in which slavery and the **Civil War** (1861–65) had a minimal effect. Free land enticed many black Americans to settle in North Dakota as permanent residents; they moved to the region as frontiersmen, farmers, construction workers, railroad workers, and cowboys.

Reconstruction: At least two dozen black men and women were part of the early-twentieth-century business world in North Dakota; they operated small cafes, hotels, livery barns, junkyards, and saloons. After North Dakota became a state in 1889, seasonal workers began arriving during early planting and at harvest time. By 1910 the African-American population in the state had reached 617; by 1920 that number had dropped to 467.

The Great Depression: North Dakota was affected by the dry years of the **Great Depression** and by **World War II** (1939–45) employment opportunities elsewhere. Residents, black and white, left by the thousands. By the mid-twentieth century, there were 257 African Americans in the state.

Civil Rights Movement to the Present: Beginning in 1957, U.S. Air Force bases at Minot and Grand Forks attracted a new surge of black personnel and their families to North Dakota; the black population rose from 777 in 1960 to 2,494 in 1970. The same period saw a modest rise in the number of college-oriented black students and professors.

Current African-American Population: According to U.S. Census Bureau estimates, the total black population in North Dakota was 4,001 (0.6 percent of the state population) as of July 1, 1998.

Key Figures: Leroy Robert "Satchel" Paige (1906–1982), baseball great who at one time played on a small-town North Dakota team.

Norton, Elenore Holmes

CIVIL RIGHTS LEADER
June 13, 1937–

Elenore Holmes Norton was an influential civil rights leader who used her legal expertise and political activism to promote equality in the United States. She is known for her firm commitment to gender and racial equality.

Born in Washington, D.C., Norton graduated from Antioch College in Ohio (1960) and received a master's degree (1963) and a law degree (1965) from Yale University (New Haven, Connecticut). Norton gained national attention when she defended the right of Alabama governor George Wallace, a vocal segregationist (supporter of separate schools and separate societies for blacks and whites), to run for president. Norton became active in civil rights groups while in college. After graduating, she worked as an attorney for the American Civil Liberties Union (ACLU), an organization that fights for citizens' rights. In 1970 she was appointed chair of New York's Human Rights Commission. Norton's success at unveiling cases of discrimination earned her a spot on a television program on civil rights. In 1975 she was co-author of a legal textbook on gender inequality called *Sex Discrimination and the Law.*

In 1977 President Jimmy Carter (1977–81) appointed Norton as chair of the Equal Employment Opportunity Commission (EEOC). At the EEOC she investigated discrimination cases and became a visible force in the administration. In 1990 Norton won a delegate seat in the House of Representatives, where she fought for women's rights. She gained the attention of the national media in 1992 when she escorted women seeking abortion information past protesters. Norton has taken on a greater role in Congress as a result of her diligence as well as a 1993 law which granted delegates limited voting rights. President Bill Clinton recognized Norton for her hard work by making her responsible for nominating candidates for U.S. attorney and federal judge.

Nursing

The first three American nurse-training schools were established in 1873, and in August 1879 Mary Eliza Mahoney (1845–1926) became the first black graduate nurse when she received her diploma from the New England Hospital for Women and Children in Boston, Massachusetts.

During the 1890s the establishment of a nationwide network of black hospitals and nursing schools grew rapidly as black physicians, educators, community leaders, and women's clubs became alarmed at the high rates of disease and death among blacks. In response, between 1891 and 1920 approximately two hundred black hospitals and thirty-six black nurse-training schools were established.

At that time, student nurses were used as an unpaid labor force. In every institution, they performed all of the housekeeping and maintenance chores, attended the patients, and dispensed medicine. In spite of the obstacles, hundreds of black women graduated from these segregated hospital nursing programs and went on to render priceless service to black communities.

Most black graduate nurses worked in private duty, usually for white families, for whom they frequently were expected to perform household chores in addition to providing nursing care—all for lower wages than were paid to white nurses. For many black female graduate nurses, however, the worst insult was the denial of membership in the American Nurses Association (ANA).

Rejecting the ANA for its discrimination, black graduate nurse Martha Franklin (1870–1968) launched a separate black nursing organization. Out of a meeting of fifty-two nurses in 1908 emerged the National Association of Colored Graduate Nurses (NACGN). Its leadership made the integration of the nursing profession a top priority.

During **World War II** (1939–45) the NACGN worked to attract public attention to the unfairness of quotas for African-American nurses (admitting only a certain number) established by the War Department. NACGN members met with politicians to describe the discrimination and disrespect black nurses suffered in the armed forces. They also encouraged nursing groups, black and white, to write letters and send telegrams protesting the discrimination against black nurses in the army and navy nurse corps. The growth of public support proved effective, and the War Department declared an end to quotas and exclusion of black nurses.

In 1948 the ANA's House of Delegates opened the gates to black membership and appointed a black nurse as assistant executive secretary in its national headquarters. Black nurse Estelle Riddle was elected to the board of directors. In response to the ANA's removal of barriers to black nurses, the NACGN decided to disband.

In December 1971 a new generation of black nurses, unhappy with limited integration, launched a new organization, the National Black Nurses Association (NBNA). Its goals are to act as an advocate for improving the health care of black people and to promote the professional development of black nurses. (*See also* **Hospitals, Black.**)

O'Leary, Hazel Rollins

CORPORATE EXECUTIVE
May 17, 1937–

Hazel Rollins O'Leary is a corporate executive who was the first woman to become U.S. secretary of energy. She is perhaps best known for her involvement in a scandal while working as energy secretary.

Born in Newport News, Virginia, O'Leary graduated from **Fisk University** (Nashville, Tennessee) in 1959 and earned a law degree from Rutgers University (New Brunswick, New Jersey) in 1966. Early in her career she served as assistant state attorney general for New Jersey. During the Ford and Carter administrations, O'Leary worked for the Department of Energy, where she met her future husband. In 1989 O'Leary earned an executive position with Northern States Power Company, one of the largest utility companies in the Midwest. While with the company she worked on environmental affairs, public relations, and fuel conservation.

O'Leary, a supporter of using nuclear energy, attempted to develop a nuclear storage facility in the Midwest. When the Sioux Indian Reservation protested building a storage facility on their land, O'Leary worked out a compromise to continue construction. Her success with Northern States Power earned her the position of energy secretary, making her the first woman to hold the position.

O'Leary was forced to resign in 1997, however, when it was discovered that she had been selling access to her office in exchange for contributions to her favorite charities. When the event was further investigated, she admitted to wrongdoing. In February 2000 O'Leary began working for a New York firm as an investment banker.

Odell Waller Case ▪▪▪

On September 27, 1940, Odell Waller, a black sharecropper (a farmer who rented the land he farmed, paying the rent with part of his crop) from Pittsylvania County in Virginia was sentenced to death for killing his landlord, a white man named Oscar W. Davis, after a hasty trial before an all-white jury. There was no doubt that Waller had shot Davis, possibly in self-defense, during a dispute arising over Davis's refusal to give the Waller family its share of the wheat crop, but otherwise the case was full of uncertainties.

Waller's plight attracted the attention of the Workers Defense League (WDL), a socialist organization (one advocating collective ownership of property and supporting the working class). After Waller's conviction the WDL led a campaign to save him that attracted national attention and won the support of many prominent Americans. For many people, Waller became a symbol of the country's racial and economic problems.

The WDL's principal argument was that Waller had not been tried by a jury of his peers. Not only were all the jurors white, six were landlords who hired sharecroppers. But the defense lawyers failed to convince either the Virginia or the federal courts that Waller's constitutional rights had been violated, and on July 2, 1942, Waller was put to death in Virginia's electric chair in Richmond.

Odetta ▪▪▪

FOLK SINGER
December 31, 1930–

Odetta (born Odetta Holmes Gordon) grew up in Los Angeles, California, and by the age of thirteen she was studying piano, singing, and playing the guitar. In the early 1950s the rich-voiced Odetta emerged as an important figure on the San Francisco and New York **folk music** scenes. She began performing and recording more widely, presenting a varied mix of spirituals, slave songs, prison and work songs, folk ballads, Caribbean songs, and blues. She also appeared in the film *Sanctuary* (1961).

In the early 1960s Odetta began to address political and social issues. She became an important advocate for civil rights and took part in the historic 1963 civil rights march in Washington, D.C. Throughout the 1960s and 1970s Odetta continued to perform internationally and record. In 1974 she appeared in the television film *The Autobiography of Miss Jane Pittman*. In 1986 she presented a concert marking forty years of her life as a performer. The concert performance was released as a live recording, *Movin' It On*, in 1987.

Odetta has received acclaim throughout the world as one of the central figures of modern folk music. In 1998 she released a CD, *To Ella*, in tribute to her late friend **Ella Fitzgerald.** In 2000 she released *Odetta: Blues Everywhere I Go.*

Ohio

First African-American Settlers: African Americans have been in Ohio at least since the eighteenth century, when the state played a crucial role in both the **Underground Railroad** and the **abolition** movement.

Slave Population: Although the Northwest Ordinance of 1787 outlawed slavery in the area, proslavery forces still tried—but failed—to make Ohio a slave state. Although slavery was prohibited, it was still common for Kentucky slaves to be hired for work on Ohio tobacco plantations and factories; slave owners were protected by law when vacationing or traveling in the state with their slaves.

Free Black Population: The state constitution, which took effect when Ohio entered the Union in 1803, denied black suffrage (voting rights) but left no other restrictions on civil rights. Black codes (laws regulating the activities of blacks) instituted in 1804, however, denied blacks the right to hold political office, to serve in the state militia or on juries, to testify against whites in court, to receive public charity, or to send their children to public schools. African Americans were still drawn to the state by agricultural work and the Ohio River trade.

Civil War: Several volunteer black companies were formed at the outset of the **Civil War** (1861–65) but were refused military service; blacks were instead organized into labor gangs. When the governor of Ohio became desperate to fill enlistment quotas, however, the 127th Ohio Volunteer Regiment was organized. Ultimately, five thousand Ohio blacks served in the Union army. During the war years the state's black population increased as escaping or emancipated (freed) slaves migrated north.

Reconstruction: Ratification of the **Fifteenth Amendment**—rejected by Ohio in 1869 and barely passed in 1870—brought blacks voting rights and the right to sit on juries. Increasing racial tension, however, led to violence that erupted at the turn of the twentieth century in **lynching**s and rioting.

The Great Depression: Black urban growth and housing discrimination led to the creation of dilapidated neighborhoods to which blacks were confined. The **Great Depression** brought widespread misery as overtaxed community institutions were unable to respond to poverty and provide adequate health care. **World War II** (1939–45) brought renewed migration to Ohio's cities; for example, between 1940 and 1960 Cincinnati's black population increased by 72,000.

Civil Rights Movement: During the 1960s, anger over chronic discrimination and police harassment led to racial uprisings. Over time, however, blacks were able to transform their population growth into political power. Carl B. Stokes of Cleveland set a landmark in African-American history in 1967 when he became the first black elected mayor of a large city.

Current African-American Population: According to U.S. Census Bureau estimates, the total black population in Ohio was 1,289,760 (11 percent of the state population) as of July 1, 1998.

Key Figures: Poet James Madison Bell (1826–1902); **Paul Laurence Dunbar** (1872–1906), writer; **Hallie Quinn Brown** (1850–1949), national

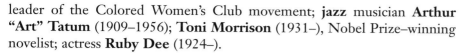

leader of the Colored Women's Club movement; **jazz** musician **Arthur "Art" Tatum** (1909–1956); **Toni Morrison** (1931–), Nobel Prize–winning novelist; actress **Ruby Dee** (1924–).

(SEE ALSO WILBERFORCE UNIVERSITY.)

Oklahoma

First African-American Settlers: The first blacks arrived in Oklahoma in the 1830s via the notorious Trail of Tears, the forced exodus of more than fourteen thousand members of the Cherokee Nation from their native lands in the southeastern United States to Indian Territory in the West. An estimated four thousand died on the journey. With them went thousands of their African-American slaves, as well as some free blacks.

Slave Population: Slaveholding American Indians transferred their agricultural system to the new land; some planted cotton but most slaves were employed growing foodstuffs and serving as domestics. Despite slave uprisings in 1841 and 1853, the social and legal status of blacks in Indian territories declined through the pre–Civil War period.

Free Black Population: Although a community of **free blacks** existed in early Oklahoma, they were denied suffrage (the right to vote) and, often, education. Racial tension increased through the nineteenth century.

Civil War: The **Civil War** (1861–65) disrupted the American Indian slave economy and caused internal warfare. In 1861 federal troops left the territory, forcing antislavery Indians and blacks alike to flee to Kansas.

Reconstruction: In 1889 the Oklahoma Territory was created and opened to non-Indian settlement. No racial barriers were created to land ownership, and Oklahoma already had a thriving black farming community. By 1890 there were 3,000 black settlers in the territory who grew cotton or food crops. Oklahoma's black population climbed to 55,000 by 1900 and 113,000 by 1910; most worked as farmers, railroad workers, cowboys, and laborers. Race relations worsened, however, and when Oklahoma was admitted to the Union in 1907, its first state legislature segregated public transportation and waiting rooms and made interracial marriage a felony.

The Great Depression: Chronic agricultural depression and soil erosion, coupled with taxation and white harassment, forced many black farmers to sell their land to white planters. Many moved to urban areas and found work as low-paid manual laborers or domestic servants. After the depression and following decades of overt racial discrimination, African Americans saw the desegregation of public universities in 1948 and public schools in 1955.

Civil Rights Movement: By the mid-1960s the **sit-in** movement had spread to Oklahoma, and by 1964 almost all state public accommodations had been forced to desegregate.

Current African-American Population: According to U.S. Census Bureau estimates, the total black population in Oklahoma was 261,945 (8 percent of the state population) as of July 1, 1998.

Key Figures: Poet **Melvin Beaunorus Tolson** (1898–1966); **Ralph Ellison** (1914–1994), writer; historian **John Hope Franklin** (1915–).

(SEE ALSO **JAZZ**.)

Opera

Opera began in Italy during the early seventeenth century as a form of musical storytelling. During the past two hundred years, African Americans have played an important role in its development as an art form.

African Americans have performed in operas since the early nineteenth century, even though they were barred from performing in major opera houses in the United States. As a result, many well-qualified singers either pursued careers in Europe or confined their performances to concerts. One of the first prominent African-American opera singers was Elizabeth Taylor Greenfield (c. 1824–1876). Born a slave in Mississippi, Greenfield was known as "the Black Swan." She performed with a troupe of African-American opera singers in the United States, Canada, and England throughout the 1850s and 1860s.

The first known African-American opera company was the Colored American Opera Company of Philadelphia, Pennsylvania, and Washington, D.C. It staged performances in 1873 and 1879. Twelve years later Theodore Drury, a highly trained opera tenor, started his own company, which performed full operas by the turn of the twentieth century. Between 1900 and 1910, his company appeared in New York City; Boston, Massachusetts; Providence, Rhode Island; and Philadelphia, Pennsylvania.

One of the most famous African-American opera singers of the twentieth century was **Marian Anderson** (1897–1993). Barred from the opera stage in the United States, Anderson became a famous concert singer. The most dramatic moment in her career occurred in 1939, when she was barred from performing in a Washington, D.C., concert hall. This act of racial discrimination drew protests from First Lady Eleanor Roosevelt (1884–1962) and others. Anderson was invited to give an outdoor recital on the steps of the Lincoln Memorial, where she performed to an audience of 75,000.

Although some major companies, such as the New York City Opera, cast African Americans as early as the 1940s, the Metropolitan Opera in New York City did not allow African-American performers until 1955, when Anderson sang a starring role in an opera by Italian composer Verdi (1813–1901). Outside the concert hall African-American singers were often confined to operas that had all-black casts, such as Virgil Thomson's *Four Saints in Three Acts* (1933) and American composer George Gershwin's (1898–1937) *Porgy and Bess* (1935).

African-American opera singers were not fully accepted by major American opera companies until the 1960s, when **Leontyne Price** (1927–) was welcomed by the U.S. opera establishment. In 1966 Price opened the season at the Metropolitan Opera House in New York's Lincoln Center, in a role that was written for her.

AFRICAN AMERICANS AND OPERA: THE CONCERT SPIRITUAL

One unique contribution that African-American singers made to opera and concerts was the development of the concert spiritual. This music combined melodies from African-American religious traditions with the harmonies of European opera. For many African-American singers, their first exposure to classical singing occurred in church or while listening to a recital of religious music and spirituals. Because they were not allowed on the opera stage, many classically trained African-American singers became primarily known through their concerts, and their songs frequently included spirituals as well as European opera.

The two most prominent African-American women opera singers in the 1980s and early 1990s were **Kathleen Battle** (1948–) and **Jessye Norman** (1945–). Battle began her American career at the Metropolitan Opera House (or "Met"), and Norman sang in the major opera houses of Europe throughout the 1970s before her first appearance at the Met in 1983. In 1991 the two singers performed together at New York City's Carnegie Hall. By the late 1990s another woman, Denyce Graves, was being talked about as the next African-American opera diva (principal singer). From a poverty-stricken childhood in Washington, D.C., Graves rocketed to stardom after being discovered by the famous opera singer Placido Domingo, when Graves played "Emilia" in a production of the opera *Otello*.

Male African-American singers have not enjoyed the same success as their female counterparts. Many believe that this is because opera companies are reluctant to cast African-American men with white women. Nevertheless, some African-American men have managed to build impressive careers in the opera, including **Simon Estes** (1938–), Kevin Short, and Vinson Cole.

African-American operatic talent has been supported by the establishment of educational programs and opera companies for aspiring singers. **Fisk University, Hampton University,** Morgan State University, Virginia State University, and **Wilberforce University** have produced major operatic talent. The 1970s saw a boom in African-American opera productions with the establishment of two major companies, Opera/South (1970) and the National Ebony Opera (1974). These were founded specifically to create professional opportunities for African-American performers, writers, conductors, and technicians.

As opera has become more available to African-American artists, major opera houses have produced new works and also revived older works by African-American composers. In 1993 bandleader and composer **Duke Ellington**'s (1899–1974) unfinished opera, *Queenie Pie*, was performed for the first time at the Brooklyn Academy of Music. African-American singers are widely recognized both for their artistic excellence and their popular appeal. However, male performers continue to claim that they are not cast as readily as women in opera productions, and African-American composers continue to encounter resistance to works about African-American subjects.

(See also **M. Sissieretta "Black Patti" Jones, Dorothy Maynor, Mattiwilda Dobbs, Anthony Davis, Scott Joplin.***)*

Oregon

First African-American Settlers: The first documented African American in Oregon arrived in 1788 as a member of a fur-trading crew. Other blacks soon arrived as explorers and pioneers.

Slave Population: Slaves accompanied white explorers and pioneers to Oregon. The best-known early African American in Oregon was York, a slave of William Clark's of the Lewis and Clark expedition. Slavery was banned in 1843, but when Oregon became a state in 1859, the state constitution included an article forbidding black residence, employment, property holding, and voting.

Free Black Population: During the fur-trading era (1820–1840), the western frontier provided African Americans with an appealing alternative to the rigid slave system of the South and the harsh discrimination of the North and the East. Although many endured a persistent antiblack sentiment, some blacks prospered as guides and farmers. The 1850 census listed 207 blacks in Oregon.

Civil War: Oregon supported the Union in the **Civil War** (1861–65) but instituted new laws banning African Americans from juries, forbidding interracial marriages, and establishing a black poll tax. The exclusion law was not repealed until 1926, and the marriage law was not done away with until 1955.

Reconstruction: The establishment of **Jim Crow** laws (providing for segregated accommodations and transportation) proceeded in the late nineteenth century, and in 1906 the state Supreme Court pronounced them legal. Blacks accounted for less than 0.3 percent of Oregon's population into the 1940s.

The Great Depression: The economic hardships of the **Great Depression** led to the collapse of many black-owned businesses. During **World War II** (1939–45), however, thousands of African Americans were recruited to work in Portland's shipbuilding industry; from 1940 to 1943 the area's black population increased tenfold to over twenty thousand.

Civil Rights Movement to the Present: The increase in the black population and in their economic power produced political activism that transformed African-American life in Oregon. Laws concerning fair employment (1949), public accommodations (1953), and fair housing (1957) led to a new era of black civil rights.

Current African-American Population: According to U.S. Census Bureau estimates, the total black population in Oregon was 60,949 (1.8 percent of the state population) as of July 1, 1998.

Key Figures: Moses "Black" Harris (c. 1800–1849), expert guide and explorer; George Washington Bush (1817–1905), prosperous farmer and humanitarian.

(SEE ALSO **KU KLUX KLAN.**)

Jesse Owens running a race in the 1936 Olympics (Courtesy of the Library of Congress)

Owens, James Cleveland "Jesse"

ATHLETE
September 12, 1913–March 31, 1980

James Cleveland "Jesse" Owens was known for his tremendous athletic achievements as well as his undying commitment to promoting a spirit of national pride in the United States. Born in Oakville, Alabama, Owens moved with his family to Cleveland, Ohio, for economic reasons. A talented athlete in high school, Owens was encouraged by his physical education teacher, Charles Riley, to take advantage of his extraordinary gift. Owens attended Ohio State University, where he set a world record in the 220-yard sprint, the 220-yard hurdles, and the long jump.

Owens stole the show at the 1936 Olympics, winning several gold medals and breaking world records in the 100- and 200-meter dashes, the long jump, and the relay competition. After the Olympics, Owens declined several business offers and opened a dry cleaning business. The business went bankrupt,

Hitler "Refuses" to Shake Owens' Hand

During the 1936 Olympic Games, Europe was on the verge of World War II (1939–45). The games were attended by Nazi German leader Adolf Hitler, who was known for his racist theories of German superiority. Owens was the star of the events, which essentially made a mockery of Hitler's racist beliefs. Sportswriters reported that Hitler refused to shake Owens's hand to deliberately show disrespect for his remarkable achievements. The story turned out to be false; however, because it made for a good story, it was often passed on—and is even today—as if it were true.

and Owens returned to Ohio State to finish his degree. He was unable to finish college and got a job as a supervisor at Ford Motor Company.

Owens became a popular spokesman for American patriotism during the cold war period (a period of heightened tensions and weapons rivalry between the United States and the former Soviet Union following **World War II**). He began making speeches on the importance of athletics and having pride in one's country. The U.S. State Department eventually sent him to foreign countries to improve relations. President Dwight D. Eisenhower (1890–1969) appointed Owens goodwill ambassador to the 1956 Olympics. Although Owens remained faithful to promoting pride in the United States, he was criticized by blacks during the **Civil Rights movement**. Some blacks believed that he was betraying the problem of racism by speaking favorably of the United States. Nevertheless, Owens was honored for his dedication to the United States by being awarded the Medal of Freedom Award (1976) and the Living Legends Award (1979).

Owens, Jesse. *See* Owens, James Cleveland

Page, Alan Cedric

LAWYER, FOOTBALL PLAYER
August 7, 1945–

Born in Canton, Ohio, Alan Page grew up with dreams of pursuing a career in law and developing his talent in **football**. He received his B.A. degree from the University of Notre Dame, South Bend, Indiana, in 1967, where he became an All-American defensive end. Page went on to play professionally for the Minnesota Vikings from 1967 to 1978. From 1978 to 1981, Page played for the Chicago Bears. He was inducted into the NFL Hall of Fame in 1988.

After his rookie season with Minnesota, Page enrolled in the law school at the University of Minnesota in Minneapolis. Unable to devote the necessary time to his studies, he put off law school until 1975, when he re-enrolled at the University of Minnesota. He was able to complete his degree in 1978.

"My heroes are young people who have worked their way out of circumstances others would succumb to."

(Source: Alan Page. "Thanks, Your Honor," by Steve Rushin. *Sports Illustrated,* 31 July 2000.

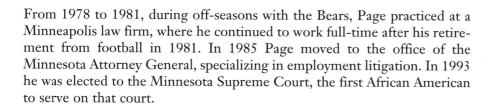
From 1978 to 1981, during off-seasons with the Bears, Page practiced at a Minneapolis law firm, where he continued to work full-time after his retirement from football in 1981. In 1985 Page moved to the office of the Minnesota Attorney General, specializing in employment litigation. In 1993 he was elected to the Minnesota Supreme Court, the first African American to serve on that court.

Paige, Leroy Robert "Satchel"

BASEBALL PLAYER
July 7, 1906–June 8, 1982

Leroy Robert "Satchel" Paige was one of the greatest **baseball** players to emerge from the Negro leagues. He is known for being the best pitcher in the Negro National League and the first African American to be inducted into the Baseball Hall of Fame on the basis of achievements outside of the major leagues.

Born in Mobile, Alabama, Paige was raised in a poor family. He earned his nickname as a boy carrying "satchels" (small bags) from the Mobile train station. At a young age Paige was sent to a reform school for stealing toy rings. While at the school he developed a knack for pitching.

In 1948 Paige was hired by the Cleveland Indians at the age of forty-two. He was the first African-American pitcher to play in the American League. Paige helped the Indians win the league pennant.

Although Paige played in the major leagues toward the end of his career, he is best known for his achievements in "independent" baseball leagues. Independent leagues were composed of players, such as blacks, who were not permitted to play in the majors because of the racist environment of the time. He played for teams in the Negro leagues in the 1920s and 1930s, where he teamed up with **Josh Gibson** to take part in one of the greatest hitting tandems in the history of baseball. He also played for teams in the Dominican Republic, Mexico, Cuba, and Venezuela. During his remarkable career Paige is believed to have pitched fifty-five no-hitters and won 2,000 out of 2,500 games

Paige was an unusually large man for a pitcher (six feet three and one-half inches tall and 180 pounds). He threw a lightening-fast ball that became known as the "bee ball" because, like a bee, it buzzed by but could not be seen. Paige's five decades of pitching went highly unnoticed by the major leagues, but he was recognized for his talents after he retired in 1967.

Painting and Sculpture

From the time of their first arrival in the New World, Africans were involved in a wide range of artistic efforts. Much of this early art was a reflection of the many craft activities that blacks were involved in, including building houses, making iron fences, weaving baskets, manufacturing pottery, and sewing quilts.

African-American participation in European styles of artwork was slower to develop. It is likely that persons of African descent first created European artworks at the command of their masters and white patrons, who wished them to make copies of works in fashionable styles. Most of the black crafts workers and artists in the eighteenth century were anonymous; a few references to them were seen in newspaper advertisements for their services or in notices for **fugitive slaves.**

The **Harlem Renaissance** (c. 1917–1935) marked the arrival of a new movement in art and culture in which African Americans were encouraged to incorporate African styles into their work. The beauty and creativity of the Harlem Renaissance flourished in places such as Cleveland, Ohio; San Francisco, California; **Atlanta, Georgia**; Philadelphia, Pennsylvania; Boston, Massachusetts; and Chicago, Illinois, in addition to New York City. These communities provided environments that gave artists a continuously rich supply of cultural material.

By 1934 the **Great Depression** had put at least ten thousand artists out of work. In 1935 President Franklin D. Roosevelt (1882–1945) formed the Works Progress Administration (WPA) to create jobs at every level of the skill ladder in order to preserve professional and technical skills while helping individuals keep their self-respect. Artists in the program were paid $15 to $90 a month for a variety of assignments. The WPA gave many artists a sense of collective purpose and provided them with the resources to develop their talent for the first time.

One of the most important forms of African-American artistic expression in the twentieth century was "folk art." Folk art refers to the work of artists who have not had the benefit of formal art-school training and whose work often appears simple and self-taught. Many folk artists took up art as a hobby later in life, as a religious call, or as a major change in their lifestyle or career.

By the 1970s, the variety of African-American art expanded greatly, partly because of the new attention and confidence black artists gained as they became more skilled in their work. Present-day African-American art represents the highest point of the work of many generations of creative black painters and sculptors. Few groups have been as important as African-American artists in directing attention to issues such as race, gender, identity, culture, and politics. (*See also* **Great Depression and New Deal; Folk Arts and Crafts.**)

Parker, Charlie Christopher "Bird"

JAZZ ALTO SAXOPHONIST
August 29, 1920–March 23, 1955

Often known as "Bird," or "Yardbird," Charlie Parker was probably the greatest American jazz alto saxophonist ever, as well as an innovative composer and a founder of the **jazz** style known as "bebop." He took saxophone playing to a level never reached before, making other musicians regard him with awe. Gifted jazz saxophonist **John Coltrane** (1926–1967) switched

Charlie "Bird" Parker (Archive Photos. Reproduced by permission)

from the alto to the tenor saxophone because he dreaded the idea of being compared with Parker.

Born in Kansas City, Missouri, Parker was eleven when his mother bought him an alto saxophone. By the time he was fifteen, he had become a professional musician and left school. He spent two years playing in bands in the Kansas City area, absorbing all he could about music. Parker went to New York City in 1939 and later began playing in a band led by Jay McShann. It was with this band that he made his first recording, in 1941.

In 1942 Parker joined the **Earl Hines** (1903–1983) orchestra, which featured trumpeter **Dizzy Gillespie.** Parker and Gillespie teamed up to launch a new jazz style, bebop.

In 1944 Parker, Gillespie, and others joined the **Billy Eckstine** (1914–1993) band, one of the first to introduce new jazz developments. This band provided a platform for Parker's improvisations (new "twists" on the way a piece of music is usually played). Parker began to record heavily in 1945 and performed regularly, even though some criticized his new music.

Parker returned to New York and in 1947 formed a quintet (group of five) featuring trumpeter **Miles Davis** (1926–1991). Between 1947 and 1951 the quintet recorded some of Parker's most creative new compositions, like "Now's the Time," "Ornithology," "Scrapple from the Apple," and "Yardbird Suite."

Parker later became addicted to alcohol and the drug heroin, and his health began to deteriorate during the mid-1940s. In 1951 he was barred from performing in New York City nightclubs for two years because of his continual trouble with drug police. His finances also began a downward spiral, from which he never recovered.

Parker performed in a landmark concert in 1953 in Toronto, Canada, with Gillespie, pianist Bud Powell (1924–1966), bassist **Charles Mingus** (1922–1979), and drummer **Max Roach** (1924–). Parker's last great musical statement, the concert included many pieces he and Gillespie had created during the 1940s, such as "Night in Tunisia" and "Hot House."

After the Toronto concert, his physical and mental health became so bad that he attempted suicide. He finally committed himself to a hospital. Parker's last public performance was in March 1955 at Birdland, the New York City club named for him. He died of a heart seizure in a friend's apartment.

Parks, Gordon Sr.

PHOTOGRAPHER
November 30, 1912–

Gordon Parks has achieved international recognition in a wide variety of fields, including **photography,** filmmaking, and music. He is also the first mainstream African-American photojournalist and the first African American to direct a major Hollywood **film.**

Parks was born in Fort Scott, Kansas. His mother's death when Gordon was sixteen led to the family's breakup, and Parks moved north to live with a married sister in Minneapolis. The teenager was soon on his own, struggling to attend high school and support himself.

Parks always wrote, composed, and read, absorbing on his own what he had been unable to study in school.

A cameraman's live presentation of his battle-action footage in a Chicago, Illinois, movie theater inspired Parks to take up photography, and in 1937 he acquired his first camera. Largely self-taught, he took his earliest photographs with only a few pointers from the camera salesman. Quickly mastering technique, he intuitively found the subjects most meaningful to him. The same local Minneapolis camera store soon gave him his first exhibition.

Parks worked as a fashion photographer in Chicago and also photographed the grim poverty on the city's South Side. In 1948 he joined the staff of *Life* magazine and spent two years at the magazine's Paris, France, office.

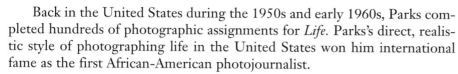

Back in the United States during the 1950s and early 1960s, Parks completed hundreds of photographic assignments for *Life*. Parks's direct, realistic style of photographing life in the United States won him international fame as the first African-American photojournalist.

Parks's longest assignment began in 1961, when he traveled to Brazil to photograph the slums of Rio de Janeiro. His story of Flavio da Silvia, a poverty-stricken Brazilian boy whom Parks found dying of asthma, attracted international attention that resulted in Flavio and his family receiving gifts, medical treatment, and, finally, a new home. At the same time, with the emerging **Civil Rights movement,** Parks undertook a new role at *Life*: interpreting the activities and personalities of the movement, in words as well as pictures, from a personal perspective. His 1971 anthology *Born Black* is a collection of these essays and images.

A gifted storyteller, Parks began his autobiographical book cycle in 1963 with *The Learning Tree*, a well-received novel that drew on the author's own childhood experiences and memories. This was followed in 1966 by *A Choice of Weapons*, which recounted the events and influences that enabled Parks to overcome prejudice and personal hardship.

Parks also gained distinction as a poet, composer, and filmmaker. In 1969 Parks became the first African American to direct a major Hollywood film, *The Learning Tree*. He also produced and wrote the script for movie and directed a number of other films, including the highly popular *Shaft* (1971), *Leadbelly* (1976), and *The Odyssey of Solomon Northup* (1984), about a free black sold into **slavery.** In addition, Parks completed the music for a ballet about **Rev. Martin Luther King Jr.** (1929–1968) and worked on a novel based on the life of J. M. W. Turner, the nineteenth-century English landscape painter.

Parks, Rosa Louise McCauley

CIVIL RIGHTS LEADER
February 4, 1913–

Rosa Louise McCauley Parks was a courageous leader of the **Civil Rights movement.** Parks is best known for her refusal to give up her seat for a white man on a segregated bus. Because of her heroic stance against racism, Parks is widely considered to be "the mother of the Civil Rights movement."

Born in Tuskegee, Alabama, Parks lived and went to high school in Montgomery, Alabama. She attended Alabama State College and worked as an insurance salesperson and a tailor before entering the **Civil Rights movement.** In 1943 she became the first woman to join the **National Association for the Advancement of Colored People (NAACP)** in Montgomery. Her early work with the NAACP focused on helping young blacks improve their lives. She also helped increase black voter registration, after which she earned a scholarship to work on integrating schools. At the time, segregated schools prevented blacks from attending the same public schools as whites. Parks's experience working on the project served to fuel her dream for racial harmony.

PARKS'S FAMOUS BUS TRIP

While taking a bus trip in Montgomery, Alabama, Parks refused to give up her seat for a white man. At the time there were separate seats for blacks and whites on buses. The reason that Parks took the seat has been widely misunderstood. Parks was characterized as simply being a tired woman who wanted to rest her feet. However, she later reported in her book *Rosa Parks: My Story* that she was not tired at all. In fact, she said "The only tired I was, was tired of giving in [to the customs of a racist society]."

In 1955 Parks set off the **Montgomery bus boycott** when she refused to give up her seat on a bus for a white man. (At the time, blacks and whites sat in separate sections in the bus.) Parks helped direct the boycott, which resulted in a Supreme Court ruling that segregating public buses was unconstitutional. After the boycott, Parks began working for Congressman **John F. Conyers** in **Detroit, Michigan**, and continued her civil rights activism. In 1987 she managed to fulfill a dream of hers to establish a youth center for blacks.

Parks gave numerous speeches on racism and won many awards for her work, including the NAACP's highest award, the Spingarn Medal, and the Martin Luther King Jr. Nonviolent Peace Prize. In the 1990s she wrote three books, including an **autobiography,** and gave a speech at the **Million Man March** (1996). In July 2000 Parks was honored by Congress when funds were granted for the creation of the Rosa Parks Library, Museum, and Learning Center in Montgomery, Alabama.

Patterson, Floyd

BOXER
January 4, 1935–

Floyd Patterson was a heavyweight champion boxer. He is known for being a "gentle giant." On one occasion he helped an opponent by picking up his mouthpiece and handing it to him.

Born in Waco, North Carolina, Patterson grew up in the slums of Brooklyn, New York. He often got into trouble as a boy, which landed him in a correctional facility for youths. While there, he learned to read and to box.

Patterson's talent for **boxing** showed instantly; he won the Golden Gloves award twice and won a gold medal in the 1952 Olympics. After becoming a professional boxer, in 1956 he won the heavyweight championship by knocking out black fighter **Archie Moore.** In 1959 Patterson was defeated in a fight he was expected to win against Ingemar Johansson. After going into seclusion he returned to the ring a year later and defeated Johansson in a five-round knockout.

Patterson's boxing career ended with two discouraging defeats by **Sonny Liston** and a career record of fifty-five wins, eight losses, and one draw. He

Walter "Sweetness" Payton in action
(AP/Wide World Photos. Reproduced by
permission)

retired in 1972 and became the head of the New York State Athletic
Commission. He was elected to the Boxing Hall of Fame in 1977 and the
Olympic Hall of Fame in 1987. In 1998 he resigned from the athletic com-
mission.

Payton, Walter Jerry "Sweetness"

FOOTBALL PLAYER
July 25, 1954–November 1, 1999

Walter Jerry Payton was one of the greatest running backs in the history
of professional **football.** He is known for his graceful footwork on the field
and for his high-class sportsmanship.

Born and raised in Columbia, Mississippi, Payton began playing football in high school. He attended Jackson State University where he earned the nickname "Sweetness," which described the elegance with which he carried the ball. He graduated from Jackson State in 1964 as the all-time leading scorer, with 464 points. He was selected in the first round of the National Football League (NFL) draft in 1975. Payton enjoyed a remarkable career with the Chicago Bears, during which he set the standard for NFL running backs. He set a record for most yards in a game in 1977 (275), rushed for more than one thousand yards ten different seasons, and was selected to the Pro Bowl ten times. Payton retired from Football in 1987 with the career record for rushing yards (16,726). He was inducted into the NFL Hall of Fame in 1993.

After retiring from football, Payton took up race car driving and opened a business called 34 Enterprises (34 was his football jersey number). On November 1, 1999, football fans across the globe were saddened by the news of Walter Payton's death; he died of a rare form of liver cancer.

Pennsylvania

First African-American Settlers: As early as 1639, Africans were recorded as being in servitude to Swedish settlers.

Slave Population: The first documented slaves arrived at the new city of Philadelphia in 1684 aboard the ship *Isabella*. Most Pennsylvania slaves worked as laborers, domestics, or craftspeople, while a few worked at charcoal iron forges. During the early 1800s the state played an important role in the **Underground Railroad.** A strong proslavery and antiblack sentiment pervaded the state, however, as evidenced by segregated facilities, race riots, and threats against black activists.

Free Black Population: By the early eighteenth century, Pennsylvania was home to a significant free black population because of the efforts of **abolition** (antislavery) societies. The 1790 state constitution conferred to freemen the right to vote, although slavery was not outlawed until the 1840s.

Civil War: Blacks were admitted to the Union (northern) army in 1863 and Camp William Penn was established to train black Union soldiers. Ten black regiments fought on Southern battlefields and served during the **Reconstruction** era.

Reconstruction: Following the end of the **Civil War** (1861–65) Pennsylvania's black population increased as a result of migration from the South. African-American communities were further transformed by the Great Migration triggered by the start of **World War I** (1914–18), leading to competition for scarce housing and leisure facilities.

The Great Depression: In response to the serious unemployment and poverty brought on by the **Great Depression,** community relief efforts were organized by African Americans. The coming of **World War II** (1939–45) brought renewed black migration and led to increased social and economic opportunity.

Civil Rights Movement to the Present: Elected black officials played prominent roles in securing such equal rights actions as the 1961 open housing law. Although campaigns led by civil rights activists helped to establish equal rights laws, frustration due to persistent discrimination sparked racial uprisings.

Current African-American Population: According to U.S. Census Bureau estimates, the total black population in Pennsylvania was 1,166,151 (10 percent of the state population) as of July 1, 1998.

Key Figures: Jazz musician **Earl "Fatha" Hines** (1903–1983); opera signer **Marian Anderson** (1897–1993); Hall of Fame catcher **Roy Campanella** (1921–1993); basketball legend **Wilt Chamberlain** (1936–); **Bill Cosby** (1937–), comedian and philanthropist; playwright **August Wilson** (1945–); **David Henry Bradley Jr.** (1950–), award-winning novelist.

(SEE ALSO **AFRICAN METHODIST EPISCOPAL (AME) CHURCH**.)

Pentecostalism

From its beginning at the Azusa Street Revival in Los Angeles, California, in 1906, black Pentecostalism has grown to become the second-largest religious movement among African Americans and one of the fastest-growing religions in the United States.

Founders and Early Movements

Charles Parham (1873–1929) of Topeka, Kansas, was one of the early founders of Pentecostalism, a Christian religious sect. He placed great importance on the baptism of the apostles, early followers of Jesus Christ, by God's Holy Spirit, as described in the biblical Book of Acts, Chapter 2. This is said to have occurred about two thousand years ago, on the fiftieth day after Christ arose from the tomb after being crucified (known as the Day of Pentecost; hence, the name of the movement). The apostles began speaking in languages that they did not understand but that were understood by people from other lands who were present at the time, because the languages were their own native tongues.

Parham, along with many others in the Pentecostal movement, associated the spiritual experience called "glossolalia," or "speaking in tongues," with the original event on the Day of Pentecost. Pentecostals saw speaking in tongues as evidence of baptism by God's Holy Spirit. Parham began preaching this new doctrine in 1901 among "Holiness" groups (followers of a movement started in the 1800s and based on the baptism of the Holy Spirit).

Parham was white, and his school in Houston, Texas, like most institutions during the early 1900s, was segregated. A black man named William J. Seymour (1870–1922) enrolled in 1905, even though he was not allowed to sit with white students. Seymour did not have the experience of speaking in tongues himself, but he adopted the school's teachings and carried them in 1906 to Los Angeles, where he was invited to serve as minister in a small Holiness church. Its leader, however, rejected Seymour's Pentecostal teachings and barred him from the church. Seymour began preaching in a member's home. After he and other members began speaking in tongues, they moved to larger facilities at 312 Azusa Street, the former home of the First African Methodist Episcopal (AME) Church.

Soon, Holiness movement members from across the United States came by the thousands to the religious revival on Azusa Street to learn about the new doctrine and experience speaking in tongues. Within twelve months, the Azusa Street Mission had created an international movement and begun publishing the journal *Apostolic Faith*. This center helped Pentecostalism spread throughout the United States and to Great Britain, Scandinavia, Brazil, Egypt, and India.

Early Pentecostalism was an interracial (with both blacks and whites) movement and one in which both men and women could serve as ministers. The Pentecostal leadership was strongly against the white terrorist **Ku Klux Klan,** and leaders and churches were often the target of Klan violence. As time went on, however, racism crept in, with both whites and blacks leaving congregations whose members were largely of the other race.

Pentecostal Denominations

Pentecostalism split into two beliefs over the doctrine of God: "Trinitarian" and "Oneness." Trinitarians hold the classic Christian belief in God as three beings—the Father, the Son, and the Holy Spirit—in one. Some black Pentecostal Trinitarian denominations are the Church of God in Christ—which in 2000 was the major African-American Pentecostal denomination—the United Holy Church, and the Church of the Living God.

Oneness groups—who began to call themselves "Apostolic" churches—claim that Jesus Christ is God, who expresses himself as the Father, Son, and Holy Spirit but is not three beings in one. A leader of this movement was black minister Garfield Thomas Haywood (1880–1931), who led the Pentecostal Assemblies of the World. Other leaders were Robert C. Lawson (1881–1961), who organized the Church of Our Lord Jesus Christ of the Apostolic Faith in 1919, and Smallwood Williams (1907–1991), who founded the Bible Way Church of Our Lord Jesus Christ Worldwide in 1957.

Overlapping the Trinitarian and Apostolic divisions is the "Deliverance" movement, with which Arturo Skinner (1924–1975), who established the Deliverance Evangelistic Centers in 1956, is associated. Skinner expanded the traditional black Pentecostal emphasis on healing to include exorcism (driving out evil spirits) and an increasing focus on miracles.

Black Pentecostals have been social as well as religious leaders of African Americans. Some joined the Fraternal Council of Negro Churches and participated in marches for black employment during the 1930s. Other groups participated in civil rights campaigns in the South in the late 1950s. Smallwood Williams was a leader in the legal battle in Washington, D.C., against segregated public schools during the 1950s

Pentecostalism in the Late Twentieth Century

During the 1970s black Pentecostals took part in the "Word of Faith" movement, with a message of healing, prosperity, and positive confession. In the late twentieth century black Pentecostalism also influenced the historic

PENTECOSTALISM AND AFRICAN-AMERICAN GOSPEL MUSIC

Pentecostals have been leaders in black religious music since the early 1900s, beginning with black religious folk music. Blind singer and pianist Arizona Juanita Dranes, one of the most popular gospel singers of the 1920s, started a trend of Pentecostal and Baptist leadership of the **gospel music** movement. Pentecostal minister Garfield Haywood wrote many hymns.

The full and enthusiastic participation of the congregation is a major part of Pentecostal musical worship, and it is usually accompanied by shouting and hand clapping. Early in the movement guitars, tambourines, and other simple instruments were used as musical accompaniments, but as time went on electric guitars, pianos, and organs found their way into the music. In the late twentieth century, computerized keyboards and synthesizers were used to produce a modern gospel music.

Some of the most well known African-American gospel singers—including Marion Williams (1927–1994) and **"Sister" Rosetta Tharpe** (1915–1973)—got their start singing in Pentecostal churches. **Mahalia Jackson** (1911–1972), famous as "the world's greatest gospel singer," said the Pentecostal church next door to her childhood home had a powerful influence on her singing.

By the 1980s Pentecostals such as Andrae Crouch, Edwin Hawkins (who recorded the popular song "Oh Happy Day" in 1969), Walter Hawkins, "Shirley Caesar," the Clark Sisters, and BeBe and CeCe Winans dominated American gospel music.

black denominations, especially the AME Church. The World Fellowship of Black Pentecostal Churches was founded in 1984.

The 1998 Pentecostal World Conference was held in Seoul, Korea, where the Yoido Full Gospel Church, with 700,000 members in 2000, is the largest Christian congregation in the world. It was estimated that in 2000 some 470 million people worldwide had adopted Pentecostalism.

Peterson, Oscar Emmanuel

PIANIST, COMPOSER
August 15, 1925–

Oscar Peterson is a well-known pianist and composer. Born in Montreal, **Canada,** Peterson first studied music at the insistence of his father, who made all his children study an instrument in order to escape the poverty of Montreal's small black community. Peterson began piano lessons at age six, and as a teenager he played on a weekly **radio** show in Montreal. From 1944 to 1949 he worked with one of Canada's most prominent dance bands.

Peterson, one of the few Canadians to reach a position of prominence in American **jazz,** began his international career in 1949, when producer Norman Granz heard him on a radio broadcast from a Montreal club. Granz arranged for Peterson to perform that same year at New York City's Carnegie Hall with a touring group of jazz stars known as Jazz at the Philharmonic. Peterson toured regularly with the group until 1953, when he formed a trio.

Peterson settled in Toronto in 1958, helping to found and manage the Advanced School of Contemporary Music. He also continued touring with his trio until 1967. He recorded and toured, often with many great jazz performers. In addition to compositions such as "Hallelujah Time," "Children's Tune," "The Smudge," and "Lovers' Promenade," Peterson has composed longer works such as *Canadian Suite* (1965) and *Easter Suite* (1984). Although he is one of the most traveled musicians in jazz, Peterson has always maintained a home in Canada. In 1991 he was named to a three-year term as chancellor of York University in Toronto.

In 1999 Peterson released *A Summer Night in Munich* and continued a schedule of live performances.

Petry, Ann Lane

WRITER
October 12, 1908–April 30, 1997

Anne Lane was born to middle-class parents in Saybrook, Connecticut, and graduated from the University of Connecticut School of Pharmacy in 1931. She worked for a while in her father's drugstore but was convinced she could be a writer. In 1938 she married George D. Petry and moved to New York City.

In New York, Petry studied creative writing at Columbia University from 1944 to 1946, and worked as a journalist for two Harlem newspapers, the *Amsterdam News* and *The People's Voice*. This experience exposed her to the gritty world of Harlem's poverty, violence, and crime, and gave her early fiction its distinctive characters and style. Her first published stories brought Petry national attention and an award from publisher Houghton Mifflin that would enable her to complete her best-known and most-celebrated novel, *The Street* (1946), the first novel by a black woman to sell more than one million copies. The novel focuses on the misguided efforts of a young black woman to find a decent living for herself and her son on the streets of Harlem.

The novels that followed, *Country Place* (1947) and *The Narrows* (1953), both deal in some way with the themes of class conflict and social responsibility. *The Narrows* is noteworthy for the frank way in which it presents a relationship between a black man and a white woman. In 1971 Petry published her only collection of short stories, *Miss Muriel and Other Stories*. Her other works include four children's books: *The Drugstore Cat* (1949), *Harriet Tubman, Conductor of the Underground Railroad* (1955), *Tituba of Salem Village* (1964), and *Legends of the Saints* (1970). Petry died on April 30, 1997.

Philadelphia, Pennsylvania

Early History

When William Penn arrived on the shores of the Delaware River in 1682 to establish the Pennsylvania Colony, the area was inhabited by Delaware Indians, Dutch, Swedes, British settlers, and free and enslaved Africans. Penn selected and named Philadelphia to be the capital of the colony. The early city was small: 1,200 acres, two miles in length from east to west between the Delaware and Schuylkill rivers, and one mile in width. The boundaries remained unchanged until the consolidation of 1854, which connected the county of Philadelphia with the city, incorporating many districts and townships, including Northern Liberties, Spring Garden, Southwark, Moyamensing, Passyunk, and Blockley into the city of Philadelphia.

Scant references exist to the early presence of blacks in the colony; however, by 1720 they numbered at least 2,500 in Pennsylvania. Many were slaves. There is evidence of their collective activities by various acts of proposed and enacted legislation. The first restriction imposed in 1693 required that Africans carry passes. Later, other acts prohibited their assembly and determined where and when they could meet. The 1790 Census recorded 210 slaves in the city and 384 in the county, but Pennsylvania's Gradual Abolition of Slavery Act of 1780 applied only to children born after the act, freeing them after service to their enslaved mothers' owners for twenty-eight years. Therefore, in addition to apprenticeship, a number of black children were indentured servants, adding an additional element of separation and rendering them still not free. Despite these limitations, Philadelphia blacks developed a community in the eighteenth century. In 1786 a petition for a burial ground was presented. A year later, the Free African Society was formed. This was the first beneficial society, established by **Richard Allen** and **Absalom Jones** in Philadelphia and comprised of blacks and a few white Quakers. Some members of the Society were part of the group that had petitioned for a burial ground.

Richard Allen recorded that the beginning of the African Church in Philadelphia occurred in 1787. Though there is considerable scholarly disagreement on the precise sequence of events, and the date of the famous incident when Allen, Jones, and their fellow black congregants were ejected from St. George's Church, by the late 1780s a number of blacks who had previously worshipped with whites began leaving those churches to establish their own places of worship. At first they worshipped in private dwellings. Later they were able to formally dedicate their own buildings.

The African Church, later the First African Church of St. Thomas (Protestant Episcopal), was dedicated in 1794. Jones was its first pastor. Bethel Methodist Church, the oldest real estate continuously owned by blacks in the United States, was dedicated in 1796. Allen was its first pastor. In 1816 Allen and others organized the African Methodist Episcopal Church, the first black denomination. The African Zoar Methodist Church was formed in 1794 by another group of blacks who left St. George's and worshipped for some time in their homes in Campingtown, an area in Northern Liberties. Later, in 1796, on ground adjacent to property owned by Lunar Brown, a member and trustee, they formally dedicated their church. Methodists and Episcopalians were not the only groups to lose black parishioners. In 1809 nine black men and women received a letter of dismission from the First Baptist Church of Philadelphia. They established the First African Baptist Church in that year in the Spring Garden district, near Northern Liberties. The First African Presbyterian Church was established in 1811 by men and women led by John Gloucester. These and many more black churches came into existence providing for the growing black population, schools, burial grounds, and meeting places. Not only do census figures indicate an increase in the black population, but the proliferation of institutions also attests to the population's increase and potential influence. Perhaps the most notable event in the early history of black Philadelphia was the yellow fever epidemic of the summer of 1793, which claimed about one-tenth of the city's 50,000 residents. Under the mistaken belief that African Americans had natural immunity to the disease, city leaders appealed to blacks to help treat and bury the dead. Some whites criticized blacks for trying to profit from the crisis. Jones and Allen rebutted the accusations in their jointly written *Narrative of the Proceedings of the Black People During the Late Awful Calamity in Philadelphia* (1794).

Emerging Black Social Structures

Literary and secret societies also came into existence in the 1800s. Beneficial society membership increased in every area in the city and county from 1837 to 1847. Their purpose was the relief of members who were unable to work, the interments of deceased members, and the relief of widows and orphans. Occupational organizations and real property owned by blacks were seen by whites as symbols of upward mobility and power and were targeted for violence and destruction.

Prominent black Philadelphians such as sail maker James Forten, the ministers Allen and Jones, and others were influential in the formation, growth, and development of Philadelphia's black community. Many also raised their voices against slavery and became prominent early abolitionists. In 1830, with Allen as president, the first National Negro Convention was held in Philadelphia. Other Philadelphia abolitionists included the three granddaughters of James Forten: Margaretta, Sarah, and Harriet Forten, and leader of the Underground Railroad, William Still.

Individual and collective economic enterprises began as early as 1810 with the founding of the African Insurance Company. A financial panic in 1814 and a subsequent depression caused its failure. Two young black men, Derrick Johnson and Joseph Allen, initiated the African Fire Association (AFA) in 1818. There were more than 7,000 blacks in the city at that time, and its formation caused a "great excitement among the members of the [white] fire and hose companies." Whites successfully argued that black fire companies were unnecessary and would be unproductive. Thereafter the founders of the AFA, a potentially powerful political organization, were persuaded and encouraged to desist by some members of the black community.

Pennsylvania's Constitution in 1790 declared that a "freeman" 21 years of age who had resided in Pennsylvania for two years and paid a state or county tax "shall enjoy the rights of an elector." Though there was some

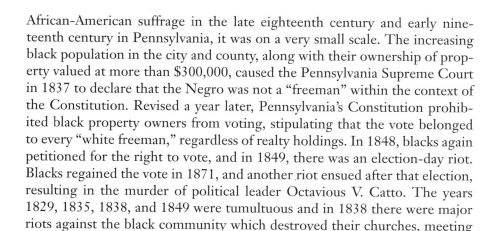

African-American suffrage in the late eighteenth century and early nineteenth century in Pennsylvania, it was on a very small scale. The increasing black population in the city and county, along with their ownership of property valued at more than $300,000, caused the Pennsylvania Supreme Court in 1837 to declare that the Negro was not a "freeman" within the context of the Constitution. Revised a year later, Pennsylvania's Constitution prohibited black property owners from voting, stipulating that the vote belonged to every "white freeman," regardless of realty holdings. In 1848, blacks again petitioned for the right to vote, and in 1849, there was an election-day riot. Blacks regained the vote in 1871, and another riot ensued after that election, resulting in the murder of political leader Octavious V. Catto. The years 1829, 1835, 1838, and 1849 were tumultuous and in 1838 there were major riots against the black community which destroyed their churches, meeting halls, residences, the African Grand Lodge of Masons Hall (Pennsylvania Hall), and the Shelter for Colored Orphans.

Despite these setbacks, black Philadelphia's institutional life grew in the second half of the nineteenth century. Businessmen and philanthropists such as Stephen Smith (1797?-1873) helped found the Institute for Colored Youth, the Home for Destitute Colored Children, the House for the Aged and Infirm Colored Persons, Mercy Hospital, and the House of Refuge. Many prominent black Philadelphians such as Robert Bogle, James LeCount, James Prosser, Jeremia Bowser, and Peter Augustine made their fortunes in the catering industry. The black community supported a number of newspapers—five by the end of the nineteenth century—including the Philadelphia *Tribune*, founded in 1884, the oldest continually published black newspaper in the United States. The artistic and intellectual attainments of Philadelphia's black middle class were considerable. Benjamin T. Tanner, a bishop in the A.M.E. Church, edited the *Christian Recorder* and *AME Church Review* and made them into important forums for black intellectual and religious thought. His son, Henry Ossawa Tanner, became the leading black artist of his generation. **Jessie Redmon Fauset** was a leading novelist of the **Harlem Renaissance**, and in novels such as *The Chinaberry Tree* (1931) provided a sensitive portrait of Philadelphia's black elite. Though originally from a poor background, **Marian Anderson** became active at an early age in the middle-class musical culture of her local church, and the Philadelphia community financially supported her training and early career. By the 1930s, she was one of the leading concert performers of her generation.

In 1899 **W. E. B. Du Bois**'s work, *The Philadelphia Negro*, was published. The book examined the history and present condition of blacks in Philadelphia. After 1900 there were considerable changes in Philadelphia's black community. Between 1900 and 1960, Philadelphia's black population increased more than 800 percent. Conditions were often difficult for the new migrants. There were jobs, but new migrants met much hostility. In 1918 there was a riot that resulted in the deaths of four blacks and many injuries. Philadelphia was not prepared to house the multitude of people who came seeking refuge. Overcrowded slums quickly developed in North and South Philadelphia, and residential segregation began. Although public housing had been available to whites, it was not until 1943 that public housing became available for blacks in North Philadelphia. In response to the increase in population, neighborhoods changed, the number of public and parochial schools increased and became more segregated, and more black churches came into existence.

Political Shifts and Changing Social Conditions

Although many black Philadelphians registered Republican, the New Deal attracted the loyalty of many who were less affluent, and the majority of black voters soon became Democrats. Blacks eventually won seats on city council and the courts. In 1938 Crystal Bird Fauset, running as a Democrat from a Philadelphia district, became the first black woman in the United States elected to a state legislature. The population continued to increase because of wartime employment opportunities. The many government installations, including the Philadelphia Navy Shipyard, provided jobs for migrants.

The 1960s and '70s were turbulent times for black Philadelphians. The emergence of a new militancy among them was evidenced by community protest meetings, race riots, and Black Panther Party rallies. Girard College, a segregated school in North Philadelphia, was established by the will of Stephen Girard for white male orphans and administered by the Board of City Trusts. Initial litigation to invalidate the will was begun in 1954 by attorney Raymond Pace Alexander. Later, another black attorney, Cecil B. Moore, not only renewed legal action, but rallied blacks to march around the wall of the college until it figuratively "came down." Moore was a criminal attorney known for representing indigent defendants pro bono. Moore increased the membership of the NAACP and eventually won election to city council. The combination of litigation and continued community pressure and moral outrage succeeded in the school's integration in 1968.

Philadelphia in the Late Twentieth Century

With more blacks in influential positions and a large, black voting population, W. Wilson Goode was elected Philadelphia's first black mayor in 1983, with 91 percent of the black vote. Although reelected four years later, his political career was marred by the bombing of the MOVE compound in May 1985. After years of sparring with a black nationalist organization, MOVE, that rejected most contact with outsiders, Philadelphia police dropped bombs into its compound, killing six, and started a fire that burned down fifty adjoining homes and left 200 people homeless. All of black Philadelphia—and most of the city's residents—were devastated at the loss of innocent lives and the destruction of a stable, black neighborhood in West Philadelphia.

Despite these difficulties, Philadelphia's black community is proud of its history as one of the centers of African-American institutional life for more than three centuries. Some of the leading monuments to black Philadelphia are the Afro-American Historical and Cultural Museum, opened in 1976, the All-Wars Memorial to Black Soldiers, unveiled in 1934, and the homes of the writer Frances Ellen Watkins Harper and the painter Henry O. Tanner. Philadelphia has been home to a number of prominent jazz musicians, including **Dizzy Gillespie, John Coltrane**, and the three Heath brothers: Percy, Al, and Jimmy. It also has been a center for black popular music. Other black Philadelphians who have achieved renown in recent decades include comedian **Bill Cosby**, and William Gray III, former congressman, ambassador to Haiti, and president of the United Negro College Fund.

The U.S. national Republican Party held its convention in Philadelphia in 2000, and attempted to create a more diverse image than it had in the past through the inclusion of numerous African Americans and other minorities in its daily programs. Outside the political realm, Dr. Emma B. Chappell was among the black Philadelphians who gained national attention; through an impressive effort to gather funding from individual small investors, Chappell established and led as president the United Bank of Philadelphia, the city's first black-owned bank in nearly four decades.

(SEE ALSO RICHARD ALLEN; MARIAN ANDERSON; BILL COSBY; W. E. B. DU BOIS; JESSIE REDMON FAUSET; ABSALOM JONES; PENNSYLVANIA)

Philosophy. *See* Afrocentricity; Conservatism

Photography

Photography began in the 1820s and 1830s with French inventors Nicéphore Niepce (1765–1833) and Louis Jacques Mandé Daguerré (1787–1851). Daguerre named his photographic process the daguerreotype (photos produced on a silver or silver-coated plate). Black lithographer and portrait painter Jules Lion (1810–1866) exhibited successful daguerreotypes in New Orleans, Louisiana, in 1839. This is considered the first exhibition of work by a black photographer.

At the beginning of the twentieth century, newspapers, journals, and books began publishing photographs, and schools and colleges began offering photography courses. Cornelius M. Battey (1873–1927), the best-known black photographer of this period, founded the photography division at **Tuskegee Institute**, Alabama, in 1916. Battey photographed African-American leaders such as **Frederick Douglass** (1817–1895), **W. E. B. Du Bois** (1868–1963), and **Booker T. Washington** (1856–1915).

New York City photographer James Augustus VanDerZee (1886–1983) worked from his studio but also photographed life in New York's Harlem district from the 1920s through the 1970s. During the black artistic revival in New York City known as the **Harlem Renaissance**, photographers exhibited their work in their communities. In 1921 the New York Public Library's 135th Street branch (now the Schomburg Center for Research in Black Culture) organized its first exhibition of work by black artists. Twin brothers Marvin Pentz Smith (1910–) and Morgan Sparks Smith (1910–1993) were well-known photographers in Harlem in the 1930s and early 1940s. They took photos of breadlines during the **Great Depression** and photographed dancers at the **Savoy Ballroom**.

The Harmon Foundation was among the first organizations to bring recognition to black photographers. In 1929 James Latimer Allen

The Pulitzer Prizes, established by American journalist and newspaper publisher Joseph Pulitzer (1847–1911), have been given each year since 1917. Over the years, new categories have been added, including photography, poetry, and music. The prizes are given to encourage excellence in public service, public morals, and education. Following are some of the African-American photographers who have received the Pulitzer Prize in journalism or photography.

Moneta J. Sleet Jr. (1969)
for his photograph of **Coretta Scott King** and her daughter at the funeral of the Reverend Dr. **Martin Luther King Jr.**

Ovie Carter (1975)
for his photographs of famine in Africa and India

Matthew Lewis (1975)
for his portrait studies of Washingtonians

John White (1982)
for work published in the Chicago *Sun Times*

Michel du Cille (1985)
for photographs of an earthquake in Colombia

Ozier Muhammad (1985)
for international reporting for the photographic essay *Africa: The Desperate Continent*

Clarence J. Williams III (1998)
for images of young children whose parents are addicted to alcohol and drugs

(1907–1977) exhibited his portraits of African-American men, women, and children in a Harmon Foundation exhibition. Allen also photographed famous African-American writers of the period, such as **Alain Leroy Locke** (1886–1954), **Langston Hughes** (1902–1967), and **Claude McKay** (1890–1948).

P. H. Polk (1898–1985), a student of Battey's, was appointed to the faculty of Tuskegee Institute's photography department in 1928, where he photographed famous African-American visitors such as **Mary McLeod Bethune** (1875–1955) and scientist-inventor **George Washington Carver** (c. 1864–1943).

Between 1935 and 1943 Farm Security Administration (FSA) photographers took photos of black migrant farmworkers in the South. In 1937 **Gordon Parks Sr.** (1912–) saw these and decided he wanted to be a photographer. He was hired by the FSA in 1941, and during **World War II** (1939–45) he worked as a war information correspondent. In 1949 he became the first African-American photographer to work on the staff of *Life* magazine.

Black photographer **Roy DeCarava** (1919–) received a Guggenheim Fellowship in 1952. He was one of the first black photographers to win the award. In 1954 he founded one of the first galleries in the United States devoted to photography as an art. In 1955 DeCarava and poet-writer Langston Hughes produced a book called *The Sweet Flypaper of Life*, showing the life of a black family in Harlem. DeCarava founded the Kamoinge Workshop in 1963 to provide support and guidance for black photographers. His photographs have been widely exhibited and published.

Black musicians and other performers have been the subject of photographs since 1935. **Milton Hinton** (1910–) photographed his musician friends while playing with **Cab Calloway**'s jazz band. Chuck Stewart (1927–) photographed every well-known musician and vocalist between 1950 and 1990. Bert Andrews (1931–1993) photographed black theatrical productions from the early 1960s through the early 1990s.

In the 1930s black photographers began working as photojournalists for newspapers and for magazines such as *Ebony*, *Jet*, and *Sepia*. A few black photojournalists—such as DeCarava, Gordon Parks, Richard Saunders, Roland L. Freeman (1936–), and Bertrand Miles—worked for larger magazines such as *Life*, *Look*, *Time*, *Newsweek*, and *Sports Illustrated*.

The **Civil Rights movement** and the Black Power movement of the 1960s and 1970s were documented by photographers Moneta J. Sleet Jr. (1926–1996), Howard Morehead, Miles, and Saunders. **Robert Sengstacke** (1943–), Howard Bingham, and others photographed the activities of the **Black Panther Party** and desegregation rallies. During the 1970s universities and art colleges began offering degrees in photography, and African-American photographers began creating new works for exhibitions.

The artistic photographs of the 1980s, 1990s, and early years of the twenty-first century offer insights into the past and look at social themes such as racism, unemployment, and child abuse. Among the many African Americans producing this type of photography are three women, Lorna Simpson (1960–), **Carrie Mae Weems** (1953–), and Pat Ward Williams

(1948–). Simpson, a multimedia artist, became the first African-American woman to be featured in a major international art exhibition, the Venice Biennial (held every two years), in 1990. Weems, who has degrees in folklore and photography, uses text and sculpture to accompany her photographs. Some of her projects of the 1990s are *Kitchen Table* (1990), *Sea Islands* (1992), and *From Here I Saw What Happened and I Cried* (1995–96). Williams, who works with three-dimensional constructions, uses themes such as African-American history, racism, family, and women's issues. Among her most famous works is *32 Hours in a Box . . . Still Counting*, a tribute to nineteenth-century abolitionist Henry Brown.

Well-known African-American photographer Roland L. Freeman is also a folklorist. He published a book of photographs of African-American quilters and their stories in 1996. Other well-known African-American photographers of the early-twentieth-first century are Steve Martin, Marilyn Nance, Melvin Greer, and Beuford Smith. Young black photographer Julian Okwu photographed black men for his book *Face Forward: Young African-American Men in a Critical Age* (1997).

In late 1999 and early 2000, an exhibit was held in the National Portrait Gallery featuring the work of nineteenth-century African-American daguerreotypist Augustus Washington (born c. 1820). Washington was an abolitionist who used his photographs to expose the cruelty of slavery.

Pickett, Wilson

SINGER, SONGWRITER
March 18, 1941–

Born in Alabama, Wilson Pickett was in a number of small-town gospel music groups in his youth before moving to Detroit, Michigan, in 1955. There he continued to sing gospel until 1959 when a neighbor, Willie Schofield, asked him to join the popular **rhythm-and-blues** group, the Falcons, of which Schofield was a member. Pickett wrote numerous songs for the group, including "I Found a Love," which became a hit in 1962.

In 1963 Pickett, who by that time was well known in the flourishing Detroit music scene, went solo and released two songs—"If You Need Me" and "It's Too Late." The following year Pickett signed with Atlantic Records. Known for his powerful vocal style, a strong, raspy delivery and melodic screams, Pickett often went by the name "Wicked" Wilson Pickett. He went on to make rhythm-and-blues hits for the rest of the decade.

In the early 1970s Pickett began producing more rock-influenced soul music. Pickett's popularity declined, however, throughout the 1970s. In the 1980s he continued to be active in the concert circuit but played mostly smaller venues in the United States and abroad. In the early 1990s, there was a revival of interest in Pickett's music. By this time, however, Pickett said he was ready to retire and make way for younger artists to come up in the business.

Pickett was charged for several violations of the law in the 1990s, including drunk driving and possession of cocaine. After a twelve-year absence, he

Wilson Pickett: Selected Hits

"Don't Fight It"
(1965)

"Mustang Sally"
(1966)

"634-5789"
(1966)

"Land of a Thousand Dances"
(1966)

"Funky Broadway"
(1967)

"Sugar, Sugar"
(1970)

"Engine Number Nine"
(1970)

"Hey Jude"
(1971)

"Don't Let the Green Grass Fool You"
(1971)

"Don't Knock My Love Pt. 1"
(1971)

released the album *It's Harder Now* in 1999, claiming that the bad times were behind him.

Pippin, Horace

PAINTER
February 22, 1888–July 6, 1946

One of the foremost self-taught painters of the 1900s, Horace Pippin was born in Pennsylvania. A disabled **World War I** (1914–18) veteran, he initially took up art in the 1920s to strengthen his wounded right arm. By the late 1930s Pippin's diverse images of childhood memories, war experiences, everyday life, landscapes, portraits, biblical subjects, and American historical events had found enthusiastic local supporters. **Alain Locke** (1885–1954) described Pippin as "a real and rare genius, combining folk quality with artistic maturity."

A descendant of former slaves, the artist was raised by Harriet Pippin. In 1891, the family relocated to the resort town of Goshen, New York, where they worked as domestic servants. As a boy, Pippin showed a strong interest in drawing, winning his first set of crayons and a box of watercolors for his response to an advertising contest for an art supply company. After working as a porter for seven years, he relocated to New Jersey and crated oil paintings with a moving and storage company. Before his service in World War I, Pippin worked in a coal yard, in an iron foundry, and as a used-clothing peddler.

In 1917 the twenty-nine-year-old Pippin enlisted in the New York National Guard. Pippin and his regiment first worked laying railroad track for two months prior to serving in combat. While in the trenches Pippin kept illustrated journals of his **military** service, but only six drawings from this period survive. He later wrote that World War I "brought out all the art" in him. In October 1918 Pippin was shot through the right shoulder by a German sniper and was honorably discharged the following year.

In 1920 Pippin married the twice-widowed Ora Fetherstone Wade, who had a six-year-old son. A community-spirited man, Pippin helped organize a black Boy Scouts troop and served as commander of the local American Legion for black veterans. As therapy for his injured arm, he began making pictures in 1925 by burning images on wood panels using a hot iron poker. At the age of forty he expanded to oil paints, completing his first painting.

Pippin first received public attention when he exhibited two paintings in the Chester County Art Association annual of 1937. Within a year Pippin was included in Holger Cahill's "Masters of Popular Painting" at New York's Museum of Modern Art. In the years between his first Philadelphia show in 1940 and his death in 1946, Pippin had solo exhibitions at New York's Bignou Gallery (1940), the Arts Club of Chicago (1941), the San Francisco Museum of Art (1942), and New York's Downtown Gallery (1944). Of the 137 works on paper, fabric, and wood that Pippin was known to have created, approximately ten percent are today unlocated. He once summed up his approach to paintings: "Pictures just come to my mind. I think my pictures out with my brain, and then I tell my heart to go ahead."

Platters, The

POPULAR MUSIC GROUP

Formed by Herbert Reed in Los Angeles in 1953, the Platters became one of the most successful popular music groups in the 1950s. In addition to Reed, the original members of the Platters were Tony Williams, David Lynch, and Alex Hodge. The group had little success until 1954, when Samuel "Buck" Ram, a songwriter and big band arranger, took over, adding the female vocalist Zora Taylor to the group and replacing Hodge with Paul Robi.

The group's 1955 recording of Ram's "Only You" reached number one on the **rhythm-and-blues** charts. "Only You" made the Platters the first black group to become popular with white rock-and-roll fans. Ram's "The Great Pretender" (1956) became the top-selling record in the United States and England. In 1956 the group also appeared in the films *Rock Around the Clock* and *The Girl Can't Help It*. Through the late 1960s, the Platters sang on almost forty hit records, including "Twilight Time" (1958) and "Smoke Gets in Your Eyes" (1958).

The Platters recorded just under four hundred songs, sold more than eighty-nine million records, performed in more than ninety countries, and appeared in twenty-seven U.S. movies and twenty-two more in other countries. They were inducted into the Rock and Roll Hall of Fame in 1990.

Over the years, members of the group changed, which resulted in several different music groups calling themselves the Platters. Only one original member, however, is still performing—Platter's founder, Herb Reed.

Plessy v. Ferguson

In the 1896 U.S. Supreme Court case *Plessy v. Ferguson*, the Court upheld Louisiana law that required railroads to provide separate but equal accommodations for blacks and whites and forbade persons from riding in cars not assigned to their race. It gave legal approval to virtually all forms of racial segregation in the United States until after **World War II** (1939–45).

The case arose as part of a strategy by a group of upper-class **New Orleans**, **Louisiana**, blacks to test the constitutionality of the separate-railroad-car law. The group raised money for a test case, and former judge Albion Tourgee, the nation's leading white spokesman for black rights, agreed to serve as attorney in the case, without pay.

In June 1892 Homer A. Plessy purchased a first-class ticket on the East Louisiana Railroad, sat in the "white" car, and was promptly arrested and charged before Judge John H. Ferguson. Plessy then sued to prevent Ferguson from conducting any further proceedings against him. Eventually, his challenge reached the U.S. Supreme Court.

Tourgee argued before the Court that segregation violated the Thirteenth Amendment to the U.S. Constitution and denied blacks equal protection of the laws, which was guaranteed by the Fourteenth Amendment. These amendments, along with the Declaration of Independence, Tourgee said, gave certain rights to all U.S. citizens and prohibited discrimination

The Court rejected Tourgee's arguments by a vote of seven to one. Justice Henry Billings Brown (1836–1913) agreed that the Fourteenth Amendment was adopted "to enforce the absolute equality of the two races before the law" but said that the amendment "could not have been intended" to do away with distinctions based on color or to enforce social equality and a blending of the two races. Brown believed that segregation was not discriminatory because whites were also segregated from blacks. Thus, he said, if segregation appeared to create inferiority, it was only because blacks chose to give it that meaning.

The Court declared that as long as segregated facilities were "equal" they were permissible. Segregation had received the blessing of the Supreme Court. In January 1897 Plessy pleaded guilty to attempting to board a "white" railroad car and paid a $25 fine.

THE DISSENTING VOTE IN *PLESSY V. FERGUSON*

In the *Plessy v. Ferguson* case only one judge disagreed with the idea of "separate but equal" segregation. In a bitter dissent (disagreement with the majority of the judges), Justice John Marshall Harlan (1833–1911), a former slave owner, acknowledged that the white race was the "dominant" race in the United States. But Harlan said he understood the U.S. Constitution to say that, in the eyes of the law, there is no dominant class of U.S. citizens. The Constitution, he said, is color-blind and tolerates no such class distinction—all citizens are equal before the law. Harlan said, "The law regards man as man, and takes no account of his surroundings or his color when his civil rights as guaranteed by the supreme law of the land are involved." More than fifty years passed before the Supreme Court recognized the truth of his dissent.

Pointer Sisters, The

POPULAR MUSIC GROUP

The Pointer Sisters, Ruth (March 19, 1946–), Anita (January 23, 1948–), Bonnie (July 11, 1950–), and June (November 20, 1954–), were born and raised in Oakland, California. Both of their parents were ministers. Growing up in a very religious household, the sisters were exposed to music through their church choir. As they matured, they began to perform secular (non-religious) music and were exposed to a wide variety of musical styles.

In 1969 the Pointer Sisters began working as backup singers with local San Francisco musicians such as Taj Mahal, Tower of Power, and Boz Scaggs. Their debut album, *The Pointer Sisters*, mixed **blues** and soul styles with vocal harmonies and costumes similar to those of female singing groups of the 1940s. The single "Yes We Can Can" reached number eleven on the pop music charts, and the sisters soon became popular guests on television variety shows.

Their second album, *That's A Plenty* (1974), included the Grammy Award-winning single "Fairytale." In 1974 the Pointer Sisters became the first African-American female group to appear on the country-music show the Grand Ole Opry, and the first to reach the top of country-and-western charts.

In 1977, after Bonnie left to pursue a solo career, the Pointer Sisters recorded the album *Energy*, which yielded two pop singles, "Fire" and "Happiness." In the early and mid-1980s, the trio produced a succession of highly successful singles, including "Slow Hand" (1981), and "Jump" (1983) and "Automatic" (1984), both of which won Grammy Awards.

The Pointer Sisters recorded *Right Rhythm* in 1991. In 1995 they returned to the spotlight in the musical *Ain't Misbehavin'*. They continue to record regularly and perform to large audiences.

ACTOR, DIRECTOR, FILMMAKER
February 20, 1927–

Sidney Poitier's dignity and talent made him the first African-American actor to be widely accepted for his portrayals of strong and proud men. The youngest of eight children, Sidney Poitier was born in Miami, Florida, and reared on Cat Island in the Bahamas off the southeastern coast of Florida. He was forced to leave school at fifteen to work on his parents' tomato farm. He then moved to Miami to live with his brother. Shortly thereafter, Poitier left for New York City, enlisted in the U.S. Army, and served as a physical therapist until **World War II** ended in 1945.

Upon his return to New York, Poitier supported himself with a series of menial jobs while studying to become an actor. He eventually became a member of the American Negro Theatre, for which he often played leading roles. He also won minor parts in Broadway (New York's premier theater district) plays.

Poitier's big break came when he was cast as a young doctor in the film *No Way Out* (1950). His status as an actor was further elevated with a memorable role as a black student suspected of high school troublemaking in *The Blackboard Jungle*. Leading roles followed in many films. With his performance as an escaped convict in *The Defiant Ones* (1958), Poitier became the first African American to be nominated for an Oscar Award in the best actor category.

Poitier attempted to diversify his roles by taking on such films as *They Call Me Mr. Tibbs!* (1970), *A Warm December* (1973), and *The Wilby Conspiracy* (1975) and by applying his talents to directing. In 1968 Poitier joined with actors Paul Newman, Steve McQueen, Dustin Hoffman, and Barbra Streisand to form First Artists, an independent production company. The popular western *Buck and the Preacher* (1972) marked his debut as both director and star; the hit comedy *Uptown Saturday Night* (both 1974), *Let's Do It Again* (1975), and *A Piece of the Action* (1977) all featured him in this dual role. In 1975 Poitier was elected to the Black Filmmakers Hall of Fame.

During the 1980s and early 1990s, Poitier concentrated on directing such works as *Stir Crazy* (1980), *Hanky Panky* (1982), *Fast Forward* (1985), and *Ghost Dad* (1990). He returned to acting briefly in 1988 for starring roles in *Shoot to Kill* and *Little Nikita*.

In addition to creative filmmaking, Poitier has produced a record album called *Sidney Poitier Reads the Poetry of the Black Man* and narrated two films about **Paul Robeson**, *Paul Robeson: A Tribute to the Artist* (1979) and *Man of Conscience* (1986). Poitier's *This Life*, an **autobiography,** was published in 1980.

In recognition of his artistic and humanitarian accomplishments, Poitier was knighted by Great Britain's Queen Elizabeth II, and the **National Association for the Advancement of Colored People (NAACP)** honored him with its first **Thurgood Marshall** Lifetime Achievement Award in 1993. Poitier published a second book, *The Measure of a Man*, in 2000. That same year, he was honored by the Screen Actors Guild, which bestowed on

Sidney Poitier (right) and Glenn Ford (center) in a scene from Poitier's break-out film, *The Blackboard Jungle* (Archive Photos. Reproduced by permission)

him its highest prize, the Life Achievement Award, for career achievement and humanitarian accomplishment.

Polite, Carlene Hatcher

NOVELIST
August 28, 1932–

Born in Detroit, Michigan, Carlene Hatcher Polite attended Sarah Lawrence College and the Martha Graham School of Contemporary Dance. Polite's career blended art and social activism, and included literature, dance, and politics. Polite danced with the Concert Dance Theatre of New York from 1955 to 1959. She then returned to Detroit, where she danced with the Vanguard Playhouse, taught dance, and became involved with the Democratic Party. In 1963 she served as an organizer of the Northern Negro Leadership Conference and coordinator of the Detroit Council for Human Rights.

Shortly after the Council closed in 1964, she moved to Paris, France. There, she continued to dance, but writing became her primary interest. Her first novel, *The Flagellants*, was published in the United States in 1967. The book involves a young black couple's difficult search for love and self-identity in an oppressive society.

Polite returned to the United States in 1971, but her Paris experiences shaped her second novel, which recounts the life and death of a female black dancer in Paris. The book shows in a brutal fashion the cancerous effects of racism. Polite's fiction is experimental, relying on unconventional techniques rather than more traditional means such as plot. Polite has been a member of the English Department at the State University of New York at Buffalo since 1971.

Politics

The history of African Americans within the American political system is both tragic and inspiring. It is tragic because it represents some of the most regrettable moments in U.S. history. However, it is at the same time inspiring because it shows how a group of people can achieve political, social, and economic dignity in the United States in the face of terrible adversity.

African-American Politics before the American Civil War

During the colonial period (when the American colonies were ruled by Great Britain before the **American Revolution** [1775–83]), black slaves were not considered citizens. However, this did not prevent blacks from establishing a political system of their own. Although blacks were not allowed to vote, they made political statements through community organizations and newspapers. But political expression means more than groups merely communicating how they would like society to change. At the other end there must exist the possibility that those views will be listened to and shaped into public policies. Before the **American Civil War** (1861–65), blacks tried to express their desire for freedom and equality. Unfortunately, no one was listening.

The Civil War Period

The Civil War was one of the lowest points in the history of the United States. However, for African Americans it brought a sense of hope that their dream of freedom would be realized. Many blacks therefore did everything they could to help the Union army destroy the Southern institution of **slavery.** By 1862 blacks were allowed to fight in the Union army, and thousands gratefully volunteered. The primary goal of political bodies that blacks associated with was to abolish slavery. Northern blacks therefore joined political parities such as the Liberty Party and the Free Soil Party, which had the same objective.

Politics During Reconstruction

After the Civil War the United States entered into a period of rebuilding called **Reconstruction** (1865–77). During this period, the old political structure began to crack. Amendments to the Constitution were passed, granting blacks citizenship (Fourteenth Amendment, 1868) and the right to vote (Fifteenth Amendment, 1870). Blacks began to win elections to public office with the help of the Republican Party. Blacks also got involved in local politics in the South. States such as Alabama, Georgia, and Virginia saw blacks elected to city council posts, and smaller towns elected black mayors. Between 1870 and 1900, twenty African Americans were elected to the U.S. House of Representatives, and two were elected to the Senate.

Although Republicans genuinely believed in equality, they also knew it was to their benefit to help blacks obtain political power. This was because the South was dominated by the Democratic Party, and Republicans were eager to increase their own power in the South by increasing the number of

Republican officeholders. Thus, Republicans appointed blacks to serve in various positions and prepared them to compete in elections against Democrats. However, when political appointments declined and it became clear that Republicans were doing little to combat racism and inequality, many blacks left the Republican Party.

The Period after Reconstruction

Blacks had to overcome far more than established laws to achieve equality. There were old customs and beliefs within the culture of the South that were even more difficult to overcome than laws. Conservative Democrats were not willing to give up power that had taken years to establish.

As soon as Union soldiers left their final posts in the South in 1877, Reconstruction came to an end. Southern whites did everything they could to keep political power out of the hands of blacks and to restore Southern control of government. Different methods were used to keep blacks from expressing their political views, including poll taxes, literacytests, redistricting, and violent threats. Poll taxes were unnecessary fees blacks had to pay in order to vote, and literacy tests were unreasonably difficult exams that blacks were forced to take before they could vote. Because many blacks were poor and did not have access to **education,** there was no way for the majority to break through these barriers.

In 1900 blacks in the South could not vote, and blacks in the North had little impact on political affairs. The political environment changed slightly as a result of the Great Migration, a massive movement of blacks from southern states to northern and western states, where they hoped to find greater economic and political opportunities. Although conditions for blacks were better in northern states, it would be decades before black political power began to blossom.

African Americans Move to the Democratic Party

In the 1930s many blacks were drawn into the Democratic Party because of the policies it drafted during the **Great Depression** (a period of severe economic hardship during the 1930s). In addition blacks began being elected to political posts through the help of the Democratic Party. Blacks were finally beginning to see the kind of political change they had been seeking.

World War II (1939–45) brought a wave of political participation from blacks. African Americans who had risked their lives in the name of democracy were eager to exercise democratic principles upon their return. In 1948 the Democratic Party announced a firm commitment to civil rights, which further inspired blacks to join the party.

The Supreme Court and Voting Rights

Little by little barriers to black political power were being torn down. In 1944 the U.S. Supreme Court outlawed the all-white primary. A primary is an election by the major parties to decide which candidates will represent them in a given election. At one time primary elections were closed to blacks; this made their vote in general elections meaningless. In 1960 the Supreme Court outlawed the practice of unfairly drawing district lines

THIRD-PARTY POLITICS

The two-party system in American politics helped blacks overcome numerous political obstacles. However, many of the obstacles blacks faced were, in fact, created by the two-party system. When avenues of political expression were ignored by the two major parties, blacks created third parties to bring important African-American concerns to the table.

For instance, in the 1960s blacks created parties such as the Mississippi Freedom Democratic Party (MFDP) and the National Democratic Party of Alabama (NDPA), which fought for black voting rights in the South. Although many of the early black third parties faded after achieving their primary end, the third party is becoming an important instrument in African-American politics.

Independent parties have done more to bring blacks to office than the Democratic and Republican parties. Between 1920 and 1990, seventeen out of twenty African-American candidates for the U.S. Senate ran on third-party platforms. In addition, the vast majority of blacks elected to the office of governor ran on third-party tickets.

Because of the success blacks have experienced with third parties and because of the failure of Democrats and Republicans to address African-American concerns, some scholars believe that the future of African-American politics will be best served if black politicians unify under a national third party.

(known as "gerrymandering"). At the national and local levels in the United States, political districts are drawn around population centers. Both southern and northern politicians were guilty of drawing district lines in such a way that black population centers were broken up, to prevent them from gaining a majority.

The Civil Rights Movement

The 1960s was a period of tremendous political change in the United States. During the Civil Rights movement, politics and society began opening up to African Americans on a large scale. There was a massive movement by blacks and whites to end discrimination and inequality. A wave of nonviolent demonstrations led to the passage of the Voting Rights Act of 1965, which shattered the remaining barriers to black voting. The legislation had an almost immediate impact; blacks were beginning to be elected to public office in the South in large numbers. Although minor efforts were still made to block the political expression of blacks, they were eventually overcome by the momentum of equality generated during the 1960s.

Politics in the Late Twentieth Century

Since the 1960s, a class of elite black politicians has developed. Organizations such as the Congressional Black Caucus (formed in 1971) ensure that issues important to the welfare of the black community continue to be addressed. However, racism and the poor social and economic status of African Americans remain barriers to the full development of black political power in the Untied States. These issues will have to be addressed in order for blacks to achieve their dream of full political, social, and economic equality in the United States. (*See also* **Abolition; Civil Rights Movement; Great Depression and New Deal; Suffrage**)

Pollard, Frederick Douglass "Fritz"

FOOTBALL PLAYER, COACH
January 27, 1894–May 11, 1986

Fritz Pollard was born in Chicago, Illinois, to a family of accomplished athletes. He followed in their footsteps and became a star **football** and **track-and-field** athlete in high school and college. He was a standout professional football player and the first African-American coach in the National Football League (NFL). When he died in 1986, no other African American had been named head coach of an NFL team.

Pollard was an exceptional running back in high school. He also excelled at track and played **baseball.** After he completed high school, the wealthy Rockefeller family was instrumental in getting Pollard to attend Brown University, where Pollard played football and ran track. At 5 feet 8 inches tall and 150 pounds, Pollard was a sterling running back and defensive player on the 1915 Bruins team that met Washington State in the Rose Bowl game. On January 1, 1916, Pollard became the first of many African Americans to participate in the Rose Bowl.

The next season, his elusive running propelled Brown to victory in its first eight games and to its first-ever victory over Harvard University. Following the 1916 season, Pollard was the second African American to be named All-American in football. Although he was a remarkable athlete, perhaps Pollard's greatest accomplishment was in a nonplayer position. In 1920 he coached the Akron Pros to an undefeated season and the championship of the American Professional Football Association (APFA). When the APFA became the NFL, Pollard again led the Pros to a winning season.

Throughout his athletic career, Pollard faced discrimination from hostile fans who often yelled "kill the nigger," opposing players who sought to injure him because of their antipathy toward African Americans, and restaurant and hotel owners who refused him service and lodging. Still, he excelled at every level in football and became a role model for many African Americans involved in sports.

Poussaint, Alvin Francis

PSYCHIATRIST, EDUCATOR, AUTHOR
May 15, 1934–

Born in East Harlem, Alvin Poussaint attended Stuyvesant High School and graduated from Columbia College and Cornell University Medical

College. He took postgraduate training at the University of California, where he served as chief resident in psychiatry from 1964 to 1965. From 1965 to 1967, he was southern field director of the Medical Committee for Human Rights in Jackson, Mississippi, providing medical care to civil rights workers and aiding in the desegregation of health facilities throughout the South. In 1967 Poussaint became an assistant professor at Tufts University Medical School. He remained there for four years (1965–69) before joining the faculty of the Harvard Medical School. At Boston's Judge Baker Guidance Center, he counseled families traumatized by the murder of a relative or friend.

Poussaint's research included the psychological and social adaptation of children of interracial marriages, the nature of grief, and the pharmacological treatment of smoking and bed wetting. He was a founding member of the Black Academy of Arts and Letters in 1969. Two years later Poussaint became an initial member of the Reverend **Jesse Jackson**'s (1941–) organization Operation PUSH (People United to Save Humanity). He also served as an advisor to Jackson during the 1984 presidential campaign.

One of the nation's leading psychiatrists, Poussaint has researched and written widely on such social issues of concern to African Americans as poverty, unemployment, self-esteem, parenting, and violence. He has written several books, including *Why Blacks Kill Blacks* (1972) and *Raising Black Children* (1992). Poussaint also served as a consultant to *The Cosby Show*. He reviewed script dialogue to ensure that the **television** series presented positive images of blacks and was free of stereotypes and discriminatory content. In 1993 Poussaint became professor of psychiatry and associate dean of student affairs at Harvard Medical School. A year later, he became the director of the Media Center for Children at the Judge Baker Children's Center.

Powell, Adam Clayton Jr.

CONGRESSMAN, CIVIL RIGHTS ACTIVIST, CLERGYMAN
November 29, 1908–April 4, 1972

Adam Clayton Powell Jr. devoted his life to improving conditions for African Americans. He was a preacher, a politician, and a civil rights activist.

Powell was born in New Haven, Connecticut. Shortly thereafter his father, Adam Clayton Powell Sr., left New Haven for New York City to assume the pastorship of the Abyssinian Baptist Church in **Harlem, New York.** The elder Powell sought the best for his only son, educating him at the elite Townsend Harris High School, then sending him to Colgate University, a largely white school in Hamilton, New York.

In 1937 Powell was named minister of the Abyssinian Baptist Church to succeed his father. The congregation boasted more than ten thousand members and was probably the largest Protestant church in the United States. During the next few years, Powell, in his forceful manner, became the most visible leader of the boycott campaign to break the discrimination that existed in stores. He pressured New York utilities, including Consolidated Edison, to hire blacks. His boycotting tactics forced the New York City private bus companies to hire black drivers for the first time.

In 1941 Powell became the first black to win election to the New York City Council. Before his first term was over, he decided to run for Congress from a newly created district that would, for the first time, enable a black to be elected from Harlem. Powell launched a two-year campaign that saw him elected in 1944. He was the first black elected to Congress from the Northeast.

Powell's talent for attracting attention and making enemies soon made him the congressional leader in the fight for civil rights legislation. In 1950 he offered an amendment which came to be known as the Powell Amendment, forbidding any federal support for segregated facilities. Powell would repeatedly introduce this amendment over the next several years. Powell gained sufficient seniority to become chairman of the powerful House Education and Labor Committee. He also supported increased federal aid to school programs, increased minimum wage, and the Head Start Program for preschool children. In 1964 the Civil Rights Act finally saw the core of the Powell Amendment enacted into law. From 1961 to 1967 Powell was one of the most powerful politicians in the United States and certainly the most powerful African American.

Powell's political downfall began when, in 1960, he accused a Harlem woman of corruption and was successfully sued for libel. Powell refused to pay, and before he finally agreed to settle in 1966 Powell had accumulated enormous amounts of bad publicity. The full House of Representatives voted to expel Powell from Congress in March 1967. Powell vowed to fight the case all the way to the U.S. Supreme Court.

He spent the last two years of his life on the island of Bimini, in the Bahamas, where he said he was working on his memoirs, which were never published. He died of cancer in a Miami hospital on April 4, 1972. (*See also* **Civil Rights Movement.**)

Adam Clayton Powell (AP/Wide World Photos. Reproduced by permission)

Powell, Colin Luther

ARMY OFFICER, CHAIRMAN OF THE JOINT CHIEFS OF STAFF
April 5, 1937–

Colin Luther Powell is a four-star general and the first African American to become chairman of the Joint Chiefs of Staff, the country's highest military position. He his known for his honesty, tireless work ethic, and inspirational patriotism.

Born in New York, New York, Powell grew up in family of Jamaican immigrants. He graduated from the City College of New York in 1958. In college he had been a member of the Reserve Officer Training Corps (ROTC), marking the beginning of his long, distinguished career in the military. In 1962 Powell was called to serve in the Vietnam War (1959–75). For his service in Vietnam, he was awarded the Purple Heart, given to those who are wounded in war. Upon his return to the United States, he worked as a military instructor in Georgia and attended officer training school, graduating second in a class of twelve hundred officers. In 1968 Powell was once again called to serve in Vietnam and won the Soldier's Medal for his bravery.

An African-American F I R S T

Colin Powell is one of the most highly respected military officers in American history. His record of bravery and sound leadership led to his appointment to the top military post in the country. In 1989 Powell became a four-star general (a general who has earned four medals). He was nominated by President George Bush (1989–93) to serve as chairman of the Joint Chiefs of Staff. As chairman, Powell was in charge of heading the U.S. efforts in the Persian Gulf War.

Colin Powell at the Vietnam War Memorial in Washington, D.C. (AP/Wide World Photos. Reproduced by permission)

Throughout Powell's military career he has moved in and out of various political appointments. In 1971 he earned a master's degree from George Washington University (Washington, D.C.), after which he worked for the Office of Management and Budget (OMB). Powell then attended another training class and became full colonel in 1976. In 1979 he earned the rank of general, and in 1983 he became the military assistant to the secretary of defense. Powell then took an assignment to command seventy-five thousand troops stationed in West Germany. Upon his return he served as President Ronald Reagan's (1981–89) national security adviser, helping coordinate arms-control agreements between the United States and the former Soviet Union. At the time, there was growing concern over the danger of nuclear weapons, and as tensions between the two countries began to ease, the important issue of reducing the threat of nuclear warfare was addressed

Powell served as chairman of the Joint Chiefs of Staff, and his calm and reassuring leadership during the Persian Gulf War (1991) earned him wide-

POWELL CONSIDERS RUNNING FOR PRESIDENT

Powell is widely considered to be the first African American with a realistic chance of becoming president of the United States. In 1995, after he helped calm political tension in Haiti and published a best-selling book (*My American Journey*), the public began encouraging him to run for the White House. National opinion polls indicated that Powell led all potential candidates. In December 1995, however, after announcing that he was a Republican, Powell told the public that he did not have the desire to become president and withdrew from consideration.

spread national attention. Powell retired form the military in 1993, after which he began making public appearances. Powell's reputation for honesty and integrity, as well as his remarkable record of achievement in the military, led him to consider running for president in 1996. In 2000 Powell became chair of America's Promise, a nonprofit organization committed to improving the lives of young people.

Price, Florence Beatrice Smith

COMPOSER, CONCERT PIANIST, ORGANIST
April 9, 1887–June 3, 1953

Florence Price (born Florence Smith) was the first African-American woman composer to achieve national recognition. She attended the New England Conservatory of Music from 1903 to 1906, graduating with diplomas in organ and piano. There, she also studied composition.

Smith taught for a time at the Cotton-Plant Arkadelphia Academy and Shorter College in Little Rock, Arkansas, and later headed the music department at Clark University in Atlanta, Georgia. In 1912 she returned to Little Rock and married Thomas J. Price, an attorney. After she married, Florence Price abandoned her college teaching career and set up a private studio at her home. Little Rock had become racially intolerable by the mid-1920s, and the Price family settled in **Chicago, Illinois,** in 1927. There, Price established herself as a concert pianist, teacher, and nationally acclaimed composer.

During the 1920s Price began to win awards for her compositions, and her music was published. In 1932 she achieved national recognition when she won first prize in the Wanamaker Music Composition Contest for her *Symphony in E Minor*. With its premiere in June 1933 by the Chicago Symphony Orchestra conducted by Frederick Stock, Price became the first African-American woman to have an orchestral work performed by a major American orchestra. In 1934 her *Piano Concerto in One Movement* was premiered by the Woman's Symphony Orchestra of Chicago with the black pianist Margaret Bonds (1913–1972).

Price wrote over three hundred compositions, including symphonies, concertos, chamber works, art songs, and settings of spirituals for voice and piano. Her art songs and arrangements of spirituals were sung by many of the most renowned singers of the day, including **Marian Anderson** (1897–1993). "My Soul's Been Anchored in De Lord," was recorded by Marian Anderson, Ellabelle Davis, and **Leontyne Price** (1927–). She also wrote popular music and orchestrated arrangements for the WGN radio symphony orchestra in Chicago. Price's instrumental music reflects the influence of her cultural heritage. The composer died in Chicago in 1953.

Price, Leontyne. *See* Price, Mary Violet Leontyne

Price, Mary Violet Leontyne

OPERA SINGER
February 10, 1927–

Born in Laurel, Mississippi, the soprano Leontyne Price came to be regarded as one of the world's greatest **opera** singers during her exceptionally long career (1952–85).

Her parents provided her with piano lessons from the age of four. Soon thereafter, she joined her mother in the church choir, and in 1936 she decided she wanted a career in music. Price enrolled at Central State College in Wilberforce, Ohio. Before she graduated in 1949, however, her vocal talent was so exceptional that she was encouraged to enter the Juilliard School of Music. There, she attracted the attention of composer Virgil Thomson, who put her in his 1952 production of his *Four Saints in Three Acts*, a work calling for an all-black cast.

Following this production in New York and performances at the Paris International Arts Festival, Price was engaged for the role of Bess in George Gershwin's *Porgy and Bess*, with which she toured in Berlin, Paris, and Vienna into 1954. In November of that year, she made her New York debut at Town Hall. The following February she appeared in the title role of Puccini's opera *Tosca* on television. In 1956 she sang the role of Cleopatra in Handel's opera *Giulio Cesare*.

She made her debut with the San Francisco Opera in 1957. Her debut with the Lyric Opera of Chicago was as Li in Puccini's opera *Turandot* (1959).

The Metropolitan Opera in New York City had only begun adding black singers to its cast in 1955. Price appeared in the Metropolitan Opera's production of Verdi's opera *Il Trovatore* on January 27, 1961, when she won an unprecedented forty-two-minute ovation. During the next five years she particularly excelled in the production of several operas. The new home of the Metropolitan Opera at Lincoln Center was opened in 1966 with a new opera by Samuel Barber, *Antony and Cleopatra*, written specifically for Price. When she concluded her career in opera performances on January 3, 1985, she had proved her abilities in the Italian operas. She also excelled in German, Spanish, French, and Slavic works, as well as in spirituals and works based on American literature.

In addition to many of the operatic roles in which she appeared on stage Price has recorded Samuel Barber's *Hermit Songs* and music of Fauré, Poulenc, Wolf, and R. Strauss, as well as Verdi's *Requiem* and Beethoven's *Ninth Symphony*. She has also recorded excerpts from *Porgy and Bess*, an album of popular songs, and *Swing Low, Sweet Chariot*, a collection of fourteen spirituals. In 1992 RCA reissued on compact disc forty-seven arias by Price under the title *Leontyne Price: The Prima Donna Collection*.

Primus, Pearl

DANCER, CHOREOGRAPHER
November 29, 1919–October 29, 1994

Dancer Pearl Primus was born in the Caribbean island of Trinidad and raised in New York City. She earned a degree in biology (1940) at Hunter College before attending the New School for Social Research, both located in New York. She later studied at New York University, where she received a master's degree in education (1959) and a Ph.D. in dance education (1978).

Primus made her professional dance debut in New York in 1943, performing her own *African Ceremonial*. In 1944 she gave her first solo recital, performing to poetry and the music of folksinger Josh White. The show met with such success that it moved to Broadway (New York's leading theater district).

Primus, who founded her own dance company in 1946, was best known for her "primitive" dances. She was famous for her energy and physical daring, being able to make leaps up to five feet high. During this time Primus often based her dances on the work of black writers and on racial issues.

In 1949 Primus began studying dance in Central and West Africa, followed by the Caribbean and the southern United States. In 1959 she traveled to the West African nation of Liberia, where she worked with the National Dance Company.

From 1984 to 1990 Primus served as a professor of ethnic studies and artist in residence at the Five Colleges consortium in Massachusetts. In 1990 she became the first chair of the Five Colleges Dance Consortium. Primus's original dance company grew into the Pearl Primus Dance Language Institute.

Prince (Nelson, Prince Rogers)

SINGER, COMPOSER
June 7, 1958–

Prince: Selected Works

For You
(album, 1978)

Prince
(album, 1979)

1999
(album, 1982)

Dirty Mind
(album, 1980)

Under the Cherry Moon
(film, 1987)

Graffiti Bridge
(film, 1992)

Chaos and Disorder
(album, 1996)

Emancipation
(album, 1997)

Prince Rogers Nelson, who goes by the name Prince, was born to two **jazz** musicians in an interrracial marriage and raised in Minneapolis, Minnesota. He began playing music at a very young age, alternating among piano, keyboards, guitar, and drums. He formed his own band in high school. Prince made his first demonstration record in 1976, playing all the parts of the music himself. In 1978 Prince signed a contract with Warner Brothers. Prince stirred controversy with his bold lyrics on his third album.

In 1984 Prince produced, wrote, scored, and starred in the film *Purple Rain*, whose soundtrack sold more than seventeen million copies and won an Oscar Award for best original music score, in addition to three Grammy Awards and three American Music Awards. Prince continued to pursue film projects.

Since 1987 Prince has recorded his own albums and produced music by others in Paisley Park Studios, a Minneapolis production facility built with the assistance of Warner Brothers. In 1987 he released an album which combined the rhythms of funk with **gospel music** and pop styles, but it failed to generate interest. In 1992 he released an album called *The Artist*, whose title he officially adopted as his name. The Artist spent several years in a contract dispute with Warner Brothers.

In recent years Prince has worked with many prominent figures in popular music, including Chaka Khan, Sheena Easton, Stephanie Mills, the Bangles, Stevie Nicks, Sheila E, **Patti LaBelle**, and **M. C. Hammer**. Although Prince has a huge international following, he has remained committed to his home state. He owns two nightclubs in Minneapolis and lives

with his wife, Mayte, who he married in 1996, on a thirty-acre estate in Chanhassen, a small town thirty miles from Minneapolis. He later changed his name back to Prince.

Professor Longhair (Henry Roeland "Roy" Boyd)

RHYTHM AND BLUES PIANIST, SINGER
December 19, 1918–January 30, 1980

Born in Bogalusa, Louisiana, Henry Byrd was raised in extreme poverty in New Orleans, earning spare change by street dancing. He learned about music as a child by listening to the blues played in the nightclubs of New Orleans, and in his late teens he taught himself piano after finding an abandoned instrument in an alley.

In the early 1930s Byrd worked as a dancer, but later in the decade he was supporting himself largely by boxing and gambling. He married in 1940 and served in the U.S. Army from 1942 to 1944. After the war his time was mainly spent roaming nightclubs and playing piano. Byrd led his first bands in the late 1940s and became known as "Professor Longhair" because of his collar-length hair. He had his first popular record in 1949 and shaved his hair off to honor its title, "Bald Head." In the 1950s Professor Longhair's quirky vocal style and modest personality kept his music from achieving national recognition. He was a brilliant, flashy pianist, however, who blended elements from many styles of music—including **rhythm and blues**, Tex-Mex, calypso, and Dixieland.

After a 1954 stroke, Professor Longhair was plagued with health problems, but he continued to record a number of regional hits; his 1959 song "Go to the Mardi Gras" eventually became New Orleans's unofficial anthem. He couldn't manage to become more than locally popular, however, and when his career slumped in the late 1950s, he became poverty-stricken, running a laundry with his wife out of their home. He gave up music in 1964 to make his living as a gambler and a janitor.

Professor Longhair was rediscovered in 1969 and became more popular than ever, with a busy schedule of performing and recording both in the United States and in Europe. In the 1970s he performed annually at the New Orleans Jazz and Heritage Festival. His last recording was *Crawfish Fiesta* in 1979. Despite his health problems, his playing remained as spirited as ever, and he gave his last performance three days before he died in his sleep in New Orleans.

Prosser, Nancy

ACTIVIST
c. 1780–18??

The life of Nancy Prosser is evidence that African-American women were active in slave revolts and other forms of resistance to slavery, although they are rarely mentioned in the records of such events. Nancy's husband,

Gabriel, led a rebellion that involved one thousand African-American slaves near Richmond, Virginia, in 1800. Nancy was active in making the swords and other weapons that the group planned to use in an attack on Richmond.

When the plan was exposed, key members were rounded up by the state militia. Gabriel and approximately thirty-five others were hanged. Nancy also might have been hanged, as happened to other black women who participated in slave revolts. (*See also* **Gabriel Prosser Conspiracy.**)

Pryor, Richard Franklin Lenox Thomas

COMEDIAN
December 1, 1940–

Richard Pryor is a comedian whose legendary comedy routines set the standard for many other African-American performers. Born and raised in Peoria, Illinois, Pryor used his early experiences with racism and poverty as themes in his comedy routines. Pryor overcame a troubled life in an extended family headed by his grandmother to become a famous comedian, film star, screenwriter, producer, and director. When he was at his peak, few **comedians** could match Pryor's popularity.

At age eleven, Pryor began acting at the Carver Community Center under the guidance of the drama teacher, Juliette Whittaker. Over the years she became the recipient of some of Pryor's performing awards; he also contributed to the private school she later founded, the Learning Tree.

After dropping out of school, Pryor joined the army in 1958. After military service, he worked in a factory and began performing in small clubs. By 1964 he had attracted enough attention to be booked for his first national television appearance, on singer Rudy Vallée's *Broadway Tonight* show. Three years later, after stops on the Ed Sullivan, Merv Griffin, and Johnny Carson television shows, Pryor appeared in the film *The Busy Body*, the first of more than forty films he wrote, acted in, produced, and/or directed into the early 1990s. His first major role was in *Lady Sings the Blues* (1972).

From 1970 through 1979 Pryor starred or costarred in twenty-one films. He contributed to the script of *Blazing Saddles* (1973), and in the same year wrote for and appeared on *The Flip Wilson Show* and was a cowriter for comedian Lily Tomlin's television specials. He continued to perform in clubs and theaters around the country, and these performances provided material for his two *Richard Pryor Live in Concert* films (both in 1979). The recordings of his performances earned him three Grammy Awards, the Recording Academy's most prestigious prize.

In 1980 Pryor produced his first film, *Bustin' Loose*. Two years later he wrote and produced *Richard Pryor: Live on the Sunset Strip*, which highlighted the off-color comedy that had made him famous. In 1986 Pryor, who had previously survived two heart attacks, discovered that he had multiple sclerosis. Although he continued to perform for a time, he eventually retired from public life.

Richard Pryor became the first recipient of the Mark Twain prize for humor, awarded by the John F. Kennedy Center for the Performing Arts (the Kennedy Center; the "national cultural center" of the United States, located in Washington D.C.) on October 20, 1998. In his official response, Pryor wrote, "It is nice to be regarded on a par with a great white man—now that's funny! Seriously though, two things people throughout history have had in common are hatred and humor. I am proud that, like Mark Twain, I have been able to use humor to lessen people's hatred."

Purvis, Charles Burleigh ▪▪▪

PHYSICIAN, EDUCATOR
April 14, c. 1842–1929

Charles Purvis was born in Philadelphia, Pennsylvania, and educated at Oberlin College and the Medical College of Western Reserve University. He served as an acting assistant surgeon for the U.S. Army. In 1869 he joined the staff at Freedmen's Hospital in Washington, D.C., as well as the faculty of the **Howard University** Medical School. This was the beginning of Purvis's fifty-seven-year association with the Howard University Medical School as a faculty member and administrator.

Purvis's reform activities paralleled his rising professional career. In 1869 he served as a Pennsylvania delegate to the national Convention of Colored Men of America. He also joined forces with Washington-area black physicians seeking to gain admission to the all-white Medical Society of the District of Columbia.

In 1881 Purvis gained national attention when President James A. Garfield was shot by an assassin; Purvis was one of the doctors brought in to treat the president. The following year, President Chester A. Arthur appointed Purvis surgeon-in-charge of Freedmen's Hospital in Washington. Under Purvis's leadership the hospital experienced significant growth.

Purvis's social ideas reflected those of his peers. He defended social welfare assistance for poor blacks on the grounds that class and color handicaps were at the root of their poverty. However, Purvis also stressed temperance, education, and self-reliance as the most effective means for people to end their poverty.

Although a prominent civic leader, Purvis was not without his critics. He exercised tight control over the administration of Freedmen's Hospital. Purvis opposed an attempt by Freedmen's controllers to promote the famed surgeon Dr. Daniel Hale Williams to succeed Purvis as the hospital's chief surgeon. The conflict between Purvis and Williams led to Williams's resignation in 1898.

When Purvis resigned from Howard in 1907, the university hailed his career at the school and Freedmen's Hospital. In 1908 the Howard trustees appointed him professor emeritus and made him a member of the university's board of trustees—a post Purvis held until 1926 when he was in his eighties. He died in Los Angeles in 1929. (*See also* **Hospitals, Black.**)